Crime Science

Crime Science
New approaches to preventing and detecting crime

edited by

Melissa J. Smith and Nick Tilley

WILLAN
PUBLISHING

Published by

Willan Publishing
Culmcott House
Mill Street, Uffculme
Cullompton, Devon
EX15 3AT, UK
Tel: +44(0)1884 840337
Fax: +44(0)1884 840251
e-mail: info@willanpublishing.co.uk
website: www.willanpublishing.co.uk

Published simultaneously in the USA and Canada by

Willan Publishing
c/o ISBS, 920 NE 58th Ave, Suite 300,
Portland, Oregon 97213-3786, USA
Tel: +001(0)503 287 3093
Fax: +001(0)503 280 8832
e-mail: info@isbs.com
website: www.isbs.com

First published 2005

ISBN 1-84392-089-1 (paperback)
    1-84392-090-5 (cased)

British Library Cataloguing-in-Publication Data

A catalogue record for this book is available from the British Library

Typeset by GCS, Leighton Buzzard, Bedfordshire, LU7 1AR
Project managed by Deer Park Productions, Tavistock, Devon
Printed and bound by T.J. International Ltd, Trecerus Industrial Estate, Padstow, Cornwall

Contents

Part 3: Case Studies in Preventive Crime Science

Part 4: Case Studies in Crime Science for Detection

Figures and tables

Figures

Tables

Notes on contributors

Kate J. Bowers is a Senior Lecturer in the Jill Dando Institute. She was previously Senior Research Associate at the Department of Civic Design, Liverpool University. Kate has been centrally involved in the monitoring, targeting and evaluation of crime prevention schemes on Merseyside over the past five years. She has also been involved in developing methods that identify the spatial and temporal distribution of repeat victimisation and the correlates of crime. She has published widely in the environmental criminology field.

Andrew Brock was formerly a Research Assistant at the Jill Dando Institute. While at the Institute, Andrew was involved in research on crime prevention in prisons, DNA fast-tracking and research into violence and crack markets. He is now developing, applying and evaluating crime prevention strategies on the urban rail network at the Crime Prevention Unit for Queensland Rail, Australia.

Paul Ekblom is a Principal Research Officer at the Home Office. Paul has researched and written extensively on crime prevention and its evaluation. His main interests are 'Design against Crime', and conceptual links between biological evolution and the crime reduction arms race, and the development of conceptual tools to help professional crime preventers improve their performance by thinking, communicating, acting and collaborating more rigorously and systematically.

Graham Farrell is a Professor of Criminology and Director of the Midlands Centre for Criminology and Criminal Justice at

Loughborough University. He was previously Associate Professor at the University of Cincinnati and, before that, Deputy Research Director at the Police Foundation in Washington, DC. He has worked for the United Nations in Vienna and at the Universities of Oxford and Manchester. He publishes mainly on repeat victimisation and crime prevention, policing, evaluation and drug policy.

Shane D. Johnson is a Senior Lecturer at the Jill Dando Institute. He was previously a Lecturer at the Department of Psychology, Liverpool University. His research interests focus on both crime science and forensic psychology. He has published over 30 papers within the fields of criminology and forensic psychology.

Gloria Laycock is the Director of the Jill Dando Institute of Crime Science. Prior to the establishment of the Institute, Gloria established and headed the Home Office Police Research Group and edited its publications on policing and crime prevention for seven years. She has extensive experience in the United Kingdom and has acted as a consultant on policing and crime prevention in North America, Australia, Israel, South Africa and Europe.

Ken Pease is a visiting Professor of Crime Science at the Jill Dando Institute. He was previously a Professor of Criminology at the University of Manchester and has also held a chair at the University of Saskatchewan. He has received an OBE for his work on crime prevention. Ken has published over 200 books, monographs and articles.

Chloe Smith is a Research Fellow at the Jill Dando Institute of Crime Science. Chloe's research at the Institute has focused on micro-audits, the New Deal for Communities (NDC) project, the 'Safer Cells' project and DNA fast-tracking.

Melissa J. Smith is a Research Fellow at the Jill Dando Institute of Crime Science. Her research has primarily focused on vehicle crime, including theft, vehicle excise duty evasion, abandoned vehicles and the vehicle underclass. She has also been involved in research on antisocial behaviour and crime prevention within correctional institutions.

Peter Stelfox is Head of Crime Operations in the Greater Manchester Police with responsibility for homicide investigation and operations targeting organised crime. He is a member of the Association of Chief

Police Officers (ACPO) Homicide Working Group, which develops policy and practice in homicide investigation for police forces in England and Wales. He has carried out research into the police response to gang violence and is currently researching the factors that determine outcomes in homicide investigations.

Lucía Summers is a Research Fellow at the Jill Dando Institute of Crime Science. Lucía has been involved in the 'Safer Cells' evaluation project, which focused on the use of situational prevention strategies to reduce suicides and self-harm in prisons. She is also involved in research on business and environmental crime.

Nick Tilley is a Visiting Professor at the Jill Dando Institute of Crime Science. He is also Professor of Sociology at Nottingham Trent University. His research interests lie in problem-oriented policing, crime reduction, programme evaluation methodology and evidence-based policy and practice.

Michael Townsley is a Senior Research Fellow at the Jill Dando Institute of Crime Science. Previously he was managing the crime and community safety theme for the North Huyton New Deal for Communities project, a ten-year regeneration programme to turn around deprived communities. He has worked on a range of operational policing projects focused on crime reduction in Australia and the UK.

Barry Webb is the deputy Director of the Jill Dando Institute of Crime Science. Previously, Barry was responsible for coordinating the evaluation of the government's Crime Reduction Programme at the Home Office Research Development and Statistics Directorate. He has published on a range of crime topics including car crime, burglary, violence, vandalism and credit card fraud.

Richard Wortley is from the School of Criminology and Criminal Justice, Griffith University, Brisbane, Australia. He worked as a prison psychologist before becoming an academic, and was formerly Chair of the Australian Psychological Society's College of Forensic Psychologists. His major research interest is in the role of the immediate environment in criminal behaviour and the implications that this has for crime prevention. He has published internationally in this area.

Introduction

Melissa J. Smith and Nick Tilley

All the chapters in this book have been written, at least in part, by individuals associated with the Jill Dando Institute of Crime Science (JDI). The JDI was established in 2002 as a centre for research, teaching and consultancy in crime science. Indeed, its formation marked the start of 'crime science' as a separately identifiable endeavour, though not of course the questions it addresses or the ideas on which it builds. The work brought together here is intended in part to 'show and tell' what crime science is about, and the sets of ideas with which it works. It also gives a flavour of some of the work which the Jill Dando Institute has been involved in over its brief lifetime. Some of the chapters are modest in scope and originality (for example that by Tilley on motorway service areas), and some bold in promising fresh areas of investigation and action (for example that by Johnson, Bowers and Pease on predictive mapping). If crime science is to be successful in years to come, much, if not all, of the specific thinking in this volume will have been superseded, but what will remain is a continued commitment to engaging with crime problems scientifically. The history of all sciences is the history of ideas that failed to survive the tests of time and had to be replaced by better ones.

Any claim to new disciplinary terrain is rightly subjected to critical scrutiny by those involved in and with interests in closely related turf. Johnny Upstart crime science is no different. It has made some criminologists apoplectic with rage. There may be several reasons for the rage, including the following:

1 As a moral issue crime is not thought to be susceptible to or appropriate for scientific study and technical intervention.

2 Human behaviour (including that of offenders and those responding to it) is deemed intentional and replete with meaning, again making it inappropriate for scientific investigation.

3 Crime scientists are considered to be insufficiently scientific, or to operate with a defective notion of what it is to be scientific.

4 Crime science may appear to be threatening to criminology in terms of the funding, students etc. it may attract and it may in that sense threaten the interests of criminology.

5 Crime scientists are believed to collude with policy-makers, funders, etc. rather than take a properly independent and critical view of what is done.

6 Crime scientists are generally believed to ask the wrong questions about crime and the criminal justice system, being more concerned with immediate and modifiable conditions than underlying 'root' causes.

7 Crime scientists take for granted the domain they are investigating and the methods they employ – they are in this sense unreflexive and uncritical.

8 Crime scientists are perceived to betray their main parent discipline, criminology, turning their backs on and rejecting what it does and what it has achieved.

9 because of its apparent preference for situational crime prevention, rational choice and routine activities theory, which are not the stock-in-trade of most criminological analysis, and

10 because of historical disputes with particular individuals associated with crime science.

Some of these overlap with one another (for example 1 and 2). Some are inconsistent with one another (for example 2 and 3). Some are *ad hominem* (for example 4, 5 and 10). There is no space here to go into them in detail. Here, though, are brief responses to each.

1 Crime science has no quarrel with the notion that crime is a moral issue, for instance in terms of what is classified as crime, which

crimes attract policy attention, ways of responding to crime and choices made by offenders to commit crimes. None of this, though, is deemed to preclude interest in the explanation of patterns of crime event or criminal behaviour, or in methods of preventing or detecting crime.

2 The issues raised here have a long history. Suffice it here to say that rational choice theory, one of the major approaches informing developments in crime science, focuses on how potential offenders define the situations in which they act. Moreover, as Stelfox and Pease argue in their chapter, forms of cognition are critical to the process of criminal investigation.

3 There is a long-running debate between advocates of experimental and realist evaluation, and these approaches are rooted in different conceptions of science. Each would say of the other that their practices are not properly scientific. The issues in this argument are again beyond this brief introduction. All that can be said here is that among the community identifying themselves with crime science are individuals with differing views on this debate, using different methodologies. There is no uniform line, and certainly no disposition to exclude particular techniques, as Laycock makes clear in her chapter.

4 Because crime science aspires to draw in a wide disciplinary base, as illustrated in Ekblom's chapter, there is scope for broadening the range of monetary and human resources devoted to understanding crime and its control. While there may be some competition with others involved in criminology, it is quite limited.

5 This is simply untrue. Crime scientists have come up with conclusions unexpected by and unwelcome to policy-makers and practitioners, just as have other researchers. The chapter by Webb *et al.* is a case in point.

6 The notion of 'root causes' is a tricky one. In contrast to many other criminologists, most crime scientists would see opportunity as a significant cause not only of crime events, but also of criminality. Moreover, it is true that crime scientists are especially interested in 'proximate' conditions for crime that may be open to intervention to produce short- and long-term falls in crime, and to pre-empt future crime opportunities. The chapters by Ekblom, Smith and Webb, Tilley, and Wortley and Summers in various ways illustrate this.

7 This is not true. There is no reason why crime scientists should be any less reflexive or critical than those looking at crime through other lenses. They do, though, take crime reduction and crime detection seriously and see a value in attempting better to achieve these objectives, as made clear in Laycock's chapter and elsewhere in this book.

8 There is certainly a close connection between criminology and crime science and no disposition to repudiate all that has been achieved in criminology. Indeed, most of those contributing to this book have backgrounds in criminology and work from a set of theories developed within criminology. This is not to say that crime science does not have a specific focus, as Laycock makes clear and as exemplified in the material brought together here. Moreover, as will be emphasised, crime science draws on many disciplines not normally associated with criminology.

9 It is indeed the case that crime science, as currently conducted, does draw heavily on a sub-set of criminological ideas, and does so overtly and knowingly. This is not to say that future developments will be confined to these traditions. Indeed, some chapters here use other theory, for example the cognitive theory used by Stelfox and Pease and the ideas relating to cost-benefit analysis used by Farrell, Bowers and Johnson.

10 While ubiquitous interpersonal conflicts may be unavoidable, and may animate some of the animosity shown for crime science by some criminologists, it is no substitute for bread-and-butter argument and analysis.

It may be perfectly possible and proper for some criminologists to 'deconstruct' the work of crime scientists. Moreover, specific work is certainly open to criticism, as well as the project of crime science as a whole. However, weaknesses in specific examples should not necessarily be taken to indicate weaknesses in the notion of crime science altogether. After all, were all disciplines to be condemned and rejected on the grounds of weak pieces of work conducted under their auspices, our universities would be empty. We see scope for 'cohabitation' between crime science and the rest of criminology, and plenty of room for fruitful dialogue between them. Within crime science, we also see a need for criticism and debate in the interests of better ideas driving out worse ones.

The best analogy for understanding the relationship between crime science and criminology, we think, is probably that with medicine. The sociology of medicine is concerned with understandings of medicine and the assumptions behind medical discourse. It is often critical. It highlights distinctive assumptions that are often taken for granted and suggests alternative ways of looking at the body and at ways of intervening in relation to its functioning or experience of its functioning. It may focus on the organisation of medicine, the prioritisation of one illness over another as well as the concepts of wellness and illness, and at patterns of power and authority in medical treatment, research and knowledge-claims. Much of this may ultimately be useful, for instance in medical practice, health promotion and the creation of well-being, but it is not oriented to meeting the specific needs of patients or of those who feel they may need medical attention. Research relating to specific medical problems, to medical treatments for particular conditions and to means of averting specific medical problems is generally undertaken by different people in different departments using different methods and largely published in different journals. Their activities may be topics for medical sociology, but they are not engaged in it. Their research is medical. Few would now argue that there is no value in medical sociology or that there is no value in medical research. They are, though, different from one another, with different substantive interests, different discourses and different methods. Crime science aspires to do the equivalent of medical research, while at any rate most traditional criminology largely does for crime and responses to it, the counterpart to medical sociology.

Overview of the book

This book has four parts: an introduction, a discussion of the theory and methodology used in crime science, and studies of both prevention and detection.

Part 1 gives a background to the emergence of crime science as a discipline. Gloria Laycock builds the background, nature and aspirations for crime science for the reader. She explains that crime science is about reducing crime, either by stopping it from occurring initially – prevention – or by speeding up the process of capturing those responsible after the crime has occurred – detection. It uses scientific methods to test theories and examines not only what works, but where, how and when. She addresses four critical areas:

- What can science tell us about the nature of crime?
- What can science contribute to prevention?
- How can science support detection?
- How is scientific method applicable to crime reduction?

Through these discussions she highlights the critical importance of opportunity and access as contributory factors explaining crime patterns. She also details the implications that crime science has for policy-makers.

Part 2 focuses on the theory and methodology used in crime science. Paul Ekblom describes an approach to future scanning recently developed (and still developing) for the group set up to deliver the UK Police Science and Technology Strategy. The approach enables those concerned with preventing crime and disorder to consider a range of scientific and technological innovations and to spot or anticipate upcoming crime risks and crime reduction opportunities – including countermeasures and counter-countermeasures on either side. The approach centres on the so-called 'Ms and Ss' framework and is designed to enable those working in hard science, technologies or applications to 'think thief' in a systematic way. The framework has the potential to integrate crime reduction, hard science and technology in a practical yet rigorous way which (through the Conjunction of Criminal Opportunity) connects with mainstream crime science and more general Crime Impact Assessment.

Graham Farrell, Kate Bowers and Shane Johnson discuss the concept and importance of cost-benefit analysis (CBA). CBA has been used increasingly in crime prevention and criminal justice research because it can influence decisions made at a policy level. However, it has also been criticised because little standardisation in the identification and measurement of cost items has been found. Farrell et al. suggest a more standardised method to develop and present the results of CBA, involving a limited portfolio of cost-benefit ratio outcome measures. Their measure allows CBA users to employ a wide variety of CBA parameters, including intangible costs, criminal justice costs, displacement, diffusion and anticipatory benefits over different time periods. They illustrate the theory in practice, with an example from the Reducing Burglary Initiative.

Part 3 includes case studies of crime science applied to the prevention of crime. This part of the book illustrates just how versatile and far reaching the impact of crime science can be. Each chapter describes an example of crime prevention in the real world – ranging from prevention in correctional institutions, vehicle crime and crime at motorway service areas to making accurate predictions about future locations of crime.

Richard Wortley and Lucía Summers illustrate how situational prevention strategies can prevent crime within correctional institutions. They discuss three particularly problematic behaviours at a prison in the United Kingdom – bullying, shouting from windows and scalding staff with hot water. They devised strategies to stop the opportunities for these behaviours to arise through simple yet effective measures. For example, to counter shouting out the windows, noise monitors were installed and prisoners were provided with in-cell television sets. Such strategies, although simple, proved effective in reducing these prisoner disorder problems.

Nick Tilley describes crime patterns at several motorway service areas (MSAs) around Birmingham, and considers how these opportunities have developed. He closely examined crime patterns at each MSA to determine where interventions might be best placed to reduce these crimes. Using an evidence-based problem-solving approach, he explores the potential ways to reduce these crimes through changes in design, policing and operational methods, and reveals difficulties that may be encountered when such an approach is put into practice.

Melissa Smith and Barry Webb explain how crime prevention can be used in contexts such as vehicle crime. In the United Kingdom, loopholes within the existing vehicle licensing and registration system have facilitated Vehicle Excise Duty (VED) evasion by motorists. They discuss how these VED evasion levels have changed over the past 17 years and how peculiarities such as vehicle classes, ages and regions within the UK that suffer extreme levels of VED evasion may have emerged. Through building three different scenarios, Smith and Webb demonstrate how various future changes to the existing licensing and registration system can prevent the numbers of motorists evading VED from increasing further.

Shane Johnson, Kate Bowers and Ken Pease describe how predicting more precisely where crimes will occur could assist in their prevention or detection. Over the last ten years, crime mapping has become a popular means to reduce uncertainty about where crime might occur in the future. Crime mapping makes assumptions about the future based on crime patterns in the past. Predicting these future patterns is dependent on understanding a sequence of events, which can then be described as a set of principles and put into practice. They use the example of domestic burglary to support this approach and discuss how this system can be improved further.

Part 4 includes studies relating to the detection of crime. Barry Webb, Chloe Smith, Andrew Brock and Michael Townsley examine the impact of an initiative between the police and the Forensic Science Service (FSS) to increase the speed with which domestic burglaries are investigated when DNA has been captured from the scene. The purpose of this 'fast-tracking' initiative is to decrease the time required to obtain, analyse and match the DNA sample against the database and the following police response to hits on this database. Webb *et al.* discuss the effect this initiative had on the speed of processing and solving cases, the actual outcomes of the investigations and the overall effect on crime. They discuss the challenges that fast- tracking faces and conclude by providing recommendations about how to improve the fast-tracking process.

Peter Stelfox and Ken Pease discuss the relationship between understanding our thought and reasoning patterns, and investigative tasks. Their chapter stresses the importance of the actions of front-line officers. There has been little research into how these officers investigate crime. What information is available suggests that investigators develop a range of heuristics which help them to make sense of crime scenes and victim/witness accounts. However, there may well be dangers in using this type of reasoning. Stelfox and Pease consider thought patterns and reasoning such as illusory correlations, selection of evidence, risky choices and the dangers of the 'I-knew-it-all-along' effects.

Part 1
Background

Chapter 1

Defining crime science

Gloria Laycock

Introduction

Although this book is the third in the Crime Science series, it is the first devoted to the topic of crime science itself. This chapter is specifically about what we see as a new discipline, or at least a significantly new paradigm. The chapter is a first step in defining what is described as a distinct approach to crime control, which merges prevention and detection under a scientific umbrella. It is called crime science.

In June 2002, at Ron Clarke's suggestion, six colleagues[1] and I met at University College London to discuss the definition of crime science. In some respects we were a little late – the Jill Dando Institute of Crime Science had already been launched at UCL on 26 April 2001. That date had marked the second anniversary of the death of Jill Dando, a popular UK TV presenter who had been brutally murdered on her doorstep. The Institute had been established in her memory thanks to a donation of over £1 million by the Trustees of the Jill Dando Fund. Much of that money had been raised by public subscription. I had given an inaugural lecture at the launch of the Institute, in which I set out my understanding of what we were then describing as the new discipline of crime science (Laycock 2001). This understanding had been informed by contributions from friends and colleagues as I had written the lecture during a period of four months spent at the Institute of Criminology in Canberra. But it was clearly a first step, and as time has passed I realise that there have been many misunderstandings among the recipients of our message, and that there were many nuances of meaning that even those closely involved in developing the discipline did not necessarily

3

agree upon. Ron Clarke's suggestion, therefore, that we should discuss the definition amongst ourselves was typical of his foresight!

I argued, at our meeting in 2002, that we should not be too pre-scriptive. I felt that we should set some broad parameters and then wait a few years and look back at what we had done, where and how we had worked, and how the discipline had developed. The subject would be operationally defined, rather as reinforcement is defined in Skinnerian psychology. I was aware when I said this that people are uncomfortable with operational definitions. Waiting until something develops before you can say what it is does not sit easily with our distaste for uncertainty. Interestingly this appears to have been the way in which operational research developed. Kirby (2003) quotes Sir Robert Watson-Watt, the inventor of radar, as saying that although he had been directly involved in the inauguration of Operational Research in the period to 1940, he had no recollection of any generally accepted definition emerging then or subsequently. 'The exception was his own "negative thesis", maintained with "damned iteration" that "Operational Research is not doing arithmetic for Air Staff' "(Kirby 2003: 2). I suppose an ultimately operational definition of Operational Research has a nice ring about it and, indeed, Kirby goes on to discuss the developing definition over the following years. These ranged from Sir Charles Goodeve's[2] shorthand definition as 'quantitative common sense' to that displayed on the first page of the Operational Research Society's house journal, the *Operational Research Quarterly*, from 1967 onwards. The definition begins: 'Operational Research is the application of the methods of science to complex problems ...' Kirby takes from this definition the observation that operational research is rooted in the methodology of science. Crime science, then, is the application of the methods of science to crime and disorder. Like operational research it is rooted in science.

That there should be some commonalities between operational research and crime science will come as no surprise to observers in this field. The approach to crime prevention of academics like Clarke and Pease draws heavily on that of Leslie Wilkins, whose own background was in operational research during the Second World War (Wilkins 2001). At that time Wilkins was concerned with the prevention of air accidents. One of his observations, for example, was that when combat aircraft crashed, the only survivor was often the gunner, who sat with his back to the direction of travel. This led Wilkins to the view that all aircraft seats, and for that matter train seats, should be so-facing (clearly he made some exceptions, including for the driver). If passengers sat with their back to the direction of travel, he argued, there would be fewer fatalities. His interest was in preventing accidents and the deaths that might result rather than in attributing blame to the driver or other individual who potentially caused the accident. In those days Wilkins might have described himself as an operational researcher, but he was able to apply the same reasoning to his developing postwar interest in crime. This general approach is one that we now call situational crime prevention.

In 1997, again pre-dating the establishment of the Institute of Crime Science, Leslie Wilkins invited Ken Pease, Nick Tilley, Graham Farrell and me to tea at his home in Cambridge. We discussed how we could generate more political interest in situational crime prevention and why that might be difficult. Leslie wanted to see a new organisation established to foster public knowledge and commitment to situational crime prevention. Following his death in 2000, Leslie's wife Barbara kindly sent me some of his letters and papers relating to our conversations about this new organisation. Quoting from a paper in that file, Leslie noted that:

> The problem of crime cannot be simplified to a problem of the criminal.

> Only a small proportion of offenders pass through the criminal justice system. Thus, even though these organisations might facilitate their reform, their impact on crime would be minimal.

> Methods which have reduced temptation have had more success in crime reduction than have those concerned with sin or sinners.

> Currently no British organisation has a remit to foster public interest in non-offender based methods of crime reduction. It is recognised that because situational methods do not have the pro-active elements of detection, conviction and punishment, they lack dramatic appeal. There is therefore, in view of the proven potential of these methods, a need for the public to be informed and for research to be encouraged in this unexciting area of public policy.

Some of these points are elaborated on further in later sections of this chapter, but suffice it to say that in sending Leslie's papers, Barbara rightly felt that she was initiating an archive for crime science.

Defining crime science

In 2002, Ron Clarke's view of crime science was that it should be defined by a coherent theory. He felt that with routine activity theory (Felson 2002), crime pattern analysis (Brantingham and Brantingham, 1993) and rational choice theory (Cornish and Clarke 1986), we were well on the way to having one. The approaches listed all focus on proximal circumstances, crime opportunities and situational contingencies as causes of crime. They constitute a useful beginning.

Clearly the definition of crime science will be further elaborated as time goes by but for now, rather like medical science, it is seen as outcome-focused. It is about reducing crime, as medical science is about reducing ill health. As a first step, it does this either by stopping crime[3] from happening in the first place (prevention) or by catching people more quickly and reliably after the event (detection). Crime science is also multi-disciplinary in that the physical, social, biological and computer sciences are all seen as relevant to crime control, and therefore to crime science. The relationship between medical science, and the multi-disciplinary nature of the approach, are illustrated in Figure 1.1 below.

One of the challenges of crime science is better to join these divergent disciplines. This process was given a push following the UK government's Foresight Programme on crime prevention. The programme was established to take a forward look at crime and its relationship with emerging technologies. In their final report, *Turning the Corner* (2000), they recommended that the Research Councils, which fund substantial amounts of university-based research in the UK, should consider how to fund cross-disciplinary work. This is surprisingly difficult since the Research Councils themselves are

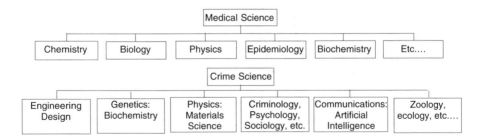

Figure 1.1   Medical science and crime science

discipline based. We have the Medical Research Council (MRC), Economic and Social Research Council (ESRC) and the Engineering and Physical Sciences Research Council (EPSRC), to name but three. They all operate similarly in inviting research bids against a sum of money set aside for a particular subject. Bids are received and assessed by peer review prior to a funding decision being made. This is a typical way of working in the university sector, which depends heavily on peer review for a number of its functions. Unfortunately, when it comes to cross-disciplinary work, it has its failings. Asking a world-class engineer to make a decision about whether or not to fund a project on a crime prevention initiative, or an economist to comment on the qualities of a new forensic tool, almost necessarily leads to distortions and some ill-feeling among the community of those assessed. Multi-disciplinary assessment panels need to reflect the composition of the bidders as well as the composition of the subject matter. This is a time-consuming process for all involved and also means that within any one panel there will be relatively few people from any given discipline.

To take a specific and fairly obvious example of cross-disciplinary work, we know that forensic science has a lot to offer policing. Fingerprint technology and the development of DNA have already made a significant impact on the way in which crime detection is approached. But the implementation of these technologies has not been as good as it might. One reason for this, as Tilley and Ford (1996) illustrated, is because insufficient attention has been paid to the social interactions between practitioners and scientists and to the training needs of the scenes of crime officers. Tilley and Ford showed, for example, that there was a considerable gap in forensic knowledge across a range of police practitioners from the police constable through to the senior investigating officer and senior scenes of crime officer. If management and implementation issues were considered at the time of introduction of these approaches then the new techniques might be more effective.

Another key feature of crime science is that the methodologies employed by crime scientists embrace the standards and values of the natural sciences. Crime science uses scientific methodologies where theories are explicit and testable and it is transparent about the degree to which it controls for chance, bias and other extraneous factors. How it does this is hotly debated. There is a powerful lobby group within criminology pressing for what it would see as a more scientific approach to the development of the discipline. This pressure, which is combined with developments in other disciplines, has led to the establishment of the Campbell Collaboration. The Campbell Collaboration is modelled on the Cochrane Collaboration, which was established in 1993 and inspired by Archie Cochrane, an epidemiologist who had been concerned at the lack of knowledge of many of his colleagues of what works in medical practice. He felt that they all too often use their experience and beliefs in making clinical decisions rather than drawing on the wealth of scientific evidence available. The Cochrane Collaboration set about the process of carrying out systematic reviews of what works and has now established a worldwide network of medical scientists to carry out these reviews and report on the outcomes. The meta-analyses which they typically conduct begin by concentrating on a review of randomised controlled trials (RCTs) in the relevant field. These are seen as the gold standard for evaluation in medical research. The Cochrane Collaboration has, however, now moved on to include other approaches than RCTs in their reviews. This is particularly appropriate if the unit of analysis is not a group of patients, who can in theory be randomly allocated, but some other unit, such as hospitals or local doctors who are operating in real-world contexts where there is much less possibility of tight experimental control.

This thinking has been carried into the Campbell Collaboration, where RCTs are held as the gold standard (Sherman *et al.* 1997). The Campbell Collaboration applies across the social science field and includes education, social welfare and criminal justice. There is a website at http://www.campbellcollaboration.org/, which sets out the way in which the Collaboration works and lists completed reviews and those in planning. There is no space in this chapter to go into the detail of the debate in this area, but suffice it to say that the crime scientist view is that there is no gold standard methodology for crime science (Laycock 2003). Rather, the appropriate methodology is that which addresses the hypothesis under review in the most acceptable manner, given the need to control for bias, to acknowledge the probability that the work is often being carried out in the community where many variables are outside the control of the experimenter, and that there we are working with probability rather than certainty. Crime science is dependent upon testing hypotheses in different contexts – addressing not only what works, but where, how and when. The context, mechanism and outcome relationships (Pawson and Tilley 1997) are vital to an understanding of crime and its control, and are necessary elements of a knowledge base in the field. If there is a gold standard then, in common with the natural sciences, it is the independent replication of results.

Although primarily focused on the outcome of crime reduction, crime science attempts to deal with crime ethically. While cutting off limbs or carrying out lobotomies, for example, might be effective in reducing crime, in our culture they could hardly be described as ethical. Similarly there are many ways to secure a conviction. Some are significantly less acceptable than others. Crime scientists are interested in working with the police and other enforcement agencies to develop effective detection methods which do not infringe human rights. And while to some extent we take as given the existing law, in terms of the definition of proscribed behaviour, that would not mean that all crime scientists would be equally content to develop methods for reducing or detecting all currently known offences.

The debates in this area are the bread and butter of criminology, and criminology is one of the many disciplines on which the crime scientist would draw. Indeed criminology, together with forensic science, are two disciplines with special claims of relevance to crime science. The former has its roots in social science and the latter in the physical sciences. Both are not only relevant but vital to this new approach. The focus on crime reduction offered by crime science, and the explicit encouragement for the involvement of other *scientific* approaches, will add value to both criminology and forensic science and help to bring elements of them together under one banner and with common cause. Ultimately, crime science aims to create a coherent body of knowledge in the field of crime reduction to guide public policy-makers, practitioners, business leaders, the media and the general public.

Perhaps most importantly, however, crime science is about applying established scientific approaches and techniques to crime control. This means using data, logic, evidence and rational thought. It specifically involves formulating and testing hypotheses and, through that process, building a body of knowledge upon which our existing theories about the proximal causes of crime can be further developed. This interest can currently be related to four questions:

- What can science tell us about the nature of crime?
- What can science contribute to prevention?
- How can science support detection?
- How is scientific method applicable to crime reduction?

This chapter touches on the four questions listed above. In answering the first question it also makes the case that reliance on the criminal justice system, as the primary means of *controlling* crime, is neither efficient nor effective (this was essentially the point made by Wilkins). Of course the criminal justice system does not exist solely for crime reduction purposes. It serves a number of other functions including the delivery of justice and the incapacitation of known offenders. It also has a declaratory function in making clear those behaviours which, it is generally agreed, should be proscribed in society. In terms of investment, however, there may be an imbalance between the amount of public money devoted to the maintenance and development of the CJS, and the encouragement of other situation-based approaches.

What can science tell us about the nature of crime?

There is a case to be made that crime in many advanced Western democracies is out of control in the sense that it is high, and in so far as it goes up further (or for that matter down) the mechanisms driving it defy simple explanation. The results of the International Crime Victim Survey, shown in Figure 1.2, illustrate the relatively high rates of crime in the UK (Van Kesteren *et al.* 2000) and the variability across a number of economically similar societies.

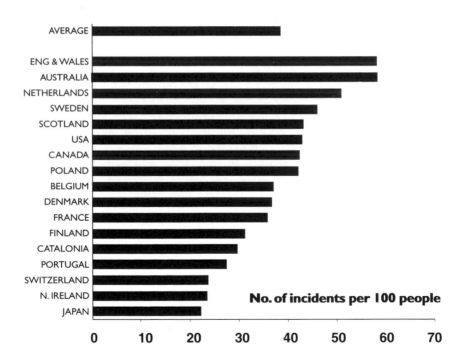

Figure 1.2 2000 International Crime Victim Survey

Looked at over time, there has been a considerable growth in the recorded crime rates, from the end of the First World War to the present day, in England and Wales specifically. This is illustrated in Figure 1.3, using police recorded figures as published by the Home Office. We know that poor educational attainment, inconsistent parenting and the increasing gap between rich and poor are all implicated as 'risk factors' for crime and disorder. This picture is consistent with the commonly held view of the criminal – criminals are not like 'us'.

This view is, however, quite incorrect. To use Thomas Gabor's (1994) phrase – 'everybody does it'. Home Office research shows that 33% of males born in 1953 had a conviction for at least one standard list offence by their 46th birthday. The cohort study also shows that half of all male offenders are only convicted once and slightly over half have a criminal career of less than one year. Nearly half were first convicted of theft or handling stolen goods – so we are probably not talking about major crime. Although a lot of people offend, they don't do it for long and it is generally not very serious.

These figures relate to known convictions. If we look at self-reported delinquency the figures are far higher. For example, in a sample of 14–21 year olds from a number of different countries, Junger-Tas et al. (1994) showed that 66% of young people in England and Wales would admit to having committed an offence at some time. The comparable figure for

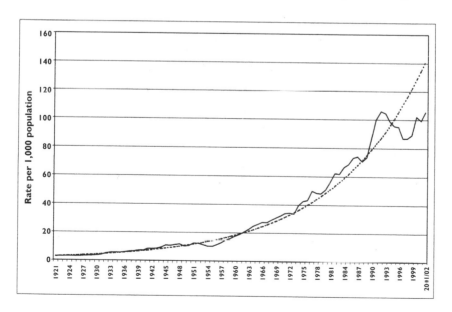

Figure 1.3 Recorded crime rates for England and Wales: 1918–2002

the Netherlands was 85%, for Portugal 81% and for Switzerland 90%. These figures are significantly higher than those shown by the police data, which reinforces Gabor's point on the prevalence of offending.

Although, as Figure 1.3 shows, the crime rate dropped in the last decade of the twentieth century, for which the government would like to take credit, it now appears to be rising again (although the data in Figure 1.3 is affected by changes in police recording rules introduced by the Home Office in 1998/9 – see Simmons *et al.* 2002). A similar fall was observed over the same timeframe in the USA although there it appeared to centre on reductions in violent crime. Blumstein and Wallman (2000) considered the possible reasons for this in some detail and could not come to a conclusive decision. To take New York City as an example, it appeared that a number of factors came together which led to a significant decline in the crime rates there. These factors included a major change in policing style (Kelling and Coles 1996) and the collapse of the crack cocaine market (Johnson et al 2000). In other parts of the United States, for example, San Diego, where similar falls have been observed over an even longer timeframe, the police approach stands in contrast to that in New York (Corner 1998). There policing is characterised as problem-solving rather than being enforcement oriented, although it still does not quite qualify as a fully fledged problem-oriented policing agency (Corner 2003).

One possible conclusion from the statistics is that there is no simple generic explanation for changes in the crime rate. There may be many ways of controlling crime and these might be locally determined, or crime may effectively rise and fall as a consequence of a whole host of pressures over which society has virtually no direct control. Both positions may be true, but there are some generalisations that can be made. For example, given the prevalence of low-level criminal behaviour, we might conclude that most people behave as they do not because they are 'wicked', but because of the situation within which they find themselves, often, in the case of young people, being influenced by their peers. Hartshorne and May's (1923) famous experiment showed that young people can be tempted to cheat in tests, particularly if they feel there is little chance of being caught out. And Farrington and Knight (1980) showed, in the 'lost letter' experiment, that otherwise 'normal' people who are assumed to be law-abiding do, under certain circumstances, steal. The atrocities in Nazi Germany, Eastern Europe, Africa and elsewhere sadly confirm that this behaviour is not restricted to the laboratory or to trivial behaviour.

So the immediate situation is important. And we have not given that fact sufficient attention in the typical, criminal justice driven approach to crime control. The opportunities provided by the immediate environment, together with the freedom to access those opportunities afforded to young people, combine to produce the high incidence of offending that we see.

Despite the clear relevance of opportunities and freedom to commit crime, our response, supported by the media and by our politicians, is to invoke the law and the supporting infrastructure of the criminal justice system: police, courts, prisons, probation, community service, etc. We arrive at this point because we consistently try to attribute blame when we discuss crime control rather than taking a lesson from the early operational researchers and trying to prevent the crimes from happening through the application of rigorous experimentation. And because we persist in seeing crime as a characteristic of the individual, we hope that the criminal justice system will deal with it successfully. But crime is not under control and indeed, as the well-known attrition table shows, it cannot be controlled in this way. Of every 100 crimes committed only about half are reported to the police and of those only about one-third are recorded. Figure 1.4 illustrates the rate of attrition through the system. Most offenders, for the more trivial offences at least, are unlikely to be caught. As Nick Ross (2002) has noted, if we dealt with accidents in this way – settling for finding out whose fault it was but not bothering to investigate whether systematic improvements might be made in the design of aircraft, cars, roads or trains – we would have a catastrophically high death rate due to accidents of one kind or another.

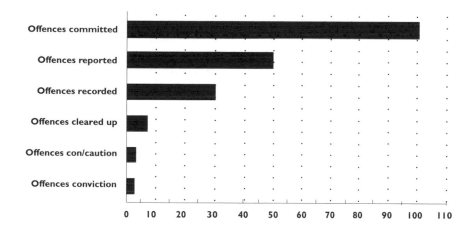

Figure 1.4 Attrition within the Criminal Justice System
Source: Home Office Research, Development and Statistics Directorate.

Although, then, the CJS cannot plausibly control the levels of crime we see today, there is no question that we need an efficient and effective system. With no such sanctions crime rates would be even higher than they are now. And the CJS performs a vital declaratory function for society in making clear the boundaries of acceptable and unacceptable behaviour. It also delivers retribution, justice and, at times, protects us from the extreme behaviour of those who need to be incarcerated for long periods. It is, therefore, necessary but not sufficient as a method of controlling crime. More is needed. What alternatives do we have? Acknowledging the limits of the CJS, we first need to prevent as many offences as possible.

What can science contribute to prevention?

In this section we are looking at ways in which crimes can be prevented, by which we mean addressing near and tangible causes rather than distant ones. What has science to offer crime prevention, so defined?

There is now a great deal of evidence that changing aspects of the immediate situation leads to measurable, and in most cases permanent, reductions in offending. Much of this work has been carried out under the heading of situational crime prevention and published in the Crime Prevention Series of books edited by Ron Clarke. Clarke (1997: 4) defines situational crime prevention as opportunity-reducing measures that: (1) are directed at highly specific forms of crime; (2) involve the management, design or manipulation of the immediate environment in as systematic and permanent way as possible; (3) make crime more difficult and risky, or less rewarding and excusable as judged by a wide range of offenders.

Taking car crime as an example, there has already been a 30% reduction in the theft of cars in recent years in England and Wales, and the government has set further targets. There is evidence that the reduction in car theft so far achieved has been due to the redesign of cars – the fitting of immobilisers and dead locks (Sallybanks and Brown 1999). These made car crime more difficult to commit, and more risky, to the generality of offenders.

The achievement in reducing car crime is a good example of what Pease (1997) calls the crime cycle. A new product is developed (in this case the motor car), it is targeted for theft or some other form of offending, and then, rather after the horse has bolted, a retrofit solution is developed. There are two problems with this: first we have to tolerate the crime wave before realising that there is a problem, and secondly, the retrofitted solution is often more expensive and less attractive than would have been the case if thought had been given to protection from crime at the design stage of the product in question. Again the car is a good example, with older vehicles having steering wheel locks which are deliberately visible and cost more than an appropriate designed-in solution would have been.

The characteristics of goods that fall into this category fit Clarke's acronym CRAVED (Clarke, 1999). They are:

- Concealable
- Removable
- Available
- Valuable
- Enjoyable and
- Disposable.

The most obvious example of a 'craved' item is cash. With the increase in credit card use and other non-cash systems of payment, such as direct transfers of wages into employees' bank accounts, there is less cash around to steal. Cash-in-transit robberies thus decline, but cash does remain in households and is a favourite target for domestic burglars as Figure 1.5, using British Crime Survey data, illustrates. It shows goods

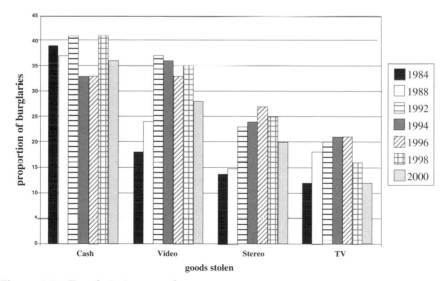

Figure 1.5 Trends in items stolen
Source: Home Office Research, Development and Statistics Directorate.

taken from burglaries – cash, videos, stereos and hi-fi equipment and TVs over the years 1984–2000. The chart shows that cash is consistently stolen in burglaries over the seven sweeps of the British Crime Survey. The loss of videos etc. seems to have built up to a peak and is now declining. There may be a number of reasons for this including the cheaper availability of new items such as videos and the fact that most households now have at least one TV. The market for second-hand electrical goods is therefore not what it once was – they are less 'disposable'. We might predict that with the increasing penetration of flat screen TVs into the market, combined with a substantial number of households without such technology, then the rate of loss of TV sets is ripe for an increase. This is where the science can assist. The most efficient way to protect that technology from subsequent theft would be to design it so that it would not work if it were to be stolen. Unfortunately, this does not appear to have been done.

The cynical observer might think that theft is good for replacement sales, so why would a company wish to design crime out? A more charitable reason for TVs not having been designed with crime in mind is that the manufacturers simply did not think of it. Whenever crime control is considered a typical response is to focus on the offender and look to the police and CJS more broadly. So it is perhaps not surprising that in general designers do not design crime out. There are, however, instances in which such an approach is more likely. This is when the manufacturers or service providers themselves are direct victims of the crime.

For example, Clarke *et al.* (2001) describe what happened to the design of mobile phones in the USA when, in 1995, they were the target of phone cloning. This practice was costing the industry $800 million per year. The solution was to redesign the phones and the industry took a whole raft of countermeasures. As a consequence such losses were all but eliminated by the end of the 1990s. The solution was not more policing or higher penalties, but redesign. Unfortunately the mobile phone manufacturers have been much slower to respond to the redesign of the mobile phone when it is the target of crime directed at the user, through street crime or other theft. In the UK the best estimate of the number of mobile phones stolen in 2000 was 700,000 (Harrington and Mayhew 2001). The exact statistics on mobile phone losses are difficult to determine partly because some phones are reported stolen when in fact they are either lost or the subject of a fraudulent insurance claim. In addition it takes some time for the losses to build up to such high levels that the issue becomes a political one. This happened in the UK when mobile phone theft was assumed to be driving the street robbery figures to unprecedented heights (Smith 2003).

Clarke *et al.*'s cloning example shows how quickly an industry can move when they are both the victim of the crime and have the expertise to deal with it. Mobile phone theft seems to be taking rather longer to reach a satisfactory solution. There are numerous similar examples where industries can act quickly in their own interests but take a little longer when the victims are more diffuse. Banks, for example, have developed the design of safes to such an extent that safe cracking is no longer a significant problem (Shover 1996). Despite a flurry of activity in the 1990s, the financial institutions have been much slower to address the vulnerable design of credit cards. Levi *et al.* (1991) first set out the extent of losses from credit card fraud in their early work, which led to the establishment of a series of initiatives by the financial institutions, including the establishment of the Association of Payment Clearing Services (APACS), but losses are now rising again and clearly a new set of initiatives is required (Levi and Handley 1998). One reason for the rise is linked to the increasing use of credit cards on the Internet, where the card owner is not present. This practice raises unique challenges to the designers of these systems, and the answers increasingly lie in science and technology (Newman and Clarke 2003).

So science, and the technological developments from it, can and do play a major role in the control of crime. At present, however, this approach is not the 'first thought' when crime prevention is considered. The profile of this agenda needs to be raised in the public and political consciousness – we need the kind of agency that Leslie Wilkins envisaged to do this.

How can science support detection?

The previous section discussed our understanding of crime and the relevance of science and technology to prevention. These perspectives influence where we look for methods of crime control, particularly the extent to which science can help in providing technical solutions to those aspects of the design of goods and services which facilitate offending. In this section we look more briefly at the potential role of science in detection.

A starting point in detecting crime is that the public need to report it. If they fail to do this, then necessarily the police cannot deal with it, but perhaps more importantly, it contributes to the impression given to the offender that detection is unlikely. Taking burglary as an example, the detection rate in the UK is typically given as of the order of 12% (Simmons and Dodd 2003). This is calculated by taking the number of burglary offences cleared up by the police as a proportion of the number of burglary offences recorded by them, although there are a number of caveats associated with these calculations arising from the ways in which crimes are reported, recorded and considered 'cleared'. Nevertheless, it is a reasonable measure of police performance, which is what it is intended to be. But it is often used as an illustration of the likelihood of a burglar being caught and the extent to which this is so. As such it gives a misleading impression. Looked at from the offender's perspective, the detection rate for burglary should be expressed as the number of offences cleared by the police as a proportion of the number of offences committed (not reported to the police, or recorded by them). This means that a more appropriate denominator could be taken from the British Crime Survey, which gives a better (and as it happens higher) estimate of the true number of burglaries being committed. If we do this then it becomes clear that the offender's perception of his or her invulnerability to detection is much higher. Attempts to calculate this figure from official data have proved difficult because, although the BCS data is given for domestic burglary, most of the raw figures for police recorded burglary include non-domestic offences. The same problem applies to the detection figures, which also include non-domestic burglary. Langan and Farrington (1998) come closest to determining the figure we are seeking in their comparative study of crime and justice in the United States and England and Wales (1981–96). There they calculate that the probability of an offender being convicted for burglary is 0.006, or 6 in 1,000. This is clearly a more worrying (but probably more accurate) figure than 12 in 100 implied by the detection rate.

Science is relevant here in two senses; it is simple mathematics to think through the nature of a denominator when calculating proportions. The choice of denominator in the example given above makes a significant difference to the end figure and to its interpretation. Science and technology can also assist in improving the reporting rate to the police. The advent of the telephone and the extent to which phones are available in homes affect the reporting rate of crime. The mobile phone has affected this further and the Internet is being developed in many police areas as a crime-reporting tool. Technology, in the broadest sense, has facilitated the reporting of crime in the margins of its development for other purposes. Clearly if crimes are not reported and recorded then they cannot be detected.

But why would the police or other agency want to increase the reporting rate when the police are measured on the extent to which they reduce crime? There are some offences, which are both serious and significantly under-reported at present, such as hate crimes generally and domestic offences specifically, and the under-reporting of these needs to be addressed. They cannot be dealt with if they are not reported. But it is in the interest of those attempting to reduce crime to have all crime reported. This would make 'hotspots' clearer, it would enable interventions to take place sooner and it would increase the likelihood of offenders being caught more quickly in the course of a potential criminal career.

Of course if more crime were to be reported it would need to be recorded on an appropriate database, preferably geo-coded and then analysed. None of these stages is necessarily simple and although there are techniques from computer science, data mining, geography and other sciences that can assist the process, they are at a relatively early stage of implementation, if not development.

Once an offence has been committed, reported and appropriately recorded, what can science do to help detection? It is probably forensic science that has been most successful in supporting detection. Fingerprint technology continues to develop with the ability to search crime scene information against large databases of prints using automatic fingerprint recognition technologies. Similarly rapid advances in the ability to search DNA traces at crime scenes against datasets containing the DNA records of known offenders, or to link offences with DNA traces, is making a growing contribution to increased detection rates. This is particularly the case for the more serious offences with the UK Forensic Science Service reporting that in a typical month the database links suspects to 15 murders, 31 rapes and 770 car crimes. In 2002, 21,000 crimes were detected using DNA evidence – a 132 per cent increase on 2000 (see Forensic Science Service 2003).

So, while the new techniques offered by the development of DNA are clearly making inroads into the detection of serious crime, there are limits to the extent to which this can be done. Recent evidence suggests that DNA traces from burglary are found in about 5% of cases (Webb *et al*. this volume). So there is, at present, a limit to the extent to which burglary can be solved through the use of DNA matching. Furthermore, there is anecdotal evidence from the police that offenders are alert to the use of DNA and either contaminate crime scenes with the DNA of others or destroy the evidence by, for example, setting fire to stolen vehicles. Ekblom (1997) has argued that offenders' behaviour changes in response to the preventive efforts of society: they learn and adapt. The same is true for offenders wishing to avoid detection. When CCTV cameras were first introduced in building societies in the UK, offenders wore large hats to avoid detection (Austin 1988). They soon learned, however, that the CCTV images were so poor that they did not need the hats and stopped wearing them. As technology has improved again, the hats and other disguises are back. So we should assume that the policies and practices of crime control need to be continuously developing, as will offender behaviour continue to do.

CCTV technology is continuing to be developed with crime control specifically in mind and the picture quality is improving with the advent of digital imaging and enhancement. Facial recognition systems are being developed which can locate a known offender in time and space using CCTV but, of course, offender-tagging systems are perhaps the most recent and significant development in ensuring that known offenders are restricted to an agreed location or successfully barred from one. While open to criticism on the grounds of civil liberties, these tagging devices are much less of an infringement than a prison sentence. It is important, however, that their use is carefully controlled and that there is no 'net-widening' to include offenders in tagging schemes who were not likely to go to prison in any case.

This raises an ethical issue about the way in which emerging technologies might be used. Scientists and technologists develop their widgets and whatnots, but the use to which they are put is a political question which might benefit from much wider and more informed public debate.

How is scientific method applicable to crime reduction?

The final question to be addressed in this chapter relates to scientific method. This is the application of the standard techniques of scientific enquiry to crime control: gathering data, testing hypotheses, accumulating knowledge. In 1990 Herman Goldstein published his book on problem-oriented policing (POP) and has spent much of his professional life encouraging the police to take a problem-solving approach to crime control. In essence, POP is scientific method.

In his writing on situational crime prevention Clarke has taken a similar stance – that SCP is not only about dealing with the immediate situation in preventing crime but is about doing so in a systematic fashion that requires the detailed analysis of data around the crime incidents. Clarke's position is similar to that of Goldstein, but wider in the sense that the methodology is recommended not just to the police, but to any agency or organisation with an interest in crime prevention.

So there is nothing new in suggesting that the police, crime prevention partners, community groups or any other agencies with an interest should use science in dealing with crime. It is, however, expecting a lot of even the police if they are not given the training and support to do this. A starting point is the need for well-trained crime analysts. They need to be comfortable with the formulation of hypotheses about crime data based on what are the best current theories. This is a considerable training requirement, and one that we are only just beginning to address. Clarke and Eck (2003) have made a start with the publication of their recent guide for crime analysts. This draws on the theoretical perspectives which support situational crime prevention, and moves analysts' training on from a preoccupation with catching offenders to addressing the potentially more effective prevention agenda.

In some respects the adoption of crime science more broadly suffers from being locked into a vicious circle. Crime is seen as fundamentally about offenders rather than situations. Until that dogmatic belief is successfully challenged, there will be relatively little enthusiasm for the kinds of approaches discussed here.

Notes

1   They were Professors Ron Clarke and Marcus Felson from Rutgers, Professor Ken Pease from the University of Huddersfield and Professor Nick Tilley from Nottingham Trent, Dr Paul Ekblom from the Home Office, and the broadcaster and journalist, Nick Ross, who had coined the term 'crime science'.
2   Sir Charles was former Deputy Controller of Research and Development at the Admiralty.
3   The word 'crime' is used through this chapter but it should be read as including disorder at one extreme and terrorism at the other. The approach of crime science is seen as relevant across a broad spectrum.

References

Austin, C. (1988) *The Prevention of Robbery at Building Society Branches*, Crime Prevention Unit Paper 14. London: Home Office.
Blumstein, A. and Wallman, J. (eds) (2000) *The Crime Drop in America*. Cambridge: Cambridge University Press.

Brantingham, P.L. and Brantingham, P.J. (1993) Environment, routine and situation: toward a pattern theory of crime, in R.V. Clarke and M. Felson (eds), *Routine Activity and Rational Choice Advances in Criminological Theory*, Vol. 5. New Brunswick, NJ: Transaction Press.

Clarke, R.V. (1997) 'Introduction', in R.V. Clarke (ed.), *Situational Crime Prevention: Successful Case Studies, 2nd edn.* New York: Harrow and Heston.

Clarke, R.V. (1999) *Hot Products: Understanding, Anticipating and Reducing Demand for Stolen Goods*, Police Research Series Paper 112. London: Home Office Research Development and Statistics Directorate.

Clarke, R.V. and Eck, J. (2003) *Become a Problem-Solving Crime Analyst*, Jill Dando Institute of Crime Science, UCL. Available from Willan Publishing, Cullompton.

Clarke, R.V., Kemper, R. and Wyckoff, L. (2001) 'Controlling cell phone fraud in the US: lessons for the UK "Foresight" Prevention', *Initiative Security Journal*, 14(1): 7–22.

Corner, G. (1998) 'Problem-oriented policing vs. zero tolerance', in T. O'Connor Shelley and A.C. Grant (eds), *Problem Oriented Policing: Critical Issues, Crime Specific Problems and the Process of Making POP Work.* Washington, DC: Police Executive Research Forum, pp. 303–314.

Corner, G. (2003) *Problem-Oriented Policing in Practice.* Paper presented at the annual meeting of the Academy of Criminal Justice Sciences in Boston, MA, March.

Cornish, D.B. and Clarke, R.V. (1986) *The Reasoning Criminal.* New York: Springer Verlag.

Ekblom, P. (1997) 'Gearing Up Against Crime: a Dynamic Framework to Help Designers Keep up with the Adaptive Criminal in a Changing World', *International Journal of Risk, Security and Crime Prevention*, 2(4): 249–265.

Farrington, D.P. and Knight, B.J. (1980) 'Stealing from a "Lost" Letter', *Criminal Justice and Behaviour*, 7: 423–436.

Felson, M. (2002) *Crime and Everyday Life*, 3rd edn. Thousand Oaks, CA: Sage Publications.

Forensic Science Service (2003) *The National DNA Database Annual Report 2002–03.* Forensic Science Service Communications Department.

Foresight Programme (2000) *Turning the Corner.* London: Department of Trade and Industry.

Gabor, T. (1994) *Everybody Does It: Crime by the Public.* Toronto: University of Toronto Press.

Goldstein, H. (1990) *Problem-Oriented Policing.* New York: McGraw-Hill.

Hartshorne, H. and May, M.A. (1923) *Studies in Deceit.* New York: Macmillan.

Harrington, V. and Mayhew, P. (2001) *Mobile Phone Theft*, Home Office research Study 235. London: Home Office Research, Development and Statistics Directorate.

Johnson, B., Golub, A. and Dunlap, E. (2000) 'The Rise and Decline of Hard Drugs, Drug Markets, and Violence in Inner-City New York', in A. Blumstein and J. Wallman (eds), *The Crime Drop in America.* Cambridge: Cambridge University Press.

Junger-Tas, J., Terlouw, G.-J. and Klien, M.W. (eds) (1994) *Delinquent Behaviour Among Young People in the Western World: First Results of the International Self-Report Delinquency Study.* Amsterdam/New York: Kugler.

Kelling, G.L. and Coles, C.M. (1996) *Fixing Broken Windows*: *Restoring Order and Reducing Crime in Our Communities.* New York: Free Press.

Kirby, M.W. (2003) *Operational Research in War and Peace: The British Experience from the 1930s to 1970.* London: Imperial College Press.

Langan, P.A. and Farrington, D.P. (1998) *Crime and Justice in the United States and England and Wales, 1981–96.* Washington, DC: Bureau of Justice Statistics.

Laycock, G. (2001) *Scientists or Politicians – Who Has the Answer to Crime?* Inaugural lecture at the Jill Dando Institute of Crime Science. Available at: http://www.jdi.ucl.ac.uk/publications/inaugural_text.php.

Laycock, G. (2003) 'Methodological issues in working with policy advisers and practitioners', in N. Tilley (ed), *Analysis for Crime Prevention*, Crime Prevention Studies, Vol. 13. Cullompton: Willan, pp. 205–237.

Levi, M. and Handley, J. (1998) *The Prevention of Plastic and Cheque Fraud Revisited,* Home Office Research Study 182. London: Home Office.

Levi, M., Bissell, P. and Richardson, A. (1991). *The Prevention of Cheque and Credit Card Fraud,* Crime Prevention Unit Paper 26. London: Home Office.

Newman, G. and Clarke, R.V. (2003) *Superhighway Robbery: Preventing E-Commerce Crime*, Crime Science Series. Cullompton: Willan.

Pawson, R. and Tilley, N. (1997) *Realistic Evaluation.* London: Sage.

Pease, K. (1997) 'Predicting the Future: the Roles of Routine Activity and Rational Choice Theory', in G. Newman, R.V. Clarke and S. Shoham (eds), *Rational Choice and Situational Crime Prevention.* Aldershot: Dartmouth.

Ross, N. (2002). *Public Lecture on Crime Science.* The Royal Institution, May. Text available at: http://www.jdi.ucl.ac.uk/news_events/seminars_lectures/RI_pres.php.

Sallybanks, J. and Brown, R. (1999). *Vehicle Crime Reduction: Turning the Corner*, Police Research Series Paper 119. London: Home Office Research, Development and Statistics Directorate.

Sherman, L., Gottfredson, D., MacKenzie, D., Eck, J., Reuter, P. and Bushway, S. (1997) *Preventing Crime: What Works, What Doesn't and What's Promising*, Report to the United States Congress, US Department of Justice.

Shover, N. (1996) *Great Pretenders: Pursuits and Careers of Persistent Thieves.* London: Westview Press/HarperCollins.

Simmons, J. and Dodd. T. (2003) *Crime in England and Wales 2002/2003.* London: Home Office Research, Development and Statistics Directorate.

Simmons, J. *et al.* (2002) *Crime in England and Wales: 2001/2002*, July. London: Home Office.

Smith, J. (2003) *The Nature of Personal Robbery*, Home Office Research Study 254. London: Research, Development and Statistics Directorate.

Tilley, N. and Ford, A. (1996) *Forensic Science and Crime Investigation*, Crime Prevention and Detection Series Paper 73. London: Home Office.

Van Kesteren, J.N., Mayhew, P. and Nieuwbeerta, P. (2000). *Criminal Victimisation in Seventeen Industrialised Countries: Key-findings from the 2000 International Crime Victim Survey*. The Hague: Ministry of Justice, WODC.

Wilkins, L.T. (2001) *Unofficial Aspects of a Life in Policy Research*. Printed postumously by the widow of Leslie Wilkins, May. Available at: http://www.essex.ac.uk/psychology/overlays/policyresearch.htm.

Part 2
Theory and Methodology

Chapter 2

How to police the future: scanning for scientific and technological innovations which generate potential threats and opportunities in crime, policing and crime reduction

Paul Ekblom

Introduction and overview

This chapter aims to alert, motivate and empower the hard science and engineering community to act as 'scouts' in identifying scientific and technological innovations (STIs) which are relevant to crime. On the one hand, they could generate potential threats of crime, disorder and terrorism, jeopardise community safety and frustrate justice, on the other, they could provide opportunities to strengthen the capacity of the police and other agencies to address these problems. Such scouts are a vital asset in supporting the work of the recently-founded Future Scanning Sub-Group (FSSG) of the Police Science and Technology Group set up to deliver the Police Science and Technology Strategy (see www.policereform.gov.uk/implementation/scienceandtech.html).

The intention is also to enable those concerned with preventing crime and disorder to consider a range of scientific and technological innovations and to spot or anticipate upcoming crime risks and crime reduction opportunities – including countermeasures and counter-countermeasures (for this is an arms race).

The aim is to establish an appropriate *mindset* ('thinking crime') in the heads of individual readers and the professional communities and institutions where they work, and supply appropriate *tools for thought*. The first part of the chapter provides background, defines key concepts, identifies the distinctive challenge posed by crime to those seeking to control it and outlines broad strategies for doing so. The second describes the methodology adopted – and under test – by the FSSG and being disseminated to scientists and engineers.

Defining crime, crime reduction, crime prevention and community safety

Crime and disorder comprise a vast set of events involving behaviour formally deemed against the law and usually committed with 'evil intent'. The events range from murder to fraud, theft, vandalism, dealing in drugs, computer hacking and terrorist atrocities. Unfortunately crime is one of society's universals – it exists wherever there is material, emotional or ideological conflict between individuals or groups, and wherever there are concentrations or flows of wealth, goods and services that motivated criminals (believe they) can safely tap to yield a more congenial living. But individuals, communities, institutions and governments can take a range of responses that, over various spatial and temporal scales, can reduce the volume of crime, its rate of growth and its adverse consequences.

Crime reduction is simply about decreasing the frequency and seriousness of criminal events, by whatever (legitimate) means. *Crime prevention* is intervention in the causes of criminal and disorderly events to reduce the risk of their occurrence and/or the potential seriousness of their consequences.

Most reduction is delivered through prevention, although some involves intervening directly in unfolding events. Actions taken after the criminal event (such as arrest and punishment or tightening of legal/physical loopholes) can serve both to prevent the criminal's next act and perhaps deter other people contemplating similar crimes.

Crime reduction interventions involve both *situational* methods (treating offenders as basically rational decision-makers and making it more risky, require more effort, more guilt-inducing and less rewarding to commit crime, and controlling provocation) and *offender-oriented* ones (ranging from incarceration to treatment to what is loosely termed 'social' prevention). These methods act through causes operating at diverse levels including the individual, family and peer group, through local institutions such as schools, the community and the neighbourhood, and through markets, national and international. Crimes comprise not only simple incidents such as the brick through the window but elaborate, multi-staged and organised processes. So the causes of crime are not simple tramlines leading to the inevitable, but are many and complex – and of course, offenders (whether individual, networked or corporate) actively try to make them happen.

Justice, of course, is a societal and personal goal distinct from crime reduction. But providing fair and satisfying justice supports many crime reduction interventions and is itself directly reductive – preventing people from taking the law into their own hands and initiating a cycle of revenge, with disastrous consequences. Both justice and crime reduction are served by common institutions carrying out the criminal and penal process. The overlap is, however, partial, and to avoid confusion we can distinguish three distinct spheres in which crime reduction interventions are implemented.

Civil approaches involve reducing the opportunity and motivation for crime by changing the way we conduct everyday life, construct our environment, design products, supply services, etc. *Judicial* approaches centre exclusively on the criminal/penal process (detection, prosecution and evidence-gathering, trial, sentencing and punishment). *Parajudicial* activities are conducted by law-enforcement agencies but are outside the criminal/penal process, such as patrolling and the provision of crime prevention advice by police, or community development work by probation staff. Hard scientists can make their contributions in each of these fields – but it is important for them to be clear which they are supporting, for the context, the activities and the functions can be very different.

Generally speaking, research has shown it is more cost-effective (and humane) to make crimes harder to take place than to focus on catching, convicting, punishing and reforming criminals after crimes have occurred (only a small proportion of offences end up with a conviction – the so-called justice gap – and reconviction rates are high). But the latter, judicial sequence has an important place in crime reduction, particularly with serious and repeat offenders.

Community safety is a wider quality-of-life issue going beyond individual events. It is a state of existence in which people, individually and collectively, are sufficiently free from a range of real and perceived risks centring on crime and disorder, are sufficiently able to cope with those they nevertheless experience, and where unable to cope unaided, are sufficiently-well protected from the consequences of these risks. In all cases this is achieved to a degree which allows people to pursue the necessities of their cultural, social and economic life, to exercise their skills, to enjoy well-being and the receipt of adequate services, and to create social capital (i.e. trust and collective efficacy) and cultural and commercial wealth (Ekblom 2001a). Obviously, most community safety is delivered through consistent application of crime reduction, but this is augmented by activities centring on reassurance. Likewise, there are grounds for believing that persistent minor disorder and signs of neglect contribute disproportionally to feelings of insecurity. (Hence, materials science could play an important role in reducing 'incivilities' such as graffiti, litter and damage – and even inadequate maintenance.)

Who reduces crime?

A huge variety of people and institutions, private, public and commercial, carry out tasks which deliver or support crime reduction (CR) interventions. These tasks range from formal and professional policing, probation and the punishment and rehabilitation of offenders, to private security, to design of products and environments against crime, to surveillance and site management by employees (e.g. station staff), to self-protection and informal social control routinely done by ordinary citizens.

Foremost among preventers, of course, are the police and related law enforcement services (such as the Forensic Science Service and HM Customs & Excise) who reduce crime professionally, whether acting alone or with others, as in local Crime and Disorder Reduction Partnerships. The police also tackle many other tasks ranging from missing persons to everyday incidents, plights and hazards which come to them because no equivalent organisation is open and available to respond on a 24/7 basis.

The challenge for crime reduction

Much so-called 'volume crime' and disorder is the familiar and unsophisticated domestic burglary, theft of/from cars, minor assault and rowdyism. Volume crime is challenging by its sheer numbers and spread. But crime at the upper end of the scale of organisation and 'professionalism' has features making it especially challenging to control (see also Cohen, Vila and Machalek 1995; Ekblom 2003). It is:

- complex;
- dispersed and invisible – forming loose networks more than gangs;
- invasive and progressive;
- resistant (impervious to countermeasures);
- evasive (moving operations around to avoid detection and countermeasures in any one location), self-protective and subversive – seeking to disable and corrupt crime control systems including formal justice;
- cryptic (hard to detect that a crime is being committed) and deceptive;
- persistent;

- adaptive to different targets, places and methods (capable of being altered to circumvent countermeasures and exploit new opportunities);
- innovative and surprising;
- entrepreneurial and sometimes well-resourced;
- mobile in location and transmissible to other offenders.

Social and technological change, moreover, constantly creates new opportunities for offending – new targets (mobile phones and laptops), new environments (cash machines, shopping centres, financial networks in cyberspace), new business models (e-tailing), new tools (such as cordless drills, spray cans, colour photocopiers or easy-to-fly airliners) and new information sources (how to pick locks or make explosives, courtesy of the Internet) which may mean a wider circle of offenders acquire 'expert' techniques.

Together, these features confront us with a pernicious combination of moving targets and shifting ground, and set the scene for an arms race between preventers and offenders. (Ekblom 1997, 1999 gives examples and parallels with military, medical, agricultural and natural evolutionary arms races.) Sooner or later, even successful crime control methods lose their force as offenders learn to circumvent them or new technology (e.g. portable 12V batteries) does it for them. Legislative solutions, especially, lag behind changing crime patterns – more so when they must be agreed internationally. (The specification of proscribed drugs is a familiar example – methylation may circumvent the legal definition without loss of narcotic effect.)

Meeting the challenge

For all these reasons, the police and their partners must improve their performance against crime and disorder and in the realm of justice.

What, though, do we mean by performance? It has several aspects (adapted from Ekblom 2002):

- cost-effectiveness;
- better responsiveness to individual and area-wide crime problems, covering:
  - prioritisation of reduction relative to the consequences of different crimes, and people's needs for protection;
  - accurate targeting on the needs of the victim and wider society, and on the causes of crime;

- more complete coverage on the ground – can practitioners cost-effectively tackle all burglaries, say, or only certain types or those in worst-hit areas?
- wider scope, in the range of different crime problems preventers can tackle – highly specific or broad-spectrum?

• avoidance of significant undesirable side effects of action – such as stigmatisation of areas or people, interference with other values and policy areas such as privacy or pollution, or even displacement of crime onto more vulnerable victims;

• greater legitimacy, acceptability or understandability of CR actions within the wider population, within subgroups or even among offenders themselves;

• swifter, fairer and more efficient justice with fewer false positive and negative decisions and more appropriately targeted sentencing;

• greater sustainability – how long the implementation of the CR activity can be maintained or how long the CR effect itself lasts.

To maintain performance, preventers must innovate faster than offenders, and must be smarter in thinking ahead and making countermoves – especially those that take offenders time, effort and expense to combat. For this, we need more than incremental advances in performance – rather, we have to *gear up* (Ekblom 1997) to:

• catch up with existing crime problems that we are currently unable to prevent;

• scan for emergent crime problems and – like outbreaks of disease – stop them early;

• anticipate new crime problems and create/deploy new solutions in good time;

• make solutions as durable as possible, and strive to maintain them, but prepare for obsolescence.

These actions require us to detect gaps between crime and our capacity to reduce it, now and in the future. This means considering both new crimes and new opportunities and motivations for crime, and new opportunities for crime reduction. It means boosting the capacity and motivation for hard science to contribute to crime reduction, whether in the civil, justice or parajudicial spheres. (In this, the recent establishment of a funding stream for hard science and crime reduction via the UK's

Engineering and Physical Sciences Research Council was significant, and a welcome intermediate outcome of the UK Foresight Programme's Crime Prevention Panel (DTI 2000)). It also means having a clear and differentiated view of the capacities the police need to maintain or develop through science and technology and other means.

A Police Science and Technology Group was recently set up to deliver the *Police Science and Technology Strategy*.[1] Aim 3 of that strategy is:

    a.   … to encompass and evaluate scientific and technological innovations, techniques and processes which can be deployed in pursuit of police purpose and aims.

    b.   Seek to identify and prepare for the opportunities and threats presented by new technology emerging onto the commercial market both for direct criminal use or as a focus for criminal activity (e.g. mobile phone thefts). (p. 16 of Appendix 1)

The police, themselves, clearly have no leading-edge expertise in these spheres. Likewise, few hard scientists and technologists are well-versed in police and crime issues. The important task is to help them not just get together, but think together. The Future Scanning Sub-Group was therefore inaugurated in 2003. Its function is to act as a bridge to the expert scientific and technical community, a filter of information crossing that bridge and an amplifier to the Strategy Group of those actual and potential STIs requiring attention and action. This entails several activities:

- identification and prioritisation of a core cluster of risk and opportunity;

- working sequentially and systematically through each risk/ opportunity area to identify specific projects requiring attention;

- reporting to the Strategy Group with recommendations on the nature of the threat and/or opportunity and the relevant action to be taken by the stakeholders comprising the Strategy Group;

- developing and refining its methodology in light of experience and documenting it in transferable form.

A wide range of stakeholders and experts participate in the FSSG.[2] Professional experience and disciplines include policing, forensic science (chemistry, physics, biology/pathology), criminological research, operational research and general technology. The Sub-Group's coverage of science and technology is inevitably incomplete and not necessarily cutting-edge. It also has a finite capacity for scanning and thinking about crime, science and technology. It therefore needs to create, and link to, a diverse network of scouts in the field. For the *scouts* to be useful, and to find the scouting task interesting and rewarding themselves, they need empowering to think systematically about crime and policing in relation to their own field. That is the main purpose of this paper – sharing the methodology with this wider audience, and in effect *transforming* their thinking. But this is a two-way affair, also serving to help professional crime preventers envisage how they can more systematically mesh with technological developments that threaten or promise.

Methodology for future scanning

The FSSG seeks to identify STIs that (a) may be deployed by the police or (b) that may be attacked or exploited by criminals. The methodology adopted is still evolving, but the broad (and unsurprising) approach is to: identify STIs that may either be deployed by the police or exploited by criminals; conduct risk and benefit analyses; and recommend a response. Identification is discussed last.

Risk analysis

Standard risk assessment techniques are employed on the STIs identified – multiplying approximate estimates (high, medium or low) of harm by the probability of the occurrence or escalation of particular types of criminal events. The risk analysis is accompanied by a matching benefit analysis – calculating the estimated level of benefit by the probability of the benefit being realised. The aim is to allow a small number of high likelihood/high impact items to be considered in more detail at any one time. The analysis focuses on:

- the *credibility* of the innovation in theory;
- the *likelihood* of its being deployed in practice;
- the potential *impact* (positive or negative) of the deployed innovation on crime, its reduction and wider policing performance;
- initial assessment of possible *countermeasures/exploitations* by offenders which could disable or circumvent existing crime reduction and/or justice strategies.

Timescale of risk

We must also identify *when* the STI will start to be used or become available. This provides a measure of the 'urgency' of response (which could benefit from a long lead time – i.e. act now to prevent a later problem emerging). Bands are as follows:

- *Short/present* – monitoring for risks and opportunities which are present, but not yet prevalent (e.g. new MOs which some police forces are experiencing and new technologies some forces are already using).

- *Medium/emerging* – risks and opportunities of new technologies we can anticipate appearing on the mass market, e.g. third generation mobile phones.

- *Longer/future* – science and technology with potential future implications for policing, e.g. quantum cryptography.

Response

A simple response framework covers the following:

- *Action* – ignore, revisit after *x* years, investigate further, monitor, act after *x* years, act now.

- *Nature and scale of action* – including taking account of counter-measures/arms races.

- *Delivery of action* – who is competent to intervene to reduce the risk/ help exploit the crime reduction opportunity? What specific tasks or general roles should they be asked to take on? How might they be mobilised – alerted, motivated, empowered, directed? What are the constraints on their action?

- *Lead time for action* – the timescale cannot be arbitrarily fixed: it is whatever is the lead time judged necessary (a) to decide on the validity/seriousness of the risk and (b) to marshal the response (if the response is itself technological, that could require several years of R&D and roll-out).

- *Risk-handling dimension* – these are risky decisions with potentially costly false positives and negatives (like earthquake prediction). These need to be explicitly declared and owned.

- *Ethical dimension* – e.g. human rights implications of response/non-response.

- *International dimension* – e.g. is this a problem in the EU or worldwide, with potential for joint action?

Identification of scientific and technological innovations posing crime risks and crime reduction opportunities

As stated, criminal events are exceedingly diverse. Specific threats are often highly particular, but to get a grip on the problem it is useful to think in generic terms which can readily be grasped by our scouts.

For this reason, the FSSG devised the 'M and S' methodology (M for Misdeeds and S for Security).

The Ms test for crime risks

Each selected STI is considered in relation to the possibility that it is at risk of being:

- *misappropriated* – property stolen;

- *mistreated* – property damaged, people assaulted, self-harm;

- *misused* – as tools/weapons for crime to support a specific modus operandi, or to be consumed as illegal drugs; this heading includes countermeasures against police or forensic tactics, and in particular those which *mislead* attempts to identify people or property;

- *mishandled* – property subject to deception, counterfeiting and smuggling, or information illegally divulged to third party;

- *misbehaved with* – creating an environment conducive to disorder, or a product conducive to conflict (e.g. over noise);

… where the targets, settings and resources for crime (whether they are the STI itself or at the receiving end of crime involving the STI) are persons, physical goods and buildings, means of payment, physical environments or electronic systems, intellectual property or information.

Also:

- *mistaken* – errors are also made by the public or police which, while not illegal, serve to constrain or misdirect crime reduction activity (e.g. false alarms, arresting the wrong person). This is obviously central to the technology of sensory systems, whether in preventing or reacting to crime – serious mistakes can of course lead to *miscarriages* of justice;

- *mistrusted* – where, for example, individual or corporate victims of crime do not report the incidents to the police due to antipathy, or reasoned judgement that there are risks such as disclosure to media or witness intimidation. The negative consequences of this include not just individual crimes not being dealt with, but police lacking a strategic picture of the nature and extent of a given problem;

- *misaligned* – having unintended adverse side effects, e.g. on privacy and other human rights, exacerbating fear or creating stigma.

Note that, given the complexity of some crimes (Ekblom 2003), it may be necessary to use several Ms in conjunction to characterise the crime risk – such as 'misappropriation of information leading to its misuse'.

The Ss test for crime reduction opportunities

We identify how the STI might be exploited to make persons, physical goods and buildings, means of payment, environments or information:

- *secured* against theft – resistant to theft, indicative that theft has happened, or recoverable/restorable to owner;

- *safeguarded* against damage – resistant to, fail-safe in or indicative of damage;

- *shielded* against misuse – *resistant* to misuse, including as weapons to attack law enforcers, or *indicative* of misuse, including tamper-evident design;

- *supporting* – justice/crime reduction/community safety, covering:
  - *supporting law enforcement* – e.g. facilitating arrest/immobilisation;
  - *supporting detection* – e.g. forensics, identification;
  - *supporting punishment* – e.g. tagging/curfewing of offenders;
  - *supporting emergency action* – covering response to accidents etc.;
  - *supporting police-public relations* – e.g. IT-based tracking/ maintenance of contacts;
  - *supporting reassurance* – e.g. surveillance technology;

- *scam-proofed* – resistant to or indicative of fraud/counterfeiting/ smuggling;

- *'s'ivilised* – environment resistant or repellent to misbehaviour and conducive to good behaviour;

- *slip proofed* – resistant to mistakes;

- *'sertain'* to report;

- *straightening adverse side effects* – see 'troublesome tradeoffs' below.

Some terms need defining further. *Resistance* includes something akin to the concepts of 'primary, secondary and tertiary safety' from the accident prevention world (stopping the crime happening in the first place, limiting it once under way and limiting adverse consequences). *Indicativeness* contributes to secondary and tertiary resistance, e.g. tamper-evident food containers help people avoid poisoning or fraud and initiate law enforcement or wider preventive action.

Note that some crime reduction opportunities and crime risks emerge, not from a single STI, but from two or more in combination – for example, a new ceramic gun with a new propellant bypassing multiple security detector systems. These pose particular challenges in that knowledge from two technological or scientific fields, plus consideration of crime opportunities and risks, must get into one head or one interacting group.

The (counter)^n issue

Being an arms race, it is sometimes necessary to refer to counter-countermeasures etc. This can be confusing if not carefully related to 'goodies or baddies'. For example, our draft assessment of biometrics began by spelling out risks of crime which, we realised, were in fact risks of criminal countermeasures (e.g. guessing password) against existing security measures (the password system) intended to protect against an initial 'primitive' crime risk from unrestricted access. A convention became necessary to spell out the degree of recursion at each stage – e.g. (1) risks of crime; (2) opportunities for CR; (3) risks of criminal countermeasures; (4) security counter-countermeasures. However, schemes like this can, if too rigidly followed, hinder comprehensible story-telling.

Boosting specific policing science and technology capabilities

The Ss again give a general overview of possibilities, particularly under the *supporting* heading. The Police Science and Technology Strategy identifies specific needs for 2003–8 in the Policing Science and Technology Capabilities.[3] Within that wide-ranging list, the current Key Capabilities (paragraph 21 of the strategy) are:

- identifying and eliminating threats to public safety, taking account of the increased risk of terrorist activity;
- effective use of intelligence-gathering technology;
- secure exchange of data between forces and other agencies;
- mobile data input and retrieval;
- maximising the value of evidence;

- effective management of investigations including the use of intelligent systems to assist decision-making;
- monitoring offenders who pose a threat;
- undertaking effective surveillance;
- effective location and recovery of evidence;
- protection of officers and vulnerable individuals.

Taking it further: the Conjunction of Criminal Opportunity

The simple 'Ms and Ss' framework broadly covers the *nature* of crime and disorder and the scope of crime reduction, community safety and justice; but to help scientists 'think crime' in detail they really need a map of the *causes* of crime and corresponding preventive *interventions* in those causes. One such map is the 'crime triangle' of victim, offender, place (Clarke and Eck 2003, and see www.popcenter.org). Used here, however, is the related but more detailed and comprehensive 'Conjunction of Criminal Opportunity' (Ekblom 2001a, 2002).

Identifying risks – how to think about causes of crime

Focusing on causes is vital for devising plausible crime reduction interventions. Where possible we want interventions which are evidence-based, too, and, better still, based on tested theories. Sadly, these are rare in the crime reduction world. Many causes are complex and perhaps also remote and fairly weak – for example, the early upbringing of children in deprived or abusive families or the global marketing strategy for setting the price and the design of mobile phones. It is, though, far simpler to start with the immediate causes of criminal events, reducible to just 11 generic precursors which act through common aspects of crime situations and of criminals, and work back out into the remoter ones, parsimoniously adding emergent causes as necessary. These precursors come together as the Conjunction of Criminal Opportunity (CCO) (see Figure 2.1). The conjunction occurs when a predisposed, motivated and equipped offender encounters, seeks or engineers a suitable crime situation involving human or material targets, enclosures (such as a building), a wider environment and people (or intelligent software) acting as crime preventers or promoters. CCO can help give scientists and technologists a concise but systematic awareness of the nature and causes of crime/disorder to check through when considering STIs. The full set of causes, together with the corresponding interventions in those causes, are described in Table 2.1. This framework was developed by drawing together existing theories and approaches to crime reduction mainly on the situational

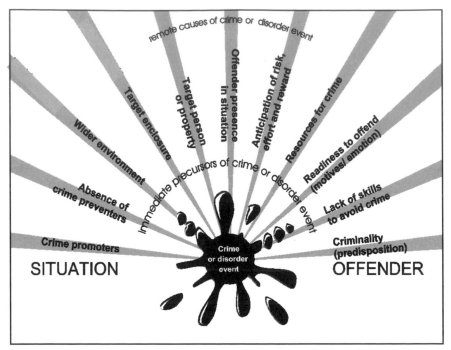

Figure 2.1 Diagnosis space: The conjunction of criminal opportunity

side, including Felson's routine activity theory (Cohen and Felson 1979), environmental criminology (Brantingham and Brantingham 1995) and Cornish and Clarke's rational offender (1986), and linking these to a range of features of the offender. A version capable of handling organised crime has also been developed (Ekblom 2003) and there is interest in doing so for terrorism.

Identifying crime reduction interventions
There is a generic family of intervention principles which disrupts, blocks or attenuates each of the 11 causes of criminal events described in Table 2.1. These principles thus reduce risk and the potential seriousness of crime (prevention), hopefully reducing the number and severity of the events that occur (reduction) and leading to wider benefits (community safety and, beyond that, economic regeneration, social inclusion, health, etc.). The principles are shown in Figure 2.2 and both causes and interventions are listed in detail in Table 2.1. CCO is an analytic framework that centres on causal *principles* or mechanisms. A useful framework for thinking specifically about tangible *methods* of situational crime prevention in particular is that of Clarke (e.g. Clarke and Eck 2003 – Step 32) who describes preventive techniques by making

it harder, riskier, less rewarding, less provocative and more guilt-inducing to commit crime. A variant of this approach focuses on design and identifies 'hot products' under the acronym CRAVED, which are predictably crime-prone due to their being Concealable, Removable, Accessible, Valuable, Enjoyable and Disposable (Clarke 1999; Clarke and Eck 2003 – Step 29).

Emergence and dynamics
Beyond these individual, 'molecular' causes and corresponding interventions we can identify some of the main processes which bring them together (Table 2.2) – effectively emergent, higher-level causes irreducibly residing in groups, networks, markets and cultures. We can also identify some of the dynamics of criminal events themselves – interactive processes *within* the unfolding criminal event, and longer-term processes *between* individual events, such as offender collaboration, adaptation and arms races. The events themselves can be linked as complex logistical scenes in a flowchart (Cornish 1994; Cornish and Clarke 2002; Ekblom 2003) in which, for example, the getaway car must be stolen, the fake pass obtained, the robbery done and the money laundered. (Newman and Clarke (2003) usefully distinguish between prime, convertible or transitional targets.) STIs will play a part in each case – for example, technology for identifying and

Table 2.1 Causes of, and interventions in, criminal and disorderly events: the conjunction of criminal opportunity

Immediate causes of criminal event	Possible interventions in cause
1. *Criminality (predisposition to offend)* Longer-term psychological features of offender including: • aggression • antisocial attitudes • criminal self-image or reputation • habits or standing decisions • drug addiction	*Reducing criminality through*: • Early/developmental intervention – tackling *risk and protective factors* • Remedial intervention (convicted/cautioned/at risk young people) At various social levels especially: • family • schools • friends • treatment in prisons, probation and medicine relating to prevention of *recidivism*

Table 2.1 continued

Immediate causes of criminal event	Possible interventions in cause
2. *Lack of resources to avoid crime* Social and intellectual skills to: • avoid conflicts • exercise self-control • de-escalate fights • earn a legitimate living and achieve esteem and social inclusion	*Supplying skills to avoid crime*: • training offenders in social skills • training in practical/work skills • contacts with preventers – mentors, minders and models

3. *Readiness to offend*
Short-term influences on people's mood or motivation
• current life circumstances including unemployment or homelessness
• needing risk, excitement, esteem
• recent events such as a domestic argument
• being in a particular emotional state such as anger
• being disinhibited through alcohol or drugs
	Reducing readiness to offend:
	• control of disinhibitors, e.g. alcohol
	• control of stressors/motivators:
	  – tackling debt, unemployment, housing problems etc
	  – resolving prior conflicts
	• satisfaction of psychological and social needs legitimately
	• esteem
	• inclusion

4. *Resources for committing crime* (See Ekblom and Tilley 2000.) These help offenders reduce risk and effort, increase reward, control conscience, by exploiting vulnerability of target, enclosure and environment, avoiding/overcoming preventers, exploiting promoters, and networking with co-offenders • skills • inside knowledge	*Restricting resources*: Control of/screening for/design of: • weapons • tools • information on target's attractiveness and vulnerability • know-how/MOs *Control of criminal organisations*: • recruitment • growth • efficiency

Immediate causes of criminal event	Possible interventions in cause
• repertoire of modus operandi • tools • weapons • transport • ability to overcome moral inhibitions • physical strength and social skills for intimidation/deceit • access to trusted network of collaborators (crime promoters)	
5. *Decision to commit offence* Offender's immediate anticipation of/ response to: • risk • effort • reward • conscience • provocation And more strategic decisions on whether this kind of crime, or the criminal career, are worthwhile	*Deterrence*: • increase perceived risk of getting caught • increase perceived costs of getting caught – formal – arrest and punishment – informal – shame – personal – guilt *Discouragement*: • increase perceived effort • reduce perceived reward
6. *Offender presence in situation* • routine activities of offender • crime attractors – motivated to look for crime there (see environment, enclosure) • free to enter or circulate in crime situation • no detectable traces left	*Excluding offenders from crime situation*: • segregating conflicting groups • closing roads and paths • attracting offenders elsewhere • exclusion of specific offenders • enhancing traceability
7a. *Target property* 'Hot product' (Clarke 1999), object, service, system or information that is:	*Reducing target vulnerability/attraction*: • target hardening • concealment • target removal

Table 2.1 continued

Immediate causes of criminal event	Possible interventions in cause
• concealable • removable • accessible • valuable • enjoyable • disposable (mobile phone = typical example)	• value reduction • reducing provocativeness • property identification
7b. *Target person* (Passive aspects of person who is the target in him/herself, as with revenge or honour assaults, or who becomes target in course of robbery of property. Active aspects are covered under 'preventers and promoters') • vulnerable • accessible • provocative (take care over this!)	*Reducing target vulnerability/ attraction* • target absence/avoidance • reducing provocation (careful)
8. *Target enclosure* Compound, building, room, container, ATM lobby that is: • vulnerable to penetration at its entry point or its boundary • has a vulnerable interior • contains attractive and vulnerable targets	*Perimeter/access security*: • adding enclosure and access • control of perimeter • control of access • screening at entrances/exits • control of interior
9. *Wider environment* Housing estates, town centres, transport interchanges, which encourage crime because they are: Logistically/tactically *favourable* for the offender and	*Environmental design and management*: • 'defensible space' principles • aiding surveillance • intelligently planned lighting • setting/communicating rules • conflict reduction (e.g. sound insulation)

Immediate causes of criminal event	Possible interventions in cause
for crime promoters, *unfavourable* for crime preventers: • concealment/surveillance (sight/sound) • rationale for legitimately being present – 'cover' • escape/pursuit • presence of promoters offering support/turning blind eye May *attract* the offence, or *motivate* it through the presence of • attractive or vulnerable targets • conflict – such as a place where rival gangs fight for control over drug outlets	
10. *Crime preventers* Potential victims, strangers, employees, police, probation, prison, private security staff, acquaintances, intimates who make crime less likely by playing active, or potentially active, roles involving: • shaping the *situation* or influencing the *offender* in advance of the criminal event (concealing phone, locking car doors when driving, etc.) • intervening during the criminal event • reacting after it (to make *next* event less likely)	*Boost preventers' presence, competence, motivation/responsibility*: • extra surveillance of enclosed and wider environments • aids for preventers – alarms, CCTV • cultivating/protecting witnesses and informants • informal social control • formal control • self-protection and avoidance

Table 2.1 continued

Immediate causes of criminal event	Possible interventions in cause
Factors which • alert • motivate and • empower preventers (with knowledge, skills, tools, e.g. forensic kit, CCTV) and perhaps • direct them (objectives, standards, regulations)	
11. *Crime promoters* Make crime *more* likely, by unwittingly, carelessly or deliberately • shaping the situation or influencing the offender (supplying weapons, tools or information, inducing the offender's cooperation by illegal threat or reward, promising to buy stolen goods, promising to look away (corruption). • intervening during the criminal event (giving encouragement, distracting the victim or preventers) • reacting after it (helping dispose of stolen goods and weapons, providing an alibi, etc.) Factors which: • lull • deter and discourage • hinder promoters	Discouraging/deterring promoters: • naming and shaming • civil/criminal liability • tackling a criminal subculture • market reduction for stolen goods • procedural controls

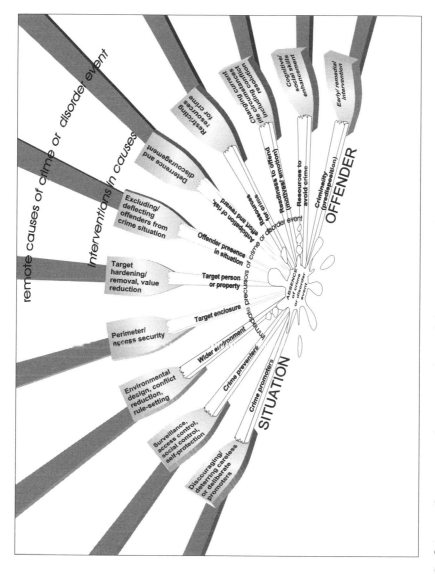

Figure 2.2 Intervention space: crime prevention and the conjunction of criminal opportunity

Table 2.2 Dynamic and emergent causes

Factors bringing the conjunction of criminal opportunity together –
emergent causes

- Environmental processes – hot spots
- Lifestyles and routine activities of offenders and victims
- Market processes – demand for goods or illegal services
- Niches for offending careers and criminal service providers such as fences
- Planning and action by the offender or offending organisation – creating
  the opportunity
- Social relations between the roles – including conflict, gang turf

Crime as a process

- Mutual perceptions, expectations and interdependent decisions (as in
  game theory) of the roles of offender, preventer and promoter
- Move and countermove in pursuit of goals
- Displacement
- Longer-term arms races
- Offender replacement
- Scenes – complex, multi-stage crimes:
  - preparation (e.g. steal getaway car, forge passport)
  - execution (e.g. rob bank)
  - escape and covering tracks (e.g. destroy DNA evidence, launder
    money)
  - consummation (spend/enjoy)
  - crime 'businesses' – repeated, organised offending

tracking stolen goods or money may help 'market reduction' in these
commodities (Sutton 1998, 2001), and methods and concepts from other
sciences may help understand, measure and manipulate them (e.g. the
niche concept is lifted from ecology – see Brantingham and Brantingham
1995). But it is difficult to name families of interventions alongside these
causes and processes.

Applying the principles

How should scientists and technologists apply the 'requirements map'
that is the Ms and Ss, the principles of the CCO and the practical
framework of methods in particular covering situational crime
prevention? Essentially, they must ask of each family of intervention
principles – can my field of expertise contribute to developing or
strengthening this particular set of interventions? Does my field of

expertise currently generate threats to the effectiveness of any of these interventions (e.g. a new portable cutting technology jeopardising existing target-hardening materials and construction)? Will it do so in the future?

Resolving troublesome tradeoffs: a key challenge for science and technology

Retrofitted steering locks exemplify rather narrowly conceived security products, where crime prevention is the top priority. However, the greatest scope and potential exists for designing goods, systems and services that are inherently secure products (such as bus shelters made from resistant material or cars with security functions designed into the engine management computer).[4] But security, protecting against the Ms and delivering the Ss, is just *one* inherent feature which must be incorporated without jeopardising the product's main function or wider usability. Troublesome tradeoffs for crime resistance (Ekblom 2001b) include:

- safety
- liability
- convenience
- reliability
- capital/running costs
- electromagnetic compatibility
- privacy and freedom
- profit
- social inclusion
- sustainable environment
- legal/ethical norms
- design freedom.

The normal response to tradeoffs is to *compromise*. Far better is to make a creative leap. New York fire escapes let residents out while blocking access to burglars by a swing-down mechanism on the last run of stairs, which serves both functions perfectly. New technology, including new materials and sometimes new science, can help relax or unlock such tradeoffs (see Ekblom 1999, 2002). The internal combustion engine ended the tradeoff between armour and mobility – tanks have both. As with engineering science, innovation comes from being equipped with sound theory – and evidence-based principles capable of being applied rationally and combinatorially to many problems, rather than fixed expertise in any one field of technology that could sooner or later be bypassed by offenders (or by military or commercial rivals).

A special challenge comes when a product's criminogenic features are very close to its main *raison d'être*. Consider the mobile phone: its portability, style, convenience and high value make it attractive to legitimate users and thieves alike. There is thus little point in making it heavier and larger to carry off or more complex to use through some demanding security routine – or the very benefit of the product vanishes. The Royal Society of Arts recently had a winner of the Student Design Award 'Less Crime Through Design' competition which demonstrated this to an extreme. A diamond ring is meant to display its value and beauty or it is pointless, but as recent 'Rolex watch' robberies have shown, these features can be highly criminogenic. The winning design involved a rotating platinum housing which hid the diamonds in risky circumstances without looking hideous or inappropriately adding to weight and bulk. Like the anti-cancer drug designed to zap the tumour without zapping the biochemically almost identical body cells, design *in extremis* must be subtle, highly discriminating and based on leading-edge understanding of principles, especially scientific and technological ones.

One key feature of the design against crime *process* is rational design from evidence-based principles, leading to iterations of simulation, prototyping, attack-testing and adjustment. A range of sciences, and especially their methodological and computing aspects, can contribute to this. One current example is the use of virtual reality computer simulation to aid in the planning and communication of street lighting designs. More intriguing possibilities exist with simulated decision-making of groups and networks of (offending and preventing) agents.

Bypassing tradeoffs between crime prevention and other requirements happens most readily if they are considered *simultaneously* during design. More generally, crime-prevention *afterthoughts* or bolt-on security products or secure functions are rarely as resistant to counter-measures, free of drawbacks and cost-effective as those which are designed in, or at least designed as a close fit to the item protected. Sometimes, the cost requirement is only a matter of having the right thought at the right time.

Mapping science and technology

Despite this attempt at a systematic approach, serendipity will always strongly condition our efforts to link STIs with crime – although serendipity favours the prepared mind. But there is one final way of empowering those on the crime reduction side to envisage fields of science, technologies, applications and products – and to help those scientists and technologists who are confined to their single area of specialism. That is to map the entire realm of science and technology. No small task, but one such attempt was recently done for the FSSG by the Home Office Scientific Development Branch.

Conclusion

Crime and its reduction, policing, science, technology and future-scanning are each complex fields of practice and research. The aim in writing this chapter has been to stimulate and assist experts in each field to look some way into the others. The ultimate benefit is our collective success in keeping ahead of crime while doing good, and maybe exciting, science and engineering.

At the time of writing, the FSSG has produced its first six STI reports covering encryption, biometrics, 'lab-on-a-chip', 3G mobile phones, geolocation and electromagnetic imaging (a summary of which is included in the appendix to this paper). These were well-received by the Police Science and Technology Group, and after a review of methodology FSSG is working on the next round. A programme of engagement with the scientific community is also under way through workshops.

Appendix – example of a summary assessment for a scientific and technological innovation: electromagnetic imaging

Overview of innovation: Passive Millimetric Microwave (PMMW) and Gigahertz Imaging

The human body gives off small amounts of energy in the microwave to terahertz spectrum which can be detected remotely without need of a transmitter. Solar energy in this spectrum reflected from objects can also be detected. In this region of the electromagnetic spectrum (the gigahertz region), dry organic materials (like paper or clothing) are fairly transparent, wet organics (like people) fairly opaque and metals shiny and very opaque.

Several passive imaging cameras have been developed that do not need a transmitter to detect objects hidden under clothing etc. With care, this technology can be used to image people in a way that makes concealed objects obvious (For an example see www.parascope.com/articles/1296/imager.htm) – with clear security benefits. Also, microwave radiation can penetrate thin walls, so covert operation is possible. It is also possible to use low-power, people-safe transmitters to obtain enhanced images for detection of concealed weapons etc. at longer ranges and indoors.

Terahertz imaging

At even higher electromagnetic frequencies (shorter wavelength) called terahertz (THz), the visible detail, though not quite as good as in the visible (or X-ray), is enough for potential use for security screening. Terahertz radiation penetrates throughout many visually opaque objects and materials to enough depth to obtain THz-absorbency/ reflectance information inside biological, chemical or complex com-posite objects. Many gases that are characteristic of dangerous chemicals and also explosives show different absorption spectra in the THz spectrum and thus offer the prospect of their detection and identification.

- *Opportunities for law enforcement/crime reduction.* This could provide efficient *shielding* against misuse of weapons thus *safeguarding* against injury, damage or threat thereof. In practice, this means screening in semi-controlled situations, such as airports, public buildings, etc., where weapons or terrorists need to be detected. There is consider-able interest in their potential for longer-range screening, for which ideas are currently under development.
- *Risks of crime.* Criminal *misuse*: as systems become available, undercover police and security operations could be affected by operatives being scanned. Low probability but medium/high seriousness.

- *Countermeasures by offender.* Screening is possible when the subject is aware of the scanning process, in which case the system could detect anomalies resulting from the shielding which would still be useful. Remote imaging makes electromagnetic imaging less vulnerable to countermeasures than physical searches, especially since the suspect may not be aware of being scanned.

- *Counter-countermeasures by crime preventers.* Constant updating of technology, leading to multi-spectral imaging.

- *Risk analysis for introduction of innovation*:
  Credibility of innovation: *High* – though currently only demonstrators from several sources.

Likelihood of innovation: *High* – main issue is speed of image acquisition, but new systems promise TV rates.

Potential impact of innovation: *High* – when affordable systems are available.

- *Related technologies and other conditions necessary to realise the crime reduction opportunity*. Multi-spectral approaches that combine data from visible, IR, X-ray, RF and other imaging modalities could be very effective.

- *Limitations and uncertainties*. Systems are effective in that they have been demonstrated, but are currently large and slow to scan – this is expected to change with technical improvements. Non-metallic weapons, explosives, ceramic knives or other weapons can be seen through clothes, but if weapons were concealed in opaque (metallic) containers only the containers would be visible, though some new ideas for imaging even inside containers are being suggested. Mm waves are non destructive to living cells and tissues generally due to safe, lower-power, non-ionising radiation. In the case of terahertz, further research is required to establish exposure risks.

- *Public acceptability*. Could create difficulties – certain sections of the public may object to 'technological strip-searches', but if handled correctly, they should realise it is part of the 'contract' with the supplier of a service they wish to use (e.g. air transport). At the system level, imaging software can be used so that revealed concealed items can be superimposed on a standard body image for observation and display purposes.

- *Timescale (present/emerging/future)*. MMW systems are running now. Next two years for PMMW, demonstrators available today. Terahertz is further away – systems in five years depending on demand.

- *Response/intervention*. Maintain a watching brief on research, industry and existing bodies, especially those currently aiming towards production devices in the UK and abroad, with a view to engagement when equipment is available to establish optimum use.

- *Summary*. This is an emergent technology whose value to crime reduction could be great. Crime risks are limited but not entirely absent.

Acknowledgements

Thanks to colleagues on the Future Scanning Sub-Group of the Police Science and Technology Group for encouragement, willing use of the scanning framework, critical and constructive collaboration in its evolution and permission to use the example summary report. Particular thanks to Alan Pratt, chair of the Sub-Group, and Lawrence Singer, both of the UK Home Office, for substantial input in initiating the framework.

Notes

1   The quote given here is taken from the 2003–2008 version of the Strategy. See http://www.policereform.gov.uk/implementation/ scienceandtech.html for both this and the updated 2004–2009 version.
2   Membership currently includes representatives of the Scientific Development Branch, the Research, Development and Statistics Directorate and the Science Policy Unit of the Home Office; the Police Information Technology Organisation, the Forensic Science Service, the Royal Academy of Engineering, the Royal Society, the Association of Chief Police Officers, the Police Superintendents' Association, the Police Federation, Unison, the Office of Science and Technology of the Department for Trade and Industry, and the Engineering and Physical Sciences Research Council.
3   See http://www.policereform.gov.uk/implementation/ scienceandtech.html.
     Repeated unchanged in the 2004–2009 Strategy at paragraph 24.
4   Case studies are at www.designagainstcrime.org – click on 'Resources' then 'Case studies'.

References

Brantingham, P. and Brantingham, P. (1995) 'Criminality of place: crime generators and crime attractors', *European Journal on Criminal Policy and Research*, 3 (3): 5–26.

Clarke, R. (1999) *Hot Products: Understanding, Anticipating and Reducing Demand for Stolen Goods*, Police Research Series Papers 112. London: Home Office.

Clarke, R. and Eck, J. (2003) *Become a Problem-Solving Crime Analyst in 55 Small Steps*. Available at: http://www.jdi.ucl.ac.uk/publications/manual/ crime_manual_content.php.

Cohen, L. and Felson, M. (1979) 'Social change and crime rate changes: a routine activities approach', *American Sociological Review*, 44: 588–608.

Cohen, L., Vila, B. and. Machalek, R. (1995) 'Expropriative crime and crime policy: an evolutionary ecological analysis', *Studies on Crime and Crime Prevention*, 4 (2): 197–219.

Cornish, D. (1994). 'The procedural analysis of offending and its relevance for situational prevention', in R.V. Clarke (ed.), *Crime Prevention Studies*, Vol. 3. Monsey, NY: Criminal Justice Press, pp. 151–196.

Cornish, D. and Clarke, R. (1986) *The Reasoning Criminal*. New York: Springer-Verlag.

Cornish, D. and Clarke, R. (2002) 'Analyzing organised crimes', in A. Piquero and S. Tibbetts (eds), *Rational Choice*. New York: Garland, pp. 41–63.

DTI (2000) *Turning the Corner*, Report of the Foresight Programme's Crime Prevention Panel. London: Department of Trade and Industry. Downloadable from http://www.foresight.gov.uk/servlet/Controller?action=eipndisplaymenuarea&id=528.

Ekblom, P. (1997) 'Gearing up against crime: a dynamic framework to help designers keep up with the adaptive criminal in a changing world', *International Journal of Risk, Security and Crime Prevention*, 214: 249–265. Available at www.homeoffice.gov.uk/rds/pdfs/risk.pdf.

Ekblom, P. (1999) 'Can we make crime prevention adaptive by learning from other evolutionary struggles?', *Studies on Crime and Crime Prevention*, 8 (1): 27–51. Available at http://www.bra.se/extra/studies (under 'välj år' choose 1999).

Ekblom, P. (2001a) 'The conjunction of criminal opportunity: a framework for crime reduction toolkits'. Crime reduction website at: www.crimereduction.gov.uk/learningzone/cco.htm.

Ekblom, P. (2001b) *Less Crime, by Design*. Illustrated website version of paper presented at Royal Society of Arts, London, October 2000. Available at: www.e-doca.net/Resources/Lectures/Less%20Crime%20by%20Design.htm

Ekblom, P. (2002) 'From the source to the mainstream is uphill: the challenge of transferring knowledge of crime prevention through replication, innovation and anticipation', in N. Tilley (ed.), *Analysis for Crime Prevention*, Crime Prevention Studies, Vol. 13. Monsey, NY: Criminal Justice Press/Cullompton, UK: Willan Publishing, pp. 131–203.

Ekblom, P. (2003) 'Organised crime and the conjunction of criminal opportunity framework', in A. Edwards and P. Gill (eds), *Transnational Organised Crime: Perspectives on Global Security*. London: Routledge, pp. 241–263.

Ekblom, P. and Tilley, N. (2000) 'Going equipped: criminology, situational crime prevention and the resourceful offender', *British Journal of Criminology*, 40: 376–398.

Newman, R. and Clarke, R.V. (2003) *Superhighway Robbery, Preventing E-commerce crime*. Cullompton, Devon and Portland, Oregon: Willan Publishing.

Sutton, M. (1998). *Handling Stolen Goods and Theft: A Market Reduction Approach*, Home Office Research Study 178. London: Home Office.

Sutton, M. (2001) *Tackling Theft with the Market Reduction Approach*, Crime Reduction Research Series Paper 8. London: Home Office.

Chapter 3

Cost-benefit analysis for crime science: making cost-benefit analysis useful through a portfolio of outcomes

Graham Farrell,[1] Kate J. Bowers[2] and Shane D. Johnson[3]

Introduction

Cost-benefit analysis (CBA) is a technique used in most areas of public policy research including health, economics and engineering. It is becoming increasingly commonplace in crime prevention and criminal justice research, and is increasingly influential in policy-making. The Home Office mandated that all evaluations for its recent multi-year nationwide Crime Reduction Programme should incorporate cost-benefit analysis. The Home Office developed guides for evaluators to follow that encourage standardisation of method (Dhiri and Brand 1999; Legg and Powell 2000; Colledge *et al.* 1999). Similar guidance materials have been produced by the Canadian government (Hornick *et al.* 2000) and the Office of Juvenile Justice and Delinquency Prevention of the US Department of Justice (Juvenile Justice Evaluation Center 2002). The European Community recently funded cost-benefit analysis of police traffic enforcement (Elvik 2001). As of mid-2004, the first in the list of the guiding principles of the National Institute of Justice of the US Department of Justice is to 'Emphasize outcome and cost-benefit evaluations of criminal justice programs and technologies' (National Institute of Justice 2004). Estimating the costs of crime and using CBA in the evaluation of criminal justice is pursued by the New Zealand Ministry of Justice (MacCallum 1997) and the Australian Institute of Criminology (Roche 1999; Chisholm 2000; AIC 2003a, 2003b; Mayhew 2003) among others. All indicators suggest the influence of CBA in the development of crime policy will continue to increase significantly.

There has been rapid methodological progress in CBA in recent years. Significant innovation in the measurement of the intangible costs of crime (Cohen 1988; Miller *et al.* 1996) and other areas (see Cohen 2000 for a review) has spurred the inclusion of 'intangibles' in the most recent quasi-experimental evaluation research (Painter and Farrington 1999, 2001). The measurement of the costs of crime has major implications for policy-makers in many areas including crime prevention, sentencing and offender treatment policies. The reason is that, if the cost of crime is greater than previously thought, then crime prevention has commensurately greater value. For example, the high-profile debate over the value of life that pervades some areas of public policy in the United States (Seelye and Tierney 2003; Hahn and Wallsten 2003) has potential implications for criminal justice programmes addressing murder and its prevention. More generally, there are implications for resource allocation within crime-related areas of policy as well as between various areas of public policy. If the aggregate cost of crime is higher than thought, funds that previously went to defence, transport, health, education or other tax-spending policies might be better spent on crime control. Hence, while the debate surrounding cost-benefit evaluation may appear solely technical to some readers, it is of potentially profound importance for the future of government.

Previous CBAs

Brandon Welsh and David Farrington have recently reviewed cost-benefit analyses of situational crime prevention projects, child development programmes and correctional treatment programmes (Welsh and Farrington 1999, 2000). Their extensive literature searches identified only 13 situational crime prevention studies and nine correctional treatment studies. Though some studies will have been published in the interim, the reviews are a landmark in the literature as they provide a snapshot of what existed to that point. The reviews find little standardisation in either the identification or measurement of cost items. Few evaluations include estimates of the intangible costs of crime. Some evaluations, such as that of the Kirkholt burglary project (Forrester *et al.* 1988, 1990), include the benefit from 'saved' police labour that is not spent investigating burglaries that were prevented, while most crime prevention evaluations exclude such cost items (but note that for the Kirkholt project, the benefits still significantly outweigh costs even when police time is excluded).[4] Few studies included the benefits from potential long-run returns that accrue from interventions that would have an effect for many years. Similarly, there are few cost-benefit evaluations that include measures of displacement or anticipation and diffused benefits (Smith *et al.* 2002; Bowers and Johnson 2003), phenomena described later. To some extent, these issues reflect the changing state of knowledge but the more recent evaluations were not always more inclusive or sophisticated. Exceptionally, Painter and Farrington's series of cost-benefit evaluations of street lighting incorporates intangible costs, displacement and diffusion effects, and estimates of short and long-run returns (Painter and Farrington 1999, 2001).

Farrington and Welsh's reviews draw conclusions that are disarmingly understated. The studies reviewed are, on the surface, comparable via the common metric of a benefit-cost ratio. However, it is clear that those ratios were derived from radically different measures and methods relating to varying cost items. It is also clear that there were so few studies that their aggregated findings are not self-evidently representative of interventions in either of the two fields. Possibly to avoid appearing to criticise CBA itself, Farrington and Welsh expertly avoid concluding that little is known, and that what is known is uncertain. However, most readers will reasonably conclude that the discipline of CBA was floundering, characterised by an absence of studies and inconsistent methods and measures, and that CBA had made at best a minor contribution in the fields of crime prevention and correctional treatment.

Cost-benefit analysis has been used in other areas of criminal justice. It has been used in policing (see, for example, Stockdale *et al.* 1999), in the assessment of drug policy (Caulkins 2000), in a series of drug court evaluations (Roman and Harrell 2001; Harrell *et al.* 2000), in the assessment of developmental child improvement programmes (Greenwood *et al.* 1996 – see Nagin 2001 for a review), in the assessment of a broad spectrum of crime policies (Aos *et al.* 2001) and in a variety of ad hoc evaluations of policies and programmes including a range of road safety efforts (ICF Consulting Ltd 2003) and in assessing the cost-effectiveness of speed cameras and traffic lights (Hooke *et al.* 1996). Evaluations that relate to harm, suffering and quality of life such as housing, health and education can contain some crime-related element. In other crime-related areas there are few reviews of the rigour of those conducted by Farrington and Welsh for situational crime prevention and correctional treatment. However, it is likely that, with the honourable exception of some of the more recent studies cited above, the rather negative conclusions are broadly applicable.

Broadly speaking, policy-relevant knowledge deriving from CBA is the exception rather than the rule in relation to crime and criminal justice. The paucity of relevant studies perhaps reflects the problems of methodology besetting CBA. Certainly in the experience of the present authors, this evaluation tool is frequently viewed with scepticism when applied in criminology. To paraphrase, we have variously heard CBA for crime prevention and criminal justice described as incomprehensible, misleading, open to widespread abuse or even intrinsically useless.

Diverse explanations can be offered as to why CBA remains underutilised. Perhaps few criminologists have the methodological expertise to undertake the exercise – this is certainly a concern of some economists who view CBA as their rightful property. However, accessible guides such as that of Dhiri and Brand (1999) can bring CBA to a fairly broad criminological audience. Second, CBA methodology has been rapidly evolving in relation to the costs of crime, potentially leaving many previous CBAs vulnerable to questions regarding the accuracy of their method. Third, perhaps results presented as a single benefit-cost ratio are inadvertently, or perhaps wilfully, misinterpreted by sectional interests so that even rigorous CBAs remain underutilised. Greater methodological transparency in the development and presentation of results may help overcome these difficulties. The solution proposed herein is a limited portfolio of benefit-cost ratio outcome measures. A set of measures will allow different audiences with different needs to identify either the outcome measure most suited to their needs or to identify the range of estimates with parameters most suited to informing their policy-relevant decision. A portfolio could allow consumers of CBA to look at variation in the benefit-cost ratio according to whether or not intangible costs of crime are included, whether or not local or national cost estimates are used, whether or not 'saved' criminal justice costs are included, whether or not displacement, diffusion and anticipatory benefits are included, and for different anticipated rates of return over time with varying discount rates.

The mathematics of multiple outcomes

The term 'limited' portfolio is used because although several benefit-cost ratios are advocated, they constitute only a small subset of those possible. This can be illustrated via a simple thought experiment.

Consider that, in addition to some fixed capital cost, there are six cost items which can each take one of two values. One item, intangible costs, can be either included or excluded from the analysis (perhaps by an insurer who wants to concentrate solely on financial costs). Another item is displacement costs that can be either included or excluded, and so on for the other variables in our hypothetical example. Each of our six variables can be used in one of two ways, so there are 2^6 or 64 permutations of benefit-cost ratios to be calculated. However, if each cost item had three possible values, the number of permutations is 3^6 or 729 benefit-cost ratios. With multiple continuous variables and confidence intervals, the number of possible benefit-cost ratios rises exponentially. The theoretical maximal case would approximate to infinity for all practical purposes. In practice, therefore, there is a trade-off to be reached. The optimal portfolio should enhance transparency and allow a broad range of discerning readers with different interests greater information on which to base a decision. Increasing the amount of information available for decision-making is, after all, the aim of cost-benefit analysis.

It is not inconceivable that some insight, however limited, into the possible range of benefit-cost ratios is what causes scepticism among some consumers of CBA when presented with a single benefit-cost ratio. This can be characterised as the 'It just doesn't feel quite right' syndrome. Without necessarily being familiar with specific methodologies or the intricacies of the particular calculation, many consumers of CBA have a strong intuition that, with so many variables and uncertainties, no single benefit-cost ratio can be appropriate.

Given an impossibly large number of benefit-cost ratios, a limited portfolio (nine main variables are discussed below) seems a modest enterprise. Note, however, the contrast to the other theoretical limiting case which has become a widely accepted norm, that is the presentation of a single benefit-cost ratio measure.

For many of the parameters discussed below, the question regarding their inclusion or exclusion can intentionally be made into a moot point by the provision of cost-benefit information for both points of view. This is preferable not only because it allows highly opinionated readers to view the outcome from their particular perspective, but it gives transparency regarding the influence of particular variables and allows the same readers to view the results from alternative positions. Hence the provision of more information promotes transparency and, it is hoped, would facilitate a more informed debate of the relevant issues.

The thesis: a portfolio of benefit-cost ratios

This section describes key variables that we propose warrant consideration in a portfolio of benefit-cost ratio outcome measures. It briefly reviews issues that make them contentious and which mean they are sometimes included in, sometimes excluded from, the presentation of benefit-cost ratios. The portfolio discussed here, as with the case study that follows, is anchored primarily in the specific field of crime reduction. With a crime reduction backdrop, the set of variables discussed below are neither exhaustive nor directly applicable to all criminal justice evaluations (since they will vary in their specifics). We anticipate that other variables will warrant consideration in other fields. However, the notion of a portfolio of outcomes is of general application.

John Roman of the Urban Institute has identified concerns akin to those discussed herein (Roman 2004). Roman demonstrated how different impact evaluation methodologies can significantly influence outputs and outcomes. He compares the effect of changing comparison group, sample sizes and statistical analysis model (using examples for in-prison treatment evaluations where various statistical control models could be selected). Roman finds that 'Clearly, the cost-benefit model can yield wildly divergent results depending on what approach was taken' (Roman 2004: 260). However, arguably Roman's most sparkling observation is that particular rare events, such as some violent crimes (rape, murder), can sometimes wholly distort a CBA. This is due to the sheer magnitude of monetary equivalence that such crimes generate. For example, Miller *et al.* (1996: 9) estimate the 'average' murder costs $2.94 million whereas the average burglary costs $1,400, making a murder 2,100 times more costly. Similar, though perhaps less exaggerated, effects can occur if a lesser crime is, for whatever reason, reclassified as a more serious event. John Roman writes:

> By moving a single crime from a felony to a serious felony, the direction and magnitude of the cost-benefit results can be fundamentally changed. Such is the power of the rare event (Roman 2004: 267)

Roman's work also helps clarify the distinction between CBA influences that are determined at the stage of impact evaluation and those determined at subsequent stages of cost estimation for CBA. There is an important distinction between impact evaluation issues and pure cost-estimation issues. In the present study, the impact evaluation issues discussed are displacement, diffusion, anticipatory benefits, the confidence intervals around the impact size and the number of years over which crime prevention returns are estimated. Their inclusion or exclusion changes the perceived impact of the programme, which then subsequently play a role in the CBA. In contrast, those issues relating to input cost measurement, intangible costs, emotional costs and the cost of averted criminal justice expenditures are pure cost-benefit issues. To put this another way, the pure cost-benefit issues are not relevant to an impact evaluation while the impact evaluation issues will remain even in the absence of a CBA. In what follows, the issues are grouped into these two types.

Issues deriving from impact evaluation technique

Displacement and diffusion of benefits
Two areas in which the issue of agents is of major importance for many criminal justice evaluations are the diffusion of preventive benefits (Clarke and Weisburd 1994) and crime displacement (see Barr and Pease 1990; Eck 1993; Hesseling 1994; Hamilton-Smith 2003). Displacement refers to how crime can move elsewhere or adapt in the wake of preventive action, even if at a lower intensity. Diffusion generally refers to how crime in other areas or of other types is reduced as a positive knock-on effect of preventive action. When it comes to a burglary reduction initiative such as that discussed below, different agents are apparent. Local residents are primarily concerned with reducing the rate of burglary where they live. Displacement is, for them, a matter of little direct concern. Similarly, diffusion of benefits (knock-on reductions in burglary in neighbouring areas) is irrelevant to them unless they can charge a fee to neighbouring residential communities, or get the neighbouring areas to return the favour. For the local police, and perhaps local and national governments, politicians and community agencies, the concerns are different. They are more concerned with aggregate effects, that is, all such knock-on effects combined. Yet police and government will have geographical limits to their interests. They will be far more interested if they are paying for the initiative since they want to determine the returns to the investment. Hence, the judgement whether either, neither or both of displacement and the diffusion of benefits provides essential information lies in the eye of the beholder. We here distinguish diffusion and displacement as variables measured separately from input and other costs. The presentation of results with and without these items is desirable because it conveys information in a way which speaks to the interests of the different parties involved. Distinguishing between types of diffusion and displacement also allows

an informed assessment of the geographical and other variations in outcomes.

Anticipatory benefits
One further issue which is noteworthy here is a recently identified phenomenon known as *anticipatory benefit* (Smith *et al.* 2002). This occurs where reductions in crime occur in an action area in advance of preventive activity on the ground. A variety of reasons exist why such a pattern may emerge, but the most convincing explanation is that pre-scheme publicity generates a deterrent effect, discouraging offenders from committing crime in the area (see Bowers and Johnson, 2003). The importance of this finding for evaluation research relates to the selection of the units of time (before and after) used to assess impact. Where this phenomenon occurs, when estimating outcomes, is it accurate to use an historic period of time which encapsulates the anticipatory epoch? This is debatable, but the authors suggest not, as it would have the effect of lowering the baseline crime rate, thereby making any quantification of outcome more conservative. If anticipatory benefits are a direct result of an intervention, however, there is a strong argument for making them available as an aspect of the overall outcome measure.

Sustainability and returns over time?
One matter considered too infrequently in crime reduction and criminal justice research is sustainability. How long will a set of crime reduction measures maintain an impact? Will security measures fall into disuse or disrepair? Will this be a gradual decay in impact over time or a sudden one-off drop? Many quasi-experimental evaluations have fairly arbitrary 'before' and 'after' periods, typically of one year or two years. In reality, however, many interventions will have a continuing effect beyond the formal evaluation period. This can lead to an underestimation of benefits. The issue of returns over time can also be problematic when a significant capital investment has been made towards the end of a project, since the time-constraint is particularly acute.

Returns over time is primarily an issue relating to impact evaluation. However, in the present context it can be considered as a benefit-cost issue because of the role of discounting in the calculation (and so it is presented as a benefit-cost issue in Table 3.1). Discounting is an issue relevant to cost-benefit analysis which is typically not incorporated in impact evaluations. Discounting, in brief, refers to the fact that we have a preference for immediacy or a 'rate of time preference' (returns in the future are worth less so that, even with zero inflation, a pound this year is worth more than a pound in five years) as well as the fact that the interest rate means present values are greater than future values because the pound could be invested (see, for example, Gramlich 1997).

It would be useful for evaluations to generate benefit-cost ratios that incorporate potential long-run returns. The best example of such an analysis is that by Painter and Farrington (1999, 2001) in their work on street lighting. They produced benefit-cost ratios showing returns within one year, but also for a 20-year period (the estimated lifetime of the lighting). The 20-year estimate incorporated maintenance and running costs as well as discounting the value of future returns.

Are there confidence intervals?
Many 'results' in social science are estimates which embody some degree of uncertainty or imprecision. There is usually some possibility, however slight, that an outcome occurred other than the one that is our 'best estimate'. A typical means of reducing such uncertainty is the use of confidence intervals. Confidence intervals give results as a range rather than a point-estimate. The spread is key: a narrow range gives greater certainty than a broad range. While a range may seem more imprecise, in fact there is greater precision derived from the reduced uncertainty. Using the typical confidence intervals of 95%, the reader can be 95% certain that the actual outcome lies somewhere between the upper and lower boundaries. Yet relatively few crime reduction or other criminal justice evaluations produce confidence intervals that circumscribe their main outcome estimates. Since policy-makers and others are more informed in so far as they know the degree of certainty with which findings can be viewed, there is a strong argument for the production of confidence intervals which can, in a fashion akin to sensitivity analysis, become confidence intervals around a benefit-cost ratio.

Pure cost estimation issues

Who pays input costs? Who receives benefits?
We begin with the well-known and uncontroversial issue of the existence of multiple agents (touched on above in relation to displacement and diffusion). Society overall may benefit from an initiative even if those paying the costs do not. Is this a desirable outcome? A region could benefit from a major road funded by a particular city within it, even though the city itself makes a significant loss (Boardman *et al.* 1996). What if a private firm could introduce security that would benefit society as a whole but which would not have

much benefit for the firm? For example, a company may not find it profitable to produce a safer product even though its production would reduce crime. In such instances, the benefit-cost ratio that the company is examining is different from that which 'society as a whole' is examining. The producer ignores costs from crime if, say, their products are frequently stolen hot-products. Society is forced to count such crime costs, which are arguably a form of pollution like any other (see Roman and Farrell 2002 for further discussion on crime pollution). Such examples illustrate the virtues of presenting both (or more) sets of benefit-cost ratios that incorporate more than one viewpoint. Typically this does not occur, the evaluation in consequence reflecting only the perspective of the funding agent.

National or local costs?
Local crime reduction schemes will incur costs which vary according to area characteristics. Labour costs are frequently an important component of many projects, but vary hugely from one place to another. Paying a carpenter to secure households in north Manchester may be a significantly different monetary undertaking in south Wales or central London. Consider either particularly affluent or poor areas in which the average cost of a burglary is radically different from the national average: the potential returns might be significantly different elsewhere. There is thus an argument for the costing of items to, at minimum, both local and national average costs where available. This is easier for some cost items than for others. National estimates of the cost of crime are readily available and produced by the Home Office (see Brand and Price 2000), and so it should be a relatively straightforward matter to provide benefit-cost estimates that utilise local and national estimates.

While this is clearly within the realms of traditional sensitivity analysis within cost-benefit analysis, the specific instance of the costs of crime is particularly relevant to crime reduction and criminal justice evaluations. It is most appropriate where local costs vary significantly from national cost estimates in a fashion that could significantly affect the overall benefit-cost ratio. In short, however, providing benefit-cost ratios that include both local and national cost estimates where available may prove a relatively simple means of providing information to audiences with different demands.

Should intangible costs be included?
A key issue arising in CBA for criminal justice in recent years has been the estimation of intangible costs. Intangible costs include emotional and psychological costs. For some crimes such as car theft, the intangible

cost is typically low both in absolute terms and relative to the financial cost and short-lived in duration. For crimes such as rape and murder, however, the intangible costs are often huge (financial costs also often being significant) and enduring. There are two main areas of contention: the first is whether or not intangible costs *should* be estimated, and the second, if the answer to the first is in the affirmative, is *how* to produce accurate estimates.

Most previous studies do not include intangible costs simply because these have not been available for very long and because, like many new developments, they encountered some initial resistance. There is now decreasing scepticism regarding whether or not intangible costs should be estimated. Even victim advocates who initially had a knee-jerk reaction against putting a monetary value on pain and suffering have come to recognise that it is far worse to exclude such costs from evaluation exercises. To exclude them is to exclude a major part of the experience of the victims of crime. Further, exclusion of such costs means that the cost of an average burglary appears to be more than the cost of a rape – from most perspectives an indefensible position. However, when recent intangible cost estimates are included, rape is, as a statistical average, 62 times more costly than burglary (Roman and Farrell 2002: 82). This seems more tenable. It is also readily apparent that society already places a value on pain and suffering when it estimates victim compensation awards (e.g. Michigan Judicial Institute 2001). Yet there is still some understandable revulsion about placing a monetary value on rape for the impersonal purposes of cost-benefit analysis. Indeed, perhaps the only thing worse than placing a value on pain and suffering is not to do so, since this implies the default value of zero. The more intricate methodological arguments are that 'monetary value' is really only a proxy for 'utility units' (so we are not really using a monetary value at all), and that statistical averages are clearly not intended to reflect individual experience.

How to estimate intangible costs is a tricky methodological issue. Estimation methodologies are arguably in their early stages, with a need for much further research to provide competition for pioneering estimates of intangible costs such as those of Cohen (1988) and Miller *et al.* (1996). There is also a need for greater investigation of the range and confidence intervals of costs estimates and how they apply to different populations and contexts.

Although this has been only a very brief review of issues relating to intangible costs, and we do not conclude that all issues have been resolved, the key purpose of the present exercise is to propose a practical remedy, namely to make results available both with and without intangible costs. The consumer of CBA may thereby examine the variation in the results.

Criminal justice costs?

The case can be made for either the inclusion or exclusion of 'saved' criminal justice costs. The argument for their inclusion is that, if crime is prevented, then there are no police costs responding to and investigating the crime, and no subsequent criminal justice costs for those cases that would otherwise be formally processed. These costs could include prosecution, court and prison or other sentencing-related costs for that proportion of cases which result in an arrest, charges and further case processing.

Many evaluations exclude criminal justice costs, reasoning that no costs would be saved. The number of crimes prevented for any small-scale project is, relative to the overall number of crimes, so trivial that police and other criminal justice costs remain the same: the police do not employ less labour or equipment and the criminal justice system does not shrink or save any costs. Yet there is also a case for their inclusion since, if small-scale demonstration projects are extended and produced the same results then, it could be argued, they would have a significant impact upon subsequent policing and criminal justice costs. To exclude such costs could be said to be similar to arguing that crime, or any set of local crimes, does not produce any criminal justice costs. A simple means to accommodate both sides of the coin, and to view the overall effect of criminal justice costs, is to present benefit-cost ratios with and without this cost item.

Promoting consumer choice

Based upon the discussion of the variables above, the possible number of permutations of outcome measures is horrendously large. The task, therefore, is to develop an optimal set or portfolio of outcome measures that conveys the maximum amount of information in a transparent way and allows readers with different needs and perspectives to consider the most appropriate measures from their perspective.

In a world of increasing computerisation, the case can easily be made for a spreadsheet-type application that allows users to select parameters and to include or exclude various cost items. Table 3.1 shows a simplified set of relevant variables and how they might vary in such an application. It is, of course, far easier to say this than to do it, as the reader will recognise in the case study that follows where we do not

Table 3.1 A user-specified benefit-cost ratio

A. Key impact evaluation influences

1. Include displacement costs:
   a. Within project area
      i. Targeted crime-type only
      ii. Other crime-types
   b. In other areas
      i. Targeted crime-type only
      ii. Other crime-types
   c. Other (as appropriate)

2. Include diffusion of benefits:
   a. Within project area
      i. Targeted crime-type only
      ii. Other crime-types
   b. In other areas
      i. Targeted crime-type only
      ii. Other crime-types
   c. Other (as appropriate)

3. Include anticipatory benefits:
   a. Targeted crime-type only
   b. Other (as appropriate)

4. Select confidence intervals for measure of impact
   a. 95%
   b. Other (please specify)

B. Pure cost-estimation issues

5. Select input costs:
   a. Local
   b. National
   c. Other (as appropriate)

6. Select cost of crime estimate:
   a. Local cost of crime
   b. National cost of crime
   c. Other (as appropriate)

7. Include intangible costs (Yes/No)

8. Criminal justice costs:
   a. Include 'saved' police time (Yes/No)
   b. Include other 'saved' cost items (Yes/No)
   c. Other (as appropriate)

9. Returns over time
   a. Select number of years for returns
   b. Using discounting rate x (advised value within range 3–6).

---

necessarily reach all of the goals specified in this more abstract discussion.

Case study in Midtown[5]

The Midtown scheme was part of the national Reducing Burglary Initiative (RBI) which itself was a component of the Crime Reduction Programme initiated in 1999 by the Home Office. Other components of the programme included efforts to tackle domestic violence, to develop targeted (problem-oriented) policing and to evaluate the impact upon crime of closed-circuit television. The RBI was a nationwide effort evaluated by three regional consortia (see Kodz and Pease 2003 for an overview of national-level findings). The data presented here is from one project in the northern region. Results from the analysis have been presented elsewhere (e.g. Johnson *et al.* 2001; Johnson *et al.* 2004; Bowers *et al.* 2004). The interested reader is referred to those outlets for more general information as the focus of the present study is primarily upon the identification and development of benefit-cost ratio outcome measures.

This case study illustrates the limited portfolio of measures with data for one of the Reducing Burglary Initiative schemes undertaken in the area of Midtown. The scheme was selected as one for which detailed cost data and crime reduction outcomes were available. The need to select a scheme on this basis highlights the fact that the collection and collation of the range of necessary data is not necessarily straightforward: extensive data collection can be a tricky and costly research activity. Indeed, there is an irony in the possibility that, for low-budget evaluation research in an atmosphere of scepticism regarding CBA, it may not appear cost-effective to conduct a cost-benefit analysis!

The Midtown scheme undertook four different interventions:

- installation of household target-hardening security;
- an educational scheme to promote appropriate use of target-hardening measures by householders;
- the installation of other situational measures in the local environment, primarily alley-gating (that is large gates to close off paths used by burglars); and
- offender-based strategies (intelligence-led operations and disruption of the stolen goods market).

Input costs

The overall 'crude' cost of the scheme was £142,415 which was composed of £28,173 funding from the Reducing Burglary Initiative and the remainder from levered-in sources. This was converted to a common price base at a common point in time (that is April 1999), incorporating the time for which capital assets were utilised and their expected lifespan. After these adjustments, the overall economic costs of the scheme were £109,131. This allowed the use of a simple before-and-after approach to calculating burglary outcomes rather than having to account for phased implementation. Expenditures upon components of the preventive effort are detailed in Table 3.2.

Table 3.2 Input costs for Midtown burglary reduction scheme

Inputs	Cost (£)
Household target-hardening	23,699
Educational scheme for householders	89,678
Other situational measures (alley-gating)	22,595
Intelligence operations and market-disruption efforts	6,443
Total input cost	142,415
Total input cost converted to April 1999 prices	109,131

Costs of burglary

The value to society of a prevented burglary is a necessary component of the CBA. The national average cost to society of burglary in a dwelling in England and Wales was £2,344 in the year 1999, the components of which are shown in Table 3.3 which is derived from the estimates of Brand and Price (2000: viii). As the most comprehensive of such estimates currently available this estimate is used in the cost-benefit calculations that follow.

In the calculation of net benefits and benefit-cost ratios that follows, the cost of burglary was varied to account for possible different perspectives. Three measures are used: benefit measure 1 (BM1) of £2,344 being the total as shown in Table 3.4. Benefit measure 2 excludes £550 equivalent of emotional and physical costs. This was the closest proxy to the exclusion of intangible costs that could be generated. Benefit measure 2 therefore uses £1,794 as the value of each burglary prevented. Benefit measure 3 excludes, in addition, criminal justice and police costs estimated at £490, giving a value of £1,304 for BM3.

Outcomes

Impact evaluation and confidence intervals

The scheme was operational between September 1999 and September 2001. The outcome evaluation estimated that 308 burglaries were prevented over the two-year period. To increase reliability, this point-estimate of burglaries prevented was set within statistical confidence intervals. The upper and lower 95% confidence intervals set the number of burglaries as between 262 and 355 (for the calculation of the confidence intervals see Johnson *et al.* 2004). Including low or high

Table 3.3 Components of the estimated cost of a burglary

Item	Cost (£)
Property stolen and damaged	830
Emotional and physical	550
Criminal justice system (including police)	490
Security expenditure	330
Insurance administration	100
Lost output	40
Victim services	4
Health services	0
Total	2,344

Source: Brand and Price (2000).

Table 3.4 Impact measures and benefit measures used to derive limited portfolio of outcomes

Measure	Description	Estimate
Impact measure 1 (IM1)	Burglary prevented in scheme area	Mean = 308
Impact measure 1 (IM1)	IM1 plus net displacement/diffusion effect of 37 further burglaries prevented	345
Impact measure 1 (IM1)	IM2 plus net anticipatory benefit effect of 419 further burglaries prevented	764
Benefit measure 1 (BM1)	All burglary cost items shown in Table 3.3	£2,344
Benefit measure 2 (BM1)	IM1 excluding emotional and physical cost of £550	£1,794
Benefit measure 3 (BM1)	IM2 excluding criminal justice or police costs of £490	£1,304

estimates of outcome changes the magnitude of the benefit-cost ratios by 15% in either direction. For presentational simplicity, the confidence intervals are not shown in the main tables of net benefits or benefit-cost ratios as table size would triple. However, in reading those tables the reader should be aware that confidence intervals of 15% either side apply to the findings.

Displacement and diffusion

In the calculation of net benefits and benefit-cost ratios, three impact measures are used. Impact measure 1 (IM1) is the 308 burglaries prevented in the project area as described in the previous paragraph. Impact measure 2 (IM2) includes the net effect of displacement and diffusion. The net effect of displacement and the diffusion of benefits within the two years of the project was estimated to be an additional 37 burglaries prevented. When added to the 308 burglaries prevented in the project area, total burglaries prevented is 345 for impact measure 2. The anticipatory benefits generated by this project were estimated to be 419 additional burglaries prevented. Impact measure 3 (IM3) is equal to IM2 plus burglaries prevented due to the anticipation effect, for a total of 764 burglaries prevented over the two years of the project.

Returns over time

Three scenarios of returns over time were identified for the CBA. The first scenario is the two years of the project period discussed above. The impact evaluation found that 136 burglaries were prevented in year 1 and 172 in year 2 for the total of 308 over two years. There is some justification for this time-limited estimate of returns that is restricted to the duration of the project's funding period. In reality, however, the crime prevention impact would continue after the cessation of project funding. Locks, bolts, alley-gating and other security measures would continue to be used, and the education components would arguably continue to influence householders. Even if the project's police intelligence operations ceased to operate, they would have a residual effect if offenders continued to be deterred, remained incarcerated or had been nudged into desistance.

To reflect the anticipated longer lifespan of the crime reduction tactics, two further scenarios of returns over time were developed. In the second scenario, burglary continued to be prevented after the two years of the project, but at a declining rate of 10% of the original prevention rate per year. That is, the number of burglaries prevented fell from 172 by 17.2 burglaries in year 3, a further 17.2 in year 4, and so on until no more burglaries were prevented after year 11 (nine years into the future). A total of 1,082 burglaries were prevented in this scenario. Using a discounting rate of 6% the estimated total benefit from prevented burglaries ranged from £1.2m to £2.1m depending upon the value of a saved burglary that was used.

In the third returns scenario, burglary was prevented at the same rate as year 2 for a further nine years (which, although a somewhat arbitrary duration, facilitates some comparison between the second and third estimates). A total of 1,856 burglaries were prevented in this scenario. Applying a discounting rate of 6%, the estimated total benefit from prevented burglaries ranged from £4.8m to £8.6m depending upon the value of a saved burglary that was used.

Although the third scenario could be suggested to be that of an extreme optimist, Painter and Farrington (1999) assumed that crime was prevented at the same rate for 20 years. This was the anticipated lifespan of the street lighting in their experiment. While locks and bolts may fall into disuse and disrepair more rapidly than routinely maintained street lighting, it is not unfeasible that they have an extremely long lifespan in some instances. Lifetime guarantees are not uncommon for locks and other security hardware, and the lifespan of many locks will be limited only by the durability of their wooden frames.

The portfolio of benefit-cost ratios

The main variables from which the portfolio of measures were generated have been described above. The variation in the estimate of the value of a saved burglary was the benefit measures BM1, BM2 and BM3. Three impact measures were described, IM1, IM2 and IM3, and the three scenarios relating to returns over time were defined.

Table 3.4 shows a summary of the impact measures and benefit measures. Table 3.5 shows the set of net benefits from which the benefit-cost ratios shown in Table 3.6 are calculated (after the division of each total benefit estimate by the total project cost of £109,131). Recall that the 95% confidence intervals around the net benefit and benefit-cost ratios are not shown and would be 15% either side of the values in Tables 3.5 and 3.6.

There is a 21-fold variation in the benefit-cost ratio between the highest (78.75) and lowest (3.68) estimates. This is considerable. As with Painter and Farrington's findings relating to street lighting, it is the estimated extent of returns over time that appears to have the most major effect. Within the benefit-cost ratios relating solely to returns within the two years of the project, the highest estimate (16.41) is over four times the value of the lowest estimate (3.68).

Table 3.5 Multiple estimates of net benefits

	Benefit measure 1 (£2,344 per burglary)	Benefit measure 2 (£1,794 per burglary)	Benefit measure 3 (£1,304 per burglary)
Rate of returns scenario 1 (2 Years)			
Impact measure 1: Project area only (308 burglaries prevented)	£612,821	£443,421	£292,501
Impact measure 2: Including net displacement/diffusion (345 burglaries prevented)	£699,549	£509,799	£340,749
Impact measure 3: Including net displacement/diffusion and anticipatory benefits (764 burglaries prevented)	£1,681,685	£1,261,485	£887,125
Rate of return scenario 2 (10% decline p.a. in burglary prevented = 938 burglaries prevented)			
Impact measure 1: Project area only (938 burglaries prevented)	£2,089,541	£1,573,641	£1,114,021
Impact measure 2: Including net displacement/diffusion	£2,353,667	£1,775,792	£1,260,958
Impact measure 3: Including net displacement/diffusion and anticipatory benefits	£5,344,718	£4,065,018	£2,924,921
Rate of return scenario 3 (constant returns for a further 9 years = 1,478 burglaries prevented)			
Impact measure 1: Project area only (1,478 burglaries prevented)	£3,355,301	£2,542,401	£1,818,181
Impact measure 2: Including net displacement/diffusion	£3,771,483	£2,860,929	£2,049,709
Impact measure 3: Including net displacement/diffusion and anticipatory benefits	£8,484,460	£6,468,046	£4,671,604

Table 3.6 Limited portfolio of benefit-cost ratios

	Benefit measure 1 (£2,344 per burglary)	Benefit measure 2 (£1,794 per burglary)	Benefit measure 3 (£1,304 per burglary)
Rate of returns scenario 1 (2 years)			
Impact measure 1: Project area only (308 burglaries prevented)	6.62	5.06	3.68
Impact measure 2: Including net displacement/diffusion (345 burglaries prevented)	7.41	5.67	4.12
Impact measure 3: Including net displacement/diffusion and anticipatory benefits (764 burglaries prevented)	16.41	12.56	9.13
Rate of return scenario 2 (10% decline p.a. in burglary prevented)			
Impact measure 1: Project area only (938 burglaries prevented)	20.15	15.42	11.21
Impact measure 2: Including net displacement/diffusion	22.57	17.27	12.55
Impact measure 3: Including net displacement/diffusion and anticipatory benefits	49.98	38.25	27.80
Rate of return scenario 3 (constant returns for a further nine years)			
Impact measure 1: Project area only (1,478 burglaries prevented)	31.75	24.30	17.66
Impact measure 2: Including net displacement/diffusion	35.56	27.22	19.78
Impact measure 3: Including net displacement/diffusion and anticipatory benefits	78.75	60.27	43.81

The benefit-cost ratio is most sensitive to changes in the period over which returns were calculated, followed by change in the impact measure (the inclusion of displacement/diffusion and anticipatory benefits), then changes in the estimated benefits from a prevented burglary. Further sensitivity tests using other case studies will provide more information about which variables are most influential in the aggregate. However, it is clear that major variation in the cost-effectiveness of the crime reduction scheme is apparent depending on which variables are selected for inclusion in the benefit-cost ratio, and depending on which other parameters are chosen. Although this particular scheme produced positive returns in every case, it is easy to envisage a scenario in which some ratios are positive, some negative, and some close to unity.

Discussion and conclusion

Perhaps the case could be made that a limited portfolio of benefit-cost ratios is simply an extension of traditional sensitivity analysis. Certainly it has many things in common with traditional sensitivity analysis: it tests the degree to which the benefit-cost ratio varies under different conditions. Yet we would suggest it is different in so far as it is a subject-specific proposal for a reformulation of the manner in which we use CBA as a tool to inform decision-making in crime reduction and criminal justice. The evaluator providing a portfolio of outcomes becomes a service provider – providing information to policy-making customers – rather than a decision-maker contracted to one focal agency providing 'the' single answer. Although such an orientation has arguably always been part of quality cost-benefit analysis it is typically, if unfortunately, honoured in the breach. And while there will always be some degree of subjectivity in evaluation research due to the fact that there will always be some choice of variables and method, improved transparency is always to be sought.

It is clear that the lifespan of crime reduction efforts is an important topic. The benefit-cost ratio proved extremely sensitive to change in the estimated lifespan of the crime reduction effort. There is scope for empirical research into the lifespan of crime reduction efforts: perhaps questions could be included in the British Crime Survey that will shed light on the issue. It is an important issue for impact evaluation as well as cost-benefit analysis, although the orientation of CBA towards the inclusion of future costs and benefits helped identify its importance in the present instance.

There are more variables that could be varied than were included in the present case study. It was not possible to include data on national as opposed to local input costs. Likewise, only one set of estimates of the social benefit of burglary was utilised: the pioneering work of Brand and Price (2000) appears to have given them a monopoly in that field but it requires competition using alternative methods and sources if it is to prosper. Similarly, while a discount rate of 6% appears to be the default in the UK (as recommended in HM Treasury's 'Green Book'), values of 3 or 4% more typically used in the US would increase the estimated benefits for the ten-year scenarios.

The optimal set of variables that are required for a particular study will vary with the type of evaluation and the availability of data as well as the nature of the audience. As cost-benefit analysis becomes commonplace in crime reduction and criminal justice research, perhaps there will be increasing standardisation in the production of multiple cost-benefit ratio outcomes.

Crime science should aim to be practical and to facilitate choice among consumers of CBA. Different consumers demand different cost-benefit measures. Most informed readers, policy-makers or their advisors can, or should be able to, interpret multiple benefit-cost ratios and their underlying rationale. The presentation of a single 'best' benefit-cost ratio, as so often occurs, has the superficial advantage of appearing both simple and definitive. It has the disadvantage of conveying limited information. The presentation of a long list of ratios has the advantage of presenting much information but the disadvantage of being unwieldy. There is a trade-off between a confusing over-provision of technical details and the overly selective under-provision of limited information. The aim of this chapter is to suggest one direction towards a pragmatic compromise: a limited portfolio that conveys the most critical set of information in a readily comprehensible manner to a variety of audiences.

Acknowledgements

The authors thank Ken Pease. They also thank Matrix MHA consultants who directed the cost-effectiveness analysis and whose data made possible the empirical part of this chapter, as well as all the other members of the Northern Consortium. The views expressed are those of the authors and not necessarily those of the Home Office.

Notes

1 Department of Social Sciences, Loughborough University.
2 Jill Dando Institute of Crime Science, University College London.
3 Jill Dando Institute of Crime Science, University College London.
4 We thank Emily Gillespie for an unpublished cost-benefit analysis which found that Kirkholt burglary project produced a positive benefit-cost ratio when saved police time was excluded from the original calculation. The same analysis also concluded that, if savings due to the intangible costs of prevented burglary were included, then the benefit-cost ratio would be higher than that in the published report.
5 Midtown is a fictitious name to protect anonymity.

References

Aos, S., Phillips, P., Barnoski, R. and Lieb, L. (2001) *The Comparative Costs and Benefits of Programs to Reduce Crime*. Washington State Institute for Public Policy. Available at: http://www.wsipp.wa.gov/rptfiles/costbenefit.pdf.

Australian Institute of Criminology (2003a) *Measuring Crime Prevention Program Costs and Benefits*. AIC Crime Reduction Matters No. 15. Canberra: Australian Institute of Criminology. Available at http://www.aic.gov.au/publications/crm/crm015.pdf.

Australian Institute of Criminology (2003b) *Building a Policy Scorecard to Compare Crime Prevention Program Costs and Benefits*, AIC Crime Reduction Matters, no. 16. Canberra: Australian Institute of Criminology. Available at http://www.aic.gov.au/publications/crm/crm016t.html.

Barr, R. and Pease, K. (1990) 'Crime placement, displacement and deflection', in M. Tonry and N. Morris (eds), *Crime and Justice*, Vol. 12. Chicago: University of Chicago Press.

Boardman, A., Greenberg, D., Vining, A. and Weimer, D. (1996) *Cost-Benefit Analysis: Concepts and Practice*. Upper Saddle River, NJ: Prentice Hall.

Bowers, K.J. and Johnson, S. (2003) *Reducing Burglary Initiative: The Role of Publicity in Crime Prevention*, Home Office Research Series 272. London: Home Office.

Bowers, K.J., Johnson, S.D. and Hirschfield, A. (2004). 'The measurement of crime prevention intensity and its impact on levels of crime', *British Journal of Criminology*, 44(3), 419–440.

Brand, S. and Price, R. (2000) *The Economic and Social Costs of Crime*, Home Office Research Study 217. London: Home Office.

Caulkins, J.P. (2000) 'Measurement and analysis of drug problems and drug control efforts', *Measurement and Analysis of Crime and Justice. Volume 4 of Criminal Justice 2000*. Washington DC: National Institute of Justice. Available at: http://www.ncjrs.org/criminal_justice2000/vol_4/04h.pdf.

Chisholm, J. (2000) *Benefit-Cost Analysis and Crime Prevention*, AIC Trends and

Issues in Crime and Justice no. 147. Canberra: Australian Institute of Criminology. Available at http://www.aic.gov.au/publications/tandi/ti147.pdf.

Clarke, R. and Weisburd, D. (1994) 'Diffusion of crime control benefits: observations on the reverse of displacement', in R.V. Clarke (ed.), *Crime Prevention Studies*, Vol. 2. Monsey, NY: Criminal Justice Press.

Cohen, M. (1988), 'Pain, suffering and jury awards: a study of the cost of crime to victims', *Law & Society Review*, 22, 3.

Cohen, M. (2000) 'Measuring the costs and benefits of crime and justice', *Measurement and Analysis of Crime and Justice. Volume 4 of Criminal Justice 2000*. Washington DC: National Institute of Justice. Available at: http://www.ncjrs.org/criminal_justice2000/vol_4/04f.pdf.

Colledge, M., Collier, P. and Brand, S. (1999) *Programmes for Offenders: Guidance for Evaluators*, Crime Reduction Programme Guidance Note 1. London: Home Office.

Dhiri, S. and Brand, S. (1999) *Analysis of Costs and Benefits: Guidance for Evaluators*, Crime Reduction Programme Guidance Note 1. London: Home Office.

Eck, J. (1993), 'The threat of crime displacement', *Criminal Justice Abstracts*, 25: 527–546.

Elvik, R. (2001) *Cost-Benefit Analysis of Police Enforcement*, The 'Escape' Project, Working Paper 1. Finland: Technical Research Centre of Finland. Available at: http://www.vtt.fi/rte/projects/escape/escape_wp1.pdf.

Forrester, D., Chatterton, M. and Pease, K. (1988) *The Kirkholt Burglary Prevention Project, Rochdale*, Crime Prevention Unit Paper 13. London: Home Office. Available at: http://www.homeoffice.gov.uk/rds/prgpdfs/fcpu13.pdf.

Forrester, D., Frenz, S., O'Connell, M. and Pease, K. (1990) *The Kirkholt Burglary Prevention Project: Phase II*, Crime Prevention Unit Paper 23. London: Home Office. Available at: http://www.homeoffice.gov.uk/rds/prgpdfs/fcpu23.pdf.

Gramlich, E.M. (1997) *A Guide to Benefit-Cost Analysis*. 2nd edn. Prospect Heights, IL: Waveland Press.

Greenwood, P.W., Model, K.E., Rydell, C. P. and Chiesa, J. (1996) *Diverting a Life of Crime: Measuring Costs and Benefits*. Santa Monica, CA: RAND.

Hahn, R. and Wallsten, S. (2003) 'Whose life is worth more? (And why is it horrible to ask?), *Washington Post*, 1 June.

Hamilton-Smith, N. (2003) 'Anticipated consequences: developing a strategy for the targeted management of displacement and diffusion of benefits', in N. Tilley (ed.), *Evaluation for Crime Prevention*, Crime Prevention Studies, Vol. 14. New York: Criminal Justice Press.

Harrell, A., Cavanagh, S. and Roman, J. (2000) *Evaluation of the D.C. Superior Court Drug Intervention Programs*, National Institute of Justice Research in Brief. Washington, DC: National Institute of Justice. Available at: http://www.ncjrs.org/pdffiles1/nij/178941.pdf.

Hesseling, R. (1994) 'Displacement: an empirical review of the literature', in R.V. Clarke (ed.), *Crime Prevention Studies*, Vol. 3. Monsey, NY: Criminal Justice Press.

Hooke, A., Knox, J. and Portas, D. (1996) *Cost-Benefit Analysis of Traffic Light and Speed Cameras*, Police Research Series Paper 20. London: Home Office. Available at: http://www.homeoffice.gov.uk/rds/prgpdfs/fprs20.pdf.

Hornick, J.P., Paetsch, J.J. and Bertrand, L.D. (2000) *A Manual on Conducting Economic Analysis of Crime Prevention Programs*. Canadian Research Institute for Law and the Family, produced for the National Crime Prevention Centre. Available at: http://www.prevention.gc.ca/en/library/publications/reports/manual/manual.pdf.

ICF Consulting Ltd (2003) *Cost Benefit Analysis of Road Safety Improvements: Final Report*. Imperial College, London: Imperial College Centre for Transport Studies. Available at: http://www.europa.eu.int/comm/transport/road/library/icf_final_report.pdf.

Johnson, S.D., Bowers, K.J., Young, C.A. and Hirschfield, A.F.G. (2001) 'Uncovering the true picture: evaluating crime reduction initiatives using disaggregate crime data', *Crime Prevention and Community Safety: An International Journal*, 3(4): 7–24.

Johnson, S.D., Bowers, K.J., Jordan, P., Mallender, J., Davidson, N. and Hirschfield, A.F.G. (2004) 'Estimating crime reduction outcomes: how many crimes were prevented?', *Evaluation, The International Journal of Theory, Research and Practice*, 10(3), 327–348.

Juvenile Justice Evaluation Center (2002) Cost-Benefit Analysis for Juvenile Justice Programs, Program Evaluation Briefing Series No. 4. Washington, DC: Office of Juvenile Justice and Delinquency Prevention. Available at: http://www.jrsa.org/jjec/about/publications/cost-benefit.pdf.

Kodz, J. and Pease, K. (2003) *Reducing Burglary Initiative: Early Findings on Burglary Reduction*, Research Development and Statistics Directorate Findings No. 204. London: Home Office. Available at: http://www.crimereduction.gov.uk/burglary60.pdf.

Legg, D. and Powell, J. (2000) *Measuring Inputs: Guidance for Evaluators*, Crime Reduction Programme Guidance Note 3. London: Home Office.

MacCallum, M. (1997) *The Economic Analysis of Criminal Justice Policy Options*, Discussion Paper for the Strategic Responses to Crime Group. Wellington: Ministry of Justice. Available at: http://www.justice.govt.nz/pubs/reports/1997/economic/Default.htm.

Mayhew, P. (2003) *Counting the Cost of Crime in Australia. Crime Trends and Issues in Crime and Criminal Justice*. Canberra: Australian Institute of Criminology. Available at: http://www.aic.gov.au/publications/tandi/ti247.pdf.

Michigan Judicial Institute (2001) *Crime Victim Rights Manual*. Michigan: Michigan Judicial Institute. Available at: http://www.courts.michigan.gov/mji/resources/cvr/cvr.htm.

Miller, T., Cohen, M.A. and Wiersema, B. (1996) *Victim Costs and Consequences: A New Look*, National Institute of Justice Research Report. Washington DC: NIJ.

Nagin, D. (2001) 'Measuring the economic benefits of developmental prevention programs', in M. Tonry (ed.), *Crime and Justice*, 28: 347–384.

National Institute of Justice (2004) *What is NIJ?*, section of NIJ website at http://www.ojp.usdoj.gov/nij/about.htm (accessed 24 July 2004).

Painter, K.A. and Farrington, D.P. (1999) 'Street lighting and crime: diffusion of benefits in the Stoke-on-Trent project', in K.A. Painter and N. Tilley (eds.), *Crime Prevention Studies*, Vol. 10. Monsey, NY: Criminal Justice Press, pp. 77–122.

Painter, K.A. and Farrington, D.P. (2001) 'The financial benefits of improved street lighting, based on crime reduction', *Lighting Research and Technology*, 33(1): 3–12.

Roche, D. (1999) *Mandatory Sentencing*, Trends and Issues in Crime and Criminal Justice No. 138. Canberra: Australian Institute of Criminology. Available at: http://www.aic.gov.au/publications/tandi/ti138.pdf.

Roman, J. (2004) 'Can cost-benefit analysis answer criminal justice policy questions, and if so, how?' *Journal of Contemporary Criminal Justice*, 20 (3).

Roman J. and Farrell, A. (2001) 'Assessing the costs and benefits accruing to the public from a graduated sanctions program for drug-using defendants', *Law and Policy*, 23(2): 237–268.

Roman J. and Farrell, G. (2002) 'Cost-benefit analysis for crime prevention: opportunity costs, routine savings, and crime externalities', *Crime Prevention Studies*, 14: 53–92.

Seelye, K.Q. and Tierney, J. (2003) 'E.P.A. drops age-based cost studies', *New York Times*, 8 May.

Smith, M.J., Clarke, R.V. and Pease, K. (2002) 'Anticipatory benefit in crime prevention', in N. Tilley, (ed.), *Analysis for Crime Prevention*, Crime Prevention Studies 13. New York: Criminal Justice Press.

Stockdale, J., Whitehead, C. and Gresham, P. (1999) *Applying Economic Evaluation to Policing Activity*, Police Research Series Paper 103. London: Home Office.

Welsh, B.C. and Farrington, D.P. (1999) 'Value for money?', *British Journal of Criminology*, 43(3): 345–368.

Welsh, B.C. and Farrington, D.P. (2000) 'Monetary costs and benefits of crime prevention programs', in M. Tonry (ed.), *Crime and Justice: A Review of Research*, Vol. 27. Chicago: University of Chicago Press.

Part 3
Case Studies in Preventive Crime Science

Chapter 4

Reducing prison disorder through situational prevention: the Glen Parva experience

Richard Wortley and Lucía Summers

Prison disorder and situational prevention

While there is an extensive academic literature on the nature and causes of prison disorder, there are few published evaluations of attempts to reduce prison disorder. To the extent that researchers have considered the issue of preventing misbehaviour by prison inmates, for the most part suggested strategies simply involve extrapolations from epidemiological data. A correlation between prison population density and assault rates, for example, provides the usual basis for concluding that reducing overcrowding will help reduce prison violence (Cox *et al*. 1984; Gaes and McGuire 1985). Conspicuously rare in the literature are pre-test/post-test studies that demonstrate the effectiveness of such manipulations. A broad aim of the current chapter is to add to the small collection of studies that provide outcome measures for disorder-reduction initiatives in prison.

More specifically, this chapter argues for the utility of adopting a situational approach to preventing violence and other forms of misconduct in prison. To date, interpretations of prison disorder have been dominated by systemic rationales. In the tradition of deprivation theorists such as Sykes (1958) and Goffman (1961), prison disorder is believed to arise from an oppositional prisoner subculture created to protect prisoners from the harsh realities of the prison regime. Prison disorder is viewed as normative and a surface symptom of a deeper structural malaise. Adopting this logic, at a minimum prevention of disorder can only be achieved through cultural change at an institutional level, and more likely requires fundamental changes to the very nature of imprisonment.

In contrast, situational prevention involves a micro-level focus and a problem-solving method. Rather than addressing prison disorder in a global way, situational analysis examines the relationship between specific kinds of behaviour and specific aspects of the immediate environment. It requires a detailed understanding of the what, where, when and why of the problem in question. In the first instance, different categories of disorder need to be distinguished. For example, it is likely that violence towards staff will have different situational dynamics and require different prevention strategies than will violence among prisoners, and that both of these behaviours in turn will comprise distinct sub-types. An examination of the geographic characteristics of the disorder provides further clues for prevention. Are there disorder hotspots that indicate problems in certain locations within the prison or at certain times of the day/week/year, and what is it about those locations and times that are problematic? And finally, what is the perpetrator hoping to achieve? Is an assault, for example, a spontaneous outburst – the result, say, of jostling in a queue – or is it premeditated and carefully planned – perhaps revenge for an unpaid gambling debt? The desired end-point of a situational analysis is an intervention that is tailor-made to respond to the particular circumstances. It is an incremental approach whereby overall reductions in problem behaviours are achieved through the accumulation of relatively small successes.

A small number of researchers have recognised the potential that the situational prevention model offers for the control of prison disorder (e.g. Atlas 1982, 1983; Bottoms *et al.* 1995; Clarke 1980, 1987; La Vigne 1994; O'Donnell and Edgar 1996; Sparks *et al.* 1996; Wortley 2002, 2003). In particular, Wortley (2002, 2003) proposed a two-stage model of situational prison control. He argued that there were two, sometimes opposing, situational forces acting upon prisoners. First, the prison environment is the source of stresses and strains that may precipitate disorder. Overcrowding, dehumanising living conditions, depressing architecture, monotonous routines, the brutality of prison staff and fellow prisoners, lack of personal control over the environment and so forth produce frustration, boredom and fear that motivate prisoners to misbehave. Second, the prison environment provides opportunities for disorder. Lapses in security, inadequate surveillance and supervision, inconsistent discipline, access to contraband and architectural blind-spots permit prisoners to carry out their intended transgressions. These two situational elements can suggest contradictory control solutions. To reduce prison stresses it may be necessary to soften the prison environment and ease restrictions on prisoners, while reducing opportunities may require target-hardening and a tightening of security. Effective prison control requires a balance between soft and hard tactics, an approach that Clarke (1980) described as 'kind but strict' (p. 118).

Situational prevention offers prison administrators quick, practical and cost-effective interventions to control prison disorder. Moreover, since prisons are enclosed and highly controlled environments, prison administrators (in comparison with crime prevention practitioners in the community) have considerable scope in implementing whatever situational manipulations are deemed necessary. At the same time, the behaviour-specific focus means that prevention initiatives need not involve environmental changes on a grand scale, and nor need they necessarily result in harsher conditions for prisoners (they may in fact involve making conditions easier). In practice, however, the knee-jerk reaction of many prison administrators to escalating disorder is to respond with broadly applied and heavy-handed security crackdowns.

This chapter reports an exception to this rule. It describes and evaluates the efforts to reduce chronic levels of institutional misconduct at Glen Parva Young Offenders Institution. The administrators and staff who devised and introduced the initiatives at Glen Parva were not consciously working from situational theory. Nevertheless, their practical strategies to reduce disorder display the problem-solving, behaviour-specific approach that characterises the situational model.

Glen Parva

Glen Parva is a young persons' (18–21 years) prison built in the early 1960s in the suburban outskirts of Leicester (UK). It is a large institution comprising 13 units spread over a wide area. The certified normal accommodation is 664 (208 remands and 456 sentenced offenders) and on 31 January 2004 the actual prison population was 781 (212 remands and 569 sentenced offenders).

The recent history of Glen Parva has been a troubled one. An unannounced inspection in December 1997 by the Chief Inspector of Prisons resulted in a damning report (Ramsbotham 1998). That visit was itself prompted by two earlier unannounced visits in 1996 (for which published reports were not produced) that left the Inspector 'so dissatisfied' (p. 7) with what was found that the schedule of inspections was brought forward. The Inspector detailed numerous deficiencies in prisoner accommodation, health care programmes, relations between prisoners and staff, management and staff morale. Specifically on the issue of good order, he found that many young prisoners 'did not feel safe and that there was a great deal of bullying, much stealing of each other's property, and a great deal of intimidatory shouting from cell windows to threaten young prisoners' (p. 16). There was an anti-bullying policy but 'it was having very little effect on the bullying culture', while 'control and restraint techniques were used far too frequently and were not justified in many cases' (p. 16).

From 1999, the situation at Glen Parva began to turn around. A subsequent unannounced visit in 1999 (Ramsbotham 2000) reported improvements in the violence situation, noting that 'there was an impressive anti-bullying strategy in place with clear systems and procedures for identifying, recording, investigating and challenging bullying' (para. 1.19), although despite this, 'the debilitating and cruel bullying culture continued to corrupt and wreck the lives of young prisoners at Glen Parva' (para. 1.30). By 2002, substantial gains had been made. The report of the unannounced visit that year (Owers 2002), while advising that a number of institutional deficits persisted – related principally to under-resourcing – concluded that 'there had been effective work on suicide, self-harm, and bullying, with a reduction in the number of assaults and a good induction system' (p. 3). Anti-bullying was an institutional priority with the Inspector noting that 'everywhere in Glen Parva there were posters advertising the anti-bullying strategy and giving advice to young prisoners on how to get help' (p. 11). At the same time, there was a significant reduction in the use of control and restraint techniques by staff as a method of maintaining order.

The improvements at Glen Parva were achieved through a variety of strategies. In keeping with the behaviour-specific focus of situational prevention, the following analyses examine the institutional responses to three problem behaviours – bullying, excessive noise from cell windows and the scalding of staff.

Case study 1: Bullying

The problem

As detailed in the various inspection reports, Glen Parva experienced high levels of intimidatory behaviour and assaults among prisoners.

Interventions

Anti-Bullying Strategy

The current Anti-Bullying Strategy (ABS) policy was introduced in January 2001 (HMYOI Glen Parva 2001), replacing earlier, less structured versions noted by the Inspectors. The ABS was designed to identify bullies, and then monitor them through a three-stage process. Once an allegation has been made against a prisoner, he is placed under observation for up to 14 days without being informed. During this period, any available evidence is gathered which might lead the prisoner to be moved onto Stage 2, at which point he is informed that he has been placed on observation. In Stage 2, some sanctions are applied and, if the prisoner shows improved behaviour after two weeks, he might be removed from the ABS system. If the prisoner fails to respond, he might stay in Stage 2 for an extended period of time or be moved on to Stage 3. In Stage 3, the prisoner is transferred to a different unit and placed in a special bullying cell. Additional sanctions also apply. After two weeks, a review takes place. If the prisoner is deemed to have responded to the intervention and the bullying behaviour has ceased, he may be transferred to a normal cell within the unit, then sent back to his original unit after another seven days. If his behaviour is not seen to improve, however, he might stay in Stage 3 for an extended period of time, although he might be moved from unit to unit so that he cannot establish himself as a bully in any unit. In extreme cases, the prisoner may be transferred to a different, less desirable establishment.

The ABS is widely publicised among prisoners. In an example of 'rule setting' (Cornish and Clarke 2003), new arrivals are told about the system as part of their induction. The 'Glen Parva Information Book' is placed in escort vehicles for prisoners to read en route to the institution. Anti-bullying poster competitions have been held, and posters are displayed prominently throughout the institution. Prisoners can identify themselves as victims by discreetly putting a note in the unit box.

Induction packs

New arrivals to Glen Parva were a particular target of bullying. They were often approached by established prisoners who offered to provide them things until they were settled. However, the basis on which these 'gifts' were offered was deliberately not made clear to the new arrival. They were in reality loans designed to place him in the debt of the lender. This would lead to sometimes violent confrontations at a later date when the lender sought to redeem the debt or otherwise use the obligation to exploit the new arrival. An induction process was put in place that included providing new arrivals with a 'first night pack' on their arrival. The kit contained goods to get them through their first few days and reduce the need to borrow from other prisoners. This 'first night pack' was first introduced in October 2000. Each pack is worth £3.50 and there are two different versions, depending on whether the new inmate is a smoker or not. The contents of the pack are: £2 in phone credits; letter paper and a pen; a small amount of cigarette paper and tobacco (only for smokers); and sweets and chocolate (a greater quantity for non-smokers, to compensate).

TV remote controls

By April 2003, all cells had their own televisions (see Case study 2). However, many prisoners would fall asleep and leave their television on all night, a practice that caused arguments among the inmates. In February 2003, remote controls were given to prisoners to allow them to turn off their sets without getting out of bed.

PIN phone system

The PIN phone system was first introduced in March 2003 and was aimed at reducing bullying consisting of stealing or forcing other prisoners to hand over their phone cards. With the new system, each prisoner is given an individual account and is asked to declare a list of telephone numbers so that only these numbers can be dialled when using this account. The prisoner is also given a PIN number, for added security. If a prisoner is found to have used someone else's account or an unauthorised telephone number is dialled, the service for this particular prisoner is discontinued and disciplinary action may follow. With a few exceptions, all calls are recorded for security purposes. This measure, together with the fact that the numbers have to be declared in advance, also prevents offenders from calling their victims.

Evaluation

There are four available sources of data – adjudication reports[1] (i.e., records of misconduct hearings), ABS statistics, unit observation books and prisoner surveys – that monitor levels of bullying at Glen Parva. Taken together, these data indicate that a reduction in bullying at Glen Parva coincided with the combined introduction of the anti-bullying initiatives. However, it is not possible to tease out the contributions of individual prevention strategies by using these data.

Figure 4.1 shows proven adjudications for violence among prisoners ('fighting' and 'assault on inmate') between 1995 and 2001. Adjudications peaked in 1998 and have fallen steadily since, particularly for remand prisoners. Because fluctuations in the prisoner population were relatively minor over this period, adjusting for prisoner numbers makes little difference to the shape of the trend lines and so for simplicity raw data are shown here (and in subsequent analyses).

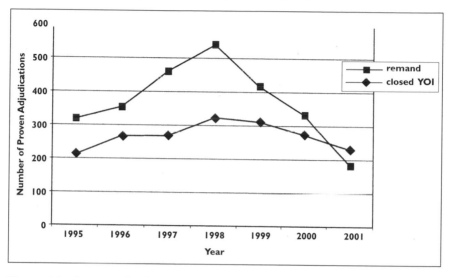

Figure 4.1   Proven adjudication for violence among prisoners

Figure 4.2 shows the number of prisoners on each stage of the ABS from January 2001 to September 2003 (excluding June–July 2003 when the anti-bullying coordinator position was unfilled and data are not available). The overall trend in the figures is downward, that is there are now fewer prisoners being identified as bullies. Within this trend there is moderate resurgence in the number of prisoners on the ABS in mid-2002. It is unclear whether this indicates anti-bullying initiatives faltered in 2002, or whether it simply reflects a seasonal variation in which more bullies are identified in the summer months (as occurred in the previous year and also in 2003).

From January 2000, officers recorded incidents of bullying in the unit observation books. These data are to some extent subjective. They include incidents where an officer observed bullying as well as their suspicions that other incidents (e.g. fighting, self-harm, an application to move to another unit, etc.) were motivated by bullying. Unfortunately, due to problems with data collation and storage, reliable

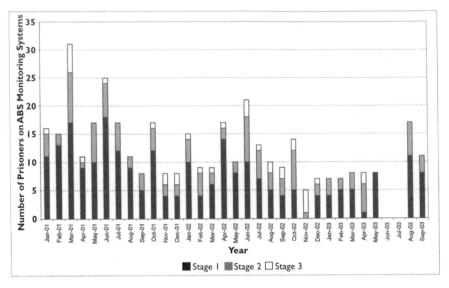

Figure 4.2 Number of prisoners on the Anti-Bullying Strategy (ABS) system by stage and month

data are only available from June 2001, with another gap between January and July 2003 (see Figure 4.3). There was an initial drop in the number of observed bullying incidents in 2001 followed by a rise in mid-2002 (mirroring the increase in the number of prisoners on the ABS at the same time). The gap in the data makes recent trends difficult to determine but based on the most recent figures, there appears to have been a drop in bullying in 2003.

Figure 4.4 shows results from bullying surveys administered to prisoners in November 1999, March 2002 and December 2003.[2] Among other questions, prisoners were asked how many times in the last month they had been called names, been asked to give another prisoner their canteen buy-up, been threatened by another prisoner and been assaulted by another prisoner.[3] Results reveal a significant downward trend on all bullying dimensions between 1999 and 2003 (called names, $X^2(6) = 21.03$, $p < 0.01$; canteen taken, $X^2(6) = 18.53$, $p < 0.01$; threatened, $X^2(6) = 26.65$, $p < 0.001$; assaulted, $X^2(6) = 18.41$, $p < 0.01$). As Figure 4.4 reveals, however, there was little improvement between 1999 and 2002, and in fact there were slight increases on two dimensions. The biggest change occurred between 2002 and 2003.

While the various measures of bullying cover different time frames, where they overlap there is a consistency in the picture they paint. Results indicate that bullying peaked in 1998 (Figure 4.1), dropping

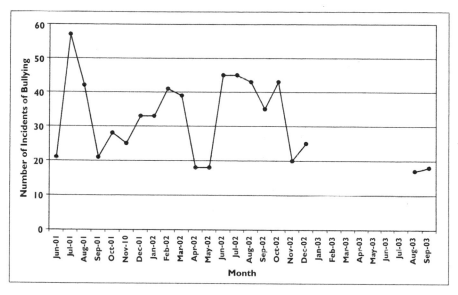

Figure 4.3 Recorded incidents of bullying from unit observation books

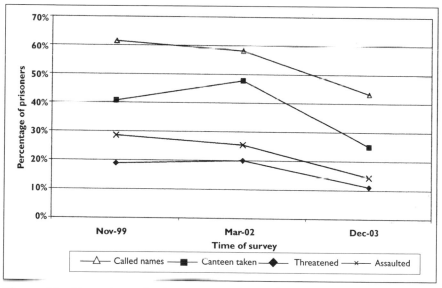

Figure 4.4 Percentage of prisoners reporting at least one experience of being bullied in the previous month

thereafter despite a slight rise again in mid 2002 (Figures 4.2, 4.3 and 4.4). By 2003 the situation had improved significantly. It is unclear why problems began to recur, albeit on a smaller scale, in 2002, but seasonal variations associated with increased bullying in summer appear to have contributed to the finding. Several initiatives were introduced after mid-2002 – including the PIN phone system and television remote controls – and these may have helped restore the momentum. When interpreting the ABS data, unit observation books and prisoner surveys, it needs to be kept in mind that the time spans involved exclude the peak problem period of 1998. That is, they are measuring bullying after the worst was over.

It should be noted that a small number of remanded juvenile prisoners (i.e., under 18 years) were held at Glen Parva until September 2001, at which time they were transferred to HMP Onley. This resulted in some change in the profile of prisoners, although the overall number did not decrease – in August 2001 there were 764 prisoners and in October 2001 there were 798. The impact of the transfer of juveniles on bullying rates appears to be minimal. Figures 4.2 and 4.3 do show dips for September 2001 but increases for the following month. Figure 4.1 shows that major improvement occurred prior to 2001 while Figure 4.4 shows the second drop in bullying did not occur until after March 2002.

Case study 2: Noise from cell windows

The problem

When locked in their cells in the evening, prisoners would shout out of their windows to other prisoners. As the Chief Inspector of Prisons noted in his report (Ramsbotham 1998), the shouting was often associated with intimidation of other prisoners and contributed to the overall atmosphere of violence that permeated the institution. The problem was concentrated in units 14 and 15. Unit 14 is a residential remand unit; unit 15 was a residential remand unit for juveniles until their transfer in September 2001, after which it became an induction unit for new arrivals. These units, then, house prisoners who are less settled and are perhaps more likely to prove troublesome. In addition, the units are also closest to the prison boundary and occupy the highest ground. The noise from these two units in particular caused numerous complaints to be made from neighbours about the noise, and significant fines were threatened by the local council for noise pollution.

Interventions

Noise monitors
In October 1999, a rugged outdoor microphone was installed in the south corner of the site between units 14 and 15, following a court case about noise disturbance. This was installed so that staff could be alerted within the unit's office of any noise occurring at the time, to ensure immediate action could be taken (prior to this, they might only find out after a resident had phoned the prison complaining about the noise). The installation was accompanied by formal disciplinary procedures aimed directly at shouting from windows.

In-cell televisions
From July 2000, there was a progressive roll-out of in-cell televisions across the institution, a process that was completed in April 2003. The principal rationale for introducing the televisions was the belief that they would reduce boredom among prisoners when they were locked in their cells and hence the level of shouting. The two most problematic units, 14 and 15, each had 13 televisions installed in the initial round (equating to 20% of cells), with the remaining cells (47 in each case) fitted in September 2002. Generally, three months were spent preparing each unit prior to these dates. This involved providing electricity to the units when required, installing the DVD electrical system, putting up shelves and so forth. This DVD system was first introduced in March 2002, and enables films to be broadcast within the prison. It is planned to adapt the system so that an information channel and an individual messaging system can be set up.

Evaluation
Data on residents' complaints are available from early 1996 to November 2003. Out of the 162 complaint calls, 136 (83.9%) were from residents living in the road closest to units 14 and 15. The number of complaints by quarter is displayed in Figure 4.5. As can be seen, there are peaks in the summer months of 1998, 1999 and 2000, with the peaks becoming smaller every year. There are no complaints in the summer of 2001 and a small number in the summer of 2002. Given the more agreeable weather conditions provided during these months, it is unsurprising that most of the calls were reported at this time of year. With extended daylight and warmer evenings, not only are inmates more likely to remain active for longer but also local residents are prone to spending more time outside and leaving their windows open, thus increasing exposure to any noise made from the institution.

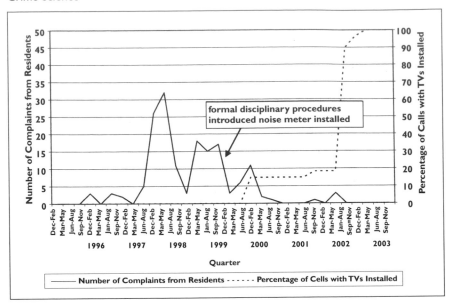

Figure 4.5 Number of complaints from residents by quarter by year and percentage of cells where TV sets had been installed

Figure 4.5 shows that a downward trend in complaints coincided with the introduction of the noise monitor. The mean number of complaints per quarter for the 15 quarters prior to the installation of the noise monitor was 7.9, and for the 15 quarters after its installation was 1.8 (t(28) = –2.18, p = 0.038). It should be noted, however, that due to technical difficulties the noise meter was not as effective as anticipated, and was often activated by noises other than those coming from the residential units. It seems that the mere threat posed by the presence of the monitor, and the tougher penalties that accompanied its installation, were sufficient to prompt behaviour change. Further reductions in complaints followed the roll-out of televisions across the institution. A drop in complaints immediately followed the initial installation. Complaints continued sporadically while the institution was only partially serviced, then ceased altogether when the rollout was completed.

Because the noise problem was concentrated in units 14 and 15, adjudication data for those units were examined.[4] If televisions helped reduce boredom, then there may have been general behavioural improvements in addition to a reduction in shouting. It can be seen in

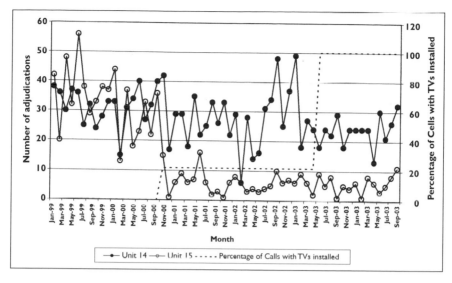

Figure 4.6 All adjudications for units 14 and 15 between January 1999 and September 2003

Figure 4.6 that there was a dramatic drop in adjudications for unit 15 in the same month that the televisions were first installed (i.e. July 2000), and this improvement has been maintained. In the 18 months (January 1999 to June 2000, inclusive) preceding the introduction of the televisions, the average number of adjudications per month was 33.3 (SD = 11.1); in the 25 months that followed the introduction of the televisions in 22% of the cells (August 2000 to August 2002, inclusive), the monthly average adjudications had fallen to 5.7 (SD = 3.3); and in the 13 months after all cells were fitted with a TV set (October 2002 to October 2003, inclusive), the monthly average number of adjudications was 5.5 (SD = 2.9). A one-way ANOVA showed an overall significant difference between these three periods (F(2,53) = 256.56, p = < 0.001), with simple contrasts showing significant differences between 0% installation and 22% installation (p < 0.001), between 0% installation and 100% installation (p < 0.001), but not between 22% installation and 100% installation. As noted earlier, unit 15 changed from a remand unit to an induction unit in September 2001, a year after the introduction of televisions. This change in function seems to have had little effect on adjudications.

The improvement is less pronounced for unit 14, although, apart from peaks in the first half of 2002, the trend is also generally downward. The monthly average adjudications in the 18 months prior to the installation of televisions (i.e. January 1999 to June 2000, inclusive) was 31.7 (SD = 6.3); the average number in the 25 months after TV sets were installed in 22% of the cells (i.e. August 2000 to August 2002, inclusive) was 27.0 (SD=9.8); in the 13 months after all cells were fitted with TV sets (i.e. October 2002 to October 2003, inclusive), the average monthly number of adjudications was 23.9 (SD = 5.0). A one-way ANOVA showed a significant difference between these three periods ($F_{(2,53)}$ = 3.95, p = 0.025 < 0.05), with simple contrasts showing a marginal significant difference between 0% installation and 22% installation (p = 0.057), a significant difference between 0% installation and 100% installation (p < 0.01), but not between 22% installation and 100% installation.

Case study 3: Staff scalding

The problem

Before being locked up at night, prisoners were issued with a can of hot water with which to make tea or coffee while in their cells. When receiving this hot water, some prisoners would throw the water over the officer, causing serious scalding.

Intervention

Thermos flasks were issued to prisoners instead of open cans of water. This intervention was first piloted in unit 14 in September 1999. Based on lessons learned in the pilot (for example that the thermoses needed to be securely sealed before handing them to the prisoners), the intervention was fully rolled out to all units in April–May 2000. The flasks were constructed from a material that was strong to ensure durability, but not tough enough to be used as a substantive weapon. The material was also difficult to break, to minimise the risk for self-harming or creating cutting instruments (although if there was judged to be a risk that a prisoner would self-harm or harm others, he was not handed out a flask).

Evaluation

Unfortunately, no records were available prior to 1999 to indicate the number of officers scalded prior to the introduction of the flasks. However, informal discussions with staff suggest it was a serious if relatively infrequent method of assault, and the policy document covering the issue of flasks invokes past incidents of scalding as the rationale for their introduction. In May 1999 (prior to the introduction of the flasks in unit 14) there is one recorded incident in unit 14 in which an officer received scalding to the face and had five days off work. After the introduction of the flasks throughout the institution, there was one further recorded incident of scalding (in September 2000). This involved a prisoner kicking a plastic flask of hot water along a landing towards a prison officer. The flask broke spraying hot water over the officer's legs. No time off work was recorded. As a result of this incident, a risk assessment was conducted on various flask designs, and a different type of plastic flask was introduced. There have been no further incidents of staff scalding since.

Discussion

By 1998, Glen Parva was experiencing a serious breakdown of order. The staff responded with a variety of situational strategies directed at different aspects of the disorder problem and substantial improvements in prisoner behaviour followed. However, the staff were not concerned with conducting a controlled piece of social scientific research, but rather with fixing a problem. It is the nature of applied social research that the link between an intervention and an observed change is notoriously difficult to establish conclusively. There is always the possibility of alternative explanations and we are left to draw inferences about most likely causes. Nevertheless, within these limitations, on the basis of the available data it seems reasonable to conclude that the interventions described above were responsible for the improved behaviour of prisoners at Glen Parva.

In the current case, the matter is complicated by the fact that numerous interventions were introduced around the same time making it difficult to isolate individual prevention effects. However, in some cases one might reasonably expect an intervention to produce a diffusion of benefits. For example, shouting from windows not only created annoying and expensive noise pollution, it generated conflict among prisoners. Thus the provision of televisions and the associated reductions in shouting probably also contributed to reductions in violence. In other cases, the diffusion of benefits may be less obvious. For example, the installation of televisions necessitated the conversion of cells to mains power (completed by June 2002). Prior to this, prisoners were issued with batteries which were also placed in socks and used as weapons in a number of assaults. The installation of televisions, then, has incidentally resulted in an additional crime prevention strategy (Cornish and Clarke's 2003 'control tools/weapons').

The strategies employed at Glen Parva help dispel the common criticism that situational prevention is a draconian approach to behaviour control. In fact, as one Inspector noted (Owers 2002), reliance on physical control and restraint by staff actually decreased at the same time that levels of misbehaviour also decreased. The interventions employed involve a combination of controlling precipitators of disorder and reducing opportunities for misbehaviour. The provision of television sets was directed at reducing the boredom that prompted prisoners to shout from windows and resulted in an improvement in prison living conditions. Even the strategies designed to reduce opportunities – first night packs, phone PINS, television remote controls and thermos flasks – cannot be said to have significantly hardened the environment. The ABS certainly resulted in some prisoners becoming the focus of additional discipline, but to the undoubted relief of most prisoners. Glen Parva is a better place now to serve a sentence than it was five years ago.

The interventions devised for Glen Parva display a problem-solving methodology but also have a commonsense quality to them. None of the interventions involves a complicated logic or depends upon esoteric theory. Replacing open cans of hot water with sealed thermoses, for example, seems an obvious thing to do and the finding that this resulted in fewer scaldings may be too easily dismissed as trivial. Yet the apparent simplicity of these strategies belies the potential potency of their impact. The fact that significant reductions in disorder can be achieved through relatively minor changes to the environment in some ways makes situational prevention all the more profound. One may speculate that the intuitive character of such interventions partly explains the lack of published accounts of attempts to reduce prison disorder. It may be that the efforts are judged (perhaps even by their implementers and wrongly so in our view) to be prosaic and of little interest to others. There are undoubtedly many innovative responses to the prison disorder problems devised by prison administrators that are never publicised.

This is not to say that situational prevention can offer a cookbook of ready-made solutions to disorder problems. The experience of situational prevention in a community setting is that what works in one location may be ineffective in another. It is not suggested, therefore, that the indiscriminate provision of televisions to prisoners will necessarily reduce problem behaviour in other institutions. What situational prevention offers is a coherent framework within which to address control problems. The lesson of situational prevention is that interventions must be designed to take account of local conditions and the specifics of the problem in question.

Acknowledgements

We are especially indebted to Glyn Griffiths, Remand and Allocation Governor, Glen Parva, and Gill Brigden, Safer Custody Group, for their invaluable role in providing the data for this chapter. We also wish to thank Clive Creese, Graham Mullis, Mark Williams, Andy Bettles, Alison Dalkin and Steve Turner from Glen Parva, and Chloe Smith and Vanessa Lee from the Jill Dando Institute, for their assistance at various stages of the project.

Notes

1 Source: Home Office.
2 These surveys were carried out by the Psychology Department at Glen Parva. See Burrows and Laurenti (1999), Bradshaw (2002) and Copson and Grennan (2003) for full descriptions of the surveys.
3 Prisoners were given the response choices of 'never', 'once or twice', 'occasionally' or 'regularly'. To simplify the graphical representation, Figure 4.4 shows the percentage of prisoners who experienced at least one case of bullying.
4 Unlike the Home Office adjudication data reported earlier, which did not show adjudications by unit, these data are drawn from the local Glen Parva records. However, they do not distinguish between proven and unproven cases.

References

Atlas, R. (1982) 'Violence in prison: architectural determinism'. Unpublished doctoral thesis, School of Criminology, Florida State University.
Atlas, R. (1983) 'Crime site selection for assaults in four Florida prisons', *Prison Journal*, 63: 59–72.
Bottoms, A.E., Hay, W. and Sparks, J.R. (1995) 'Situational and social approaches to the prevention of disorder in long-term prisons', in T.J. Flanagan (ed.), *Long-term Imprisonment*. Thousand Oaks, CA: Sage.
Bradshaw, S. (2002) *Anti-bullying Strategy Survey for HMYOI Glen Parva*. Leicester: HMYOI Glen Parva.

Burrows, J. and Laurenti, J. (1999). *Anti-bullying Strategy Survey for HMYOI & RC Glen Parva*. Leicester: HMYOI Glen Parva.

Clarke, R.V. (1980) 'Absconding from residential institutions for young offenders', in L. Hersov and I. Berg (eds), *Out of School*. Chichester, England: Wiley.

Clarke, R.V. (1987) 'Rational choice theory and prison psychology', in B.J. McGurk, D.M. Thornton and M. Williams (eds), *Applying Psychology to Imprisonment*. London: HMSO.

Copson, S. and Grennan, S. (2003) *Anti-bullying Strategy Survey for HMYOI & RC Glen Parva*. Leicester: HMYOI Glen Parva.

Cornish, D.B. and Clarke, R.V. (2003) 'Opportunities, precipitators and criminal dispositions: a reply to Wortley's critique of situational crime prevention', in M.J. Smith and D.B. Cornish (eds), *Theory and Practice in Situational Crime Prevention*. Crime Prevention Studies, Vol. 16. Monsey, NJ: Criminal Justice Press.

Cox, V.C., Paulus, P.B. and McCain, G. (1984) 'Prison crowding research: the relevance for prison housing standards and a general approach regarding crowding phenomena', *American Psychologist*, 39: 1148–1160.

Gaes, G.G. and McGuire, W.J. (1985) 'Prison violence: the contribution of crowding versus other determinants of prison assault rates', *Journal of Research in Crime and Delinquency*, 22: 41–65.

Goffman, E. (1961) *Asylums*. Garden City, NY: Anchor Books.

HMYOI Glen Parva (2001) *Anti-Bullying Strategy Policy Document*. Leicester: HMYOI Glen Parva.

La Vigne, N.G. (1994) 'Rational choice and inmate disputes over phone use on Rikers Island', in R.V. Clarke (ed.), *Crime Prevention Studies*, Vol. 3. Monsey, NY: Criminal Justice Press.

O'Donnell, I. and Edgar, K. (1996) *The Extent and Dynamics of Victimization in Prisons*. Oxford: University of Oxford.

Owers, A. (2002) *Report on an Unannounced Follow-up Inspection of HM Young Offenders Institution and Remand Centre Glen Parva, 4–6 March 2002*. London: HM Inspectorate of Prisons.

Ramsbotham, D. (1998) *HM Young Offender Institution Glen Parva: Report of an Unannounced Full Inspection, 1–5 December 1997*. London: HM Inspectorate of Prisons.

Ramsbotham, D. (2000) *Report of an Unannounced Inspection of HM Young Offender Institution and Remand Centre Glen Parva, 6–10 December 1999*. London: HM Inspectorate of Prisons.

Sparks, R., Bottoms, A. and Hay, W. (1996) *Prison and the Problem of Order*. Oxford: Clarendon Press.

Sykes, G. (1958) *The Society of Captives*. Princeton, NJ: Princeton University Press.

Wortley, R. (2002) *Situational Prison Control: Crime Prevention in Correctional Institutions*. Cambridge: Cambridge University Press.

Wortley, R. (2003) 'Situational crime prevention and prison control: lessons for each other', in M.J. Smith and D.B. Cornish (eds), *Theory and Practice in Situational Crime Prevention*. Crime Prevention Studies, Vol. 16. Monsey, NJ: Criminal Justice Press.

Chapter 5

Driving down crime at motorway service areas

Nick Tilley

Introduction

Motorway service areas (MSAs) tend to be crime hot spots. This study,[1] commissioned by the Central Motorway Police Group (CMPG), describes patterns of crime at a number of MSAs within the area around Birmingham covered by the CMPG. It explores potential means of reducing those crimes through changes in design, operating methods and policing. It also considers ways in which crime might be designed out of future MSAs.

The study broadly adopted an evidence-based problem-solving approach. An attempt was made to gauge the pattern of crime in MSAs. These patterns were then analysed in a little more detail to try to identify potential 'pinch-points', where interventions might be made to reduce opportunities or where alternative forms of design might pre-empt opportunities. The study brings out some of the practical difficulties in putting into practice an evidence-based problem-solving approach. It also reveals the ways in which opportunities for crime in hot spots are inadvertently created by a range of agencies and organisations. This has the advantage of suggesting a range of potential points of intervention. The disadvantage is that fully designing out crime is likely to call for wide-ranging changes in design and practice that may be tricky to incentivise.

Method

The main data source used to identify crime patterns in MSAs comprised police crime records. These will not, of course, include all crimes since some will not be reported or recorded. It is likely, though, to capture most of the more serious incidents, as well as many more minor ones. Four of the nine MSAs within the CMPG's area of operation were selected for detailed attention. These were believed to be broadly representative. They formed parts of three different companies, were located in three different police force areas and were in four different area types. Unfortunately, the same data were not available in all cases. Where appropriate, data were pooled for some analyses. In other circumstances, each MSA is treated individually.

For MSA 1 (close to a city) and MSA 4 (close to a small town), data were available for all crimes for 1999–2001. For MSA 2 (close to a residential area) only vehicle crime data were available, again for 1999–2001. For MSA 3, (in a rural area), data were available for all crimes but only for 2000 and 2001.

Aggregate data only were also provided for all nine MSAs across the CMPG area for mid-May 2001 to the end of February 2002. The quality of these data could not be checked. Some inaccuracies were found and recoding was necessary for the data sets examined in detail. This suggests that the figures relating to all nine MSAs can be used only to give a broad-brush overview.

Patterns of crime in motorway service areas

Table 5.1 shows the overall pattern of incidents across all nine MSAs, using the aggregate data provided for the period 15 May 2001 to 28 February 2002, which covers just over nine months. In addition to general caution over these figures because of reporting and recording rate variations and miscodings, in MSA B it is highly unlikely that only fuel drive-offs occurred. What the figures do seem to reveal, nevertheless, is considerable variation in levels of crime and incident across different MSAs. This cannot be entirely explained by police recording practices since columns 1–3 are from one force, the next three from a second force and the last three from a third. There is substantial variation in crime and incident levels between MSAs in the same police force area.

Detailed analysis of specific crime problems is needed to inform well-targeted preventive and pre-emptive strategies, and these will not

Table 5.1 Offences at CMPG force motorway service Areas 15/5/01–28/02/02

Offence/incident	Service area										
	A	B	C	D	E	F	G	H	I	Total	Average
Alarm activation	1	0	3	7	0	4	5	0	3	23	2.6
Disorder	6	1	5	17	6	21	13	0	6	75	8.3
Illegal immigrants	2	1	0	1	18	5	6	0	1	34	3.8
Misc.	11	5	6	7	26	31	9	3	14	112	12.4
Suspicious incidents	4	5	5	22	6	38	7	0	1	88	9.8
Total non-crime	24	12	19	54	56	99	40	3	25	332	
Arson	0	0	0	0	0	0	0	1	0	1	0.1
Assault	0	0	1	1	3	1	2	3	4	15	1.7
Attempted theft/ theft from gaming machines	0	0	0	2	1	19	3	18	16	59	6.6
Attempted theft/ theft from shops and stalls	2	0	0	1	1	8	11	8	3	34	3.8
Fuel drive-off	14	6	9	1	37	81	120	29	30	327	36.3
Bomb hoax	0	0	0	0	0	0	0	0	1	1	0.1
Burglary	1	0	1	3	0	0	3	1	3	12	1.3
Criminal damage	1	0	1	1	0	0	1	1	0	5	0.6
Deception	0	0	0	0	0	2	1	6	0	9	1.0
Firearms incident	0	0	0	1	0	1	0	1	1	4	0.4
Hijack/kidnap	0	0	0	0	1	2	0	0	0	3	0.3
Obstruct police	0	0	0	0	0	0	1	3	2	6	0.7
Possession drugs class A and B	1	0	0	1	3	1	3	2	2	13	1.4
Robbery	0	0	0	0	0	1	1	1	0	3	0.3
Sexual offences	0	0	0	3	0	2	0	0	1	6	0.7
Theft from motor vehicle	3	0	3	35	26	78	22	33	22	222	24.7
Employee theft	0	0	0	0	0	0	1	1	1	3	0.3
Theft (other)	7	0	4	1	2	0	11	3	12	40	4.4
Theft of motor vehicle	1	0	0	0	3	12	3	6	0	25	2.8
Total crime	30	6	19	50	77	208	183	117	98	788	

always simply follow the categories used to record crime. The following points highlight some of the more general patterns found. We then move on to a more detailed study of patterns at different locations within MSAs.

1 As seen in Table 5.1, numbers of offences vary substantially by service area. In 2001 in MSA 1 overall there were 221 recorded offences, in MSA 3 there were 155 and in MSA 4, 73. We had no consistent denominator to determine if these differences simply reflected variations in size and customer throughput.

2 Overall numbers of recorded offences at MSAs were in some cases increasing substantially and in some cases falling. In MSA 1, for example, they increased from 99 in 1999 to 124 in 2000 and 222 in 2001. In MSA 4 they decreased from 119 in 1999 to 80 in 2000 and 73 in 2001.

3 While some of the MSA operators are victims of the crimes, members of the public using the MSA facilities are also frequently the victims. Members of the public (rather than operators) were victims of approximately half the recorded offences at MSA 3 and at MSA 1 for the period over which data were available.

4 The most common recorded crimes at MSAs involved motor vehicles in one way or another. In addition, there were a smaller number of other property crimes, but very few recorded incidents involving violence. Over a three-year period, less than 2% of recorded incidents involved violence at both MSA 1 and MSA 4, and those involving vehicles in one way or another accounted for three-quarters at MSA 1 and 70% at MSA 4. In MSA 2, over a two-year period, violent crimes accounted for less than 1% and crimes involving vehicles 86%.

5 Most members of the public who are victimised are non-locals – MSAs are locations for travelling victims. Less than 10% at MSA 3, for example, were from within the county.

6 While there is some intelligence suggesting that MSAs are used by organised criminals from time to time, it was not possible to examine this systematically as part of the study reported here.

We turn now to a more detailed account of the crime patterns within MSAs. There are four main crime zones within MSAs. These comprise the car park, the lorry park, the forecourt and the main building. The forecourt includes both a sales area and a fuel pump area. The main building will typically include a games area, shop, restaurant and public lavatories as well as offices and store rooms. The patterns of crime in the four main zones are quite different from one another. Each zone is examined individually. All but seven per cent of incidents could be assigned to a location within the MSA.

Crime in MSA car parks

Theft from motor vehicles is the most common crime in MSA car parks (77% of 130 offences over three years in MSA 4, 92% of 154 offences over three years in MSA 1, 55% of 29 offences over two years in MSA 3). The numbers of thefts from vehicles in MSA car parks increased rapidly in some service stations (from 19 offences in 1999 to 83 in 2001 in MSA 1), but decreased in others (from 47 in 1999 to 27 in 2001 in MSA 4). By far the most frequently stolen item from cars in motorway service areas was laptop computers, and numbers of crimes involving their loss have been increasing. In 2001, 37% of thefts from vehicles involved laptop computers at MSA 4, compared with 19% in 1999. In MSA 1, the equivalent percentages were 71% for 2001 and 42% in 1999. The most common recorded MO was breakage of a window (70 per cent in MSA 4, and 74 per cent in MSA 1). The thefts from vehicles in MSA car parks tended to occur while the car had been left for only short periods of time. Figure 5.1 shows the cumulative proportion of incidents involving all thefts from motor vehicles at car parks in MSAs 1, 2 and 3 that occurred during time windows of different lengths. At the left end of the graph, the victim knew exactly when the offence occurred. At the right end, there was a long time window during which the offence might have been committed. For about half the incidents the time window was 15 or fewer minutes. For only 15% it was over 30 minutes. At MSA 1, only 3% of thefts from cars in the car park took place at weekends. Half took place between 4.00 pm and 8.00 pm, of which 70% overall involved loss of a computer and a further 20% bags that might have contained a computer.

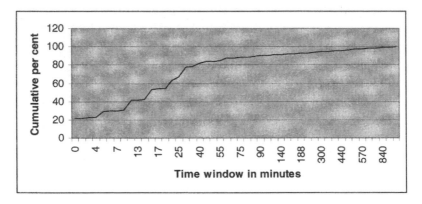

Figure 5.1 Time window for thefts from motor vehicles in MSA car parks (n = 229)

It is possible that some reports of computer thefts from cars were made fraudulently. However, the fact that quite a large number of empty computer bags were also reported stolen suggests that this is unlikely fully to explain the large numbers apparently taken.

There were eight thefts of motor vehicles from car parks across the three service areas for the periods for which data were available. There appeared to be no discernable patterns. One was taken by family members, some by unknown means and one with stolen keys.

Crime on MSA forecourts

Non-payment for fuel (referred to as 'bilking' in police circles) accounted for over 80% of recorded crimes on forecourts. Almost all incidents of bilking at all service areas involved loss of petrol – there were only a couple of cases where diesel was taken. Only one car where the registration was recorded was less than a year old and over 80% were seven or more years old. Forecourts were also sites for credit and fuel card frauds, which constituted a further 6% of incidents.

Taking and driving away motor vehicles left on forecourts while the customer was paying for fuel were infrequent but involved very substantial losses. They accounted for 6% of incidents. There were 14 recorded across three MSA forecourts: a rate of less than two per annum per MSA forecourt. All involved drivers leaving their keys in the ignition while paying for petrol. MSA 1 experienced eight of these cases over three years – substantially more than the other MSAs. Ten further vehicles were taken from MSA 1 where the site of the incident in the service area was not recorded, five of which involved keys being left in the ignition and at least some of which are likely also to have taken place on the forecourt.

In addition to bilking, card fraud and theft of vehicles, there was a small number of thefts from vehicles – just six across eight MSA years, half of which took place while the victim was paying for fuel.

Both bilking and card frauds typically involved relatively small costs per incident. The average volume of fuel taken in bilking was 34 litres. The total losses for the two service areas for which data were available on bilking over the varying periods included in this study amounted to less than £7,000 or an average of £1,400 per MSA per annum. Annualising the numbers of incidents at the highest fuel drive-off MSA shown in Table 5.1, and assuming a loss of 34 litres of fuel at each incident at 80 pence per litre produces a maximum loss per annum of about £4,000. The immediate victim in the case of fuel theft and card fraud is the operating company. The immediate victim where vehicles are taken is the driver. Where vehicles are taken, the losses are clearly very high indeed compared to those from bilking.

Crime in MSA lorry parks

The most common recorded offences in lorry parks were theft from and damage to the vehicles parked there. All damage to vehicles involved slashing curtains and theft also very often involved slashing the lorry curtains. Just over four in every five thefts from lorries involved slashing side curtains.

Recorded incidents in some lorry parks increased very rapidly over the study period. From 2000 to 2001 across all four MSAs the number of cases of damage to vehicles in lorry parks increased from 12 to 51 and thefts from vehicles increased from 29 to 57. Specifically:

- In MSA 3, damage to lorries increased from 10 to 44 cases and theft from lorries increased from 15 to 21.

- In MSA 1, thefts from vehicles increased from 7 to 28, and numbers of damaged vehicles increased from 1 to 6.

- In MSA 2, numbers remained low and stable, increasing jointly from 8 to 9.

- In MSA 4, numbers were low but increasing, going up overall from 1 to 4 incidents.

These offences overwhelmingly occurred overnight while the driver was asleep or in the MSA main building. In all cases the victim was the lorry park user or his/her company, not MSA operator companies.

In MSA 3, where the numbers of curtain slashing was especially high, there was an average of three incidents per night over a 15-night period in 2001 when one or more slashing occurred, the largest number being nine in one overnight period. In all but three cases there was also a theft from a lorry. Here it seems reasonable to assume the offenders were looking speculatively for a suitable target. In MSA 1, there were relatively fewer cases of damage to vehicles in relation to thefts. This may reflect variations in police recording practices or a different pattern of offending where the offenders knew which lorries to target in advance.

In MSA 1, 40% of thefts from lorries were from overseas trucks. The volume and range of goods is large and impressive. The following is a list of goods stolen from lorries at MSA 1 in 2001, where some indication of quantity was given:

- 21 DVD players
- 10 electric lawnmowers
- 10,140 computer games
- 8 boxes of tights
- 11 pallets of domestic electrical goods
- 1.5 pallets of printer toners
- 3 pallets of trainers
- 740 pairs of men's running shoes
- 20 cases of football shirts, all foreign teams
- 24 colour televisions
- 35 boxes of jogging tops
- 23 computer monitors
- 15 boxes of DVDs
- 299 cartons of babies' sleep soothers
- 200 tyres
- 40 computer printers
- 84 boxes containing 756 pairs of trainers
- 119 boxes of whisky
- 12 televisions.

It is not possible to estimate the financial losses involved in thefts from lorries. The data are inadequate for this purpose. It is clear, though, that the sums will be very large indeed, exceeding the costs of losses from most other sources.

The only crimes in lorry parks (other than those recorded as thefts of and from vehicles) were two cases of thefts of vehicles from transporters which might equally have been categorised as theft from a vehicle.

The pattern of time windows for crimes in lorry parks is very different from that for thefts from cars in car parks. As Figure 5.2 shows, the time window was under 30 minutes for less than 20% of the offences. For half it was seven hours or more. Half the victimised lorries arrived at the MSA between 8.00 pm and midnight. Thefts from lorries, thus, largely occur overnight. Drivers arrive in the evening and during the night goods are stolen from their trucks. Offences also occurred rather rarely at the weekend. They took place on Saturday or Sunday nights in just 4 per cent of cases.

Tarpaulin-covered lorries are particularly vulnerable because they offer relatively poor peripheral security. 'Stanley knives' are readily available and easily slash curtains whose contents can then easily be seen. In service areas there is a concentration of these suitable targets for crime. They are parked long enough to be accessed and for goods to be offloaded. The crimes will take a little time to commit and will also

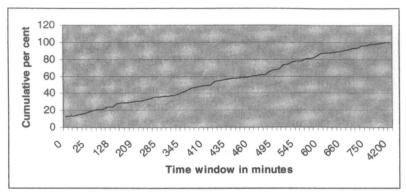

Figure 5.2 Time window for crimes in MSA lorry parks (n = 168)

require a vehicle to hand in which the goods can be taken away. The lorry parks are often not overlooked and are relatively quiet during the night. The list of goods stolen shows that the vulnerable lorries often carry goods that are, in Clarke's terms, 'CRAVED', that is goods that are Concealable, Removable, Available, Valuable, Enjoyable and Disposable (Clarke 1999). The large volumes of these goods suggest that they could not be consumed by those taking them. The thieves would need to be connected in some way to means of marketing large numbers of similar stolen products. They are, thus, likely to be relatively serious offenders.

Crime in the MSA main building

A variety of recorded crimes were committed in the MSA buildings. These included burglaries, shop theft and theft from gaming machines, in most of which the operator is the victim. There were also a number of personal thefts where staff or members of the public were victims.

Theft and attempted theft from gaming machines was the most common main building offence, at about nine per MSA per annum. The average annual loss for each MSA was a little under £2,000. Almost all incidents involved breaking or trying to break into the cash box by force.

Shop theft was the next most common recorded offence, at just over six per service area per annum. A wide range of goods was stolen. Most recorded shop thefts related to incidents where the offender was caught. It is almost certain, of course, that many more incidents also occurred, but were unnoticed and form part of 'shrinkage' (unaccounted loss) whose various possible sources cannot easily be distinguished.

The third most common offence was personal theft, at about six per service area per annum. This often involved loss of handbags and wallets. In several cases workers at the service area were victims where offenders had entered offices. Other offences most often took place in the public lavatories or restaurant area.

There was a sprinkling of burglaries, an average of 1.5 per annum per MSA. Just under half involved entry into insecure areas and just over half forced entry.

Understanding crime patterns at MSAs

Motorway service areas are very busy places. They are for this reason what Brantingham and Brantingham (1995) refer to as crime 'generators'. The Brantinghams list entertainment districts, concentrated office areas and sports stadiums as examples of crime generators. These draw together large numbers of people some of whom are liable to be tempted to commit crime alongside numerous targets for crime.

MSAs attract a substantial throughput of customers, a proportion of whom are liable to be open to temptation in the face of crime opportunities. And MSAs do throw up opportunities and temptations of various sorts. The parked car with hot products (those that are CRAVED) on view comprises one example. The petrol pump where driving away without payment is possible is another. The self-service shop is a further example.

MSAs may also comprise what the Brantinghams' refer to as 'crime attractors'. Crime attractors are places that offenders are drawn to specifically because of the supply of crime opportunities they provide. Here, rather than simply responding to crime opportunities as they arise, offenders go to the location to look for, or make use of, known opportunities to commit crimes. It appears that at least some MSAs do function as crime attractors. Night-time lorry parks may act in this way. They can be expected to furnish potential crime opportunities. The patterns of curtain slashing at some MSAs suggest that offenders are coming to look for opportunities known in advance to be likely to be available. Where particular trucks are targeted it appears that purposive visits are being made to MSAs to commit specific crimes against known vehicles. The thefts from gaming machines again suggest knowing offenders coming to MSAs with particular offences in mind.

Crime attractors and crime generators tend to overlap, of course, as in the case of MSAs. It is not always clear how the offending patterns are being produced or indeed whether they are being produced in one way. The pattern of late afternoon/early evening thefts of laptop computers from cars in MSA car parks suggests that there may be some specific targeting by offenders, though this is likely to be mixed in with opportunist offending at the same time.

Crime prevention at MSAs

It would be a mistake to suggest that MSA operators are unaware of or indifferent to crime. Many already use a range of crime prevention techniques. These include CCTV, lighting, tagging of goods and alarming of exit points, security patrols, layouts that allow for mutual surveillance within main buildings, shop layouts permitting staff guardianship of goods most at risk of theft, non-display of goods such as CDs that attract thieves, external landscaping that provides scope for surveillance, cordoning off of areas that cannot be guarded, signage, warning notices encouraging patrons to be cautious and so on. There is also guidance to staff advising them not to put themselves at risk from violence by intervening with customers or criminals who may attack them. Indeed, the low number of violent incidents at MSAs may to some degree be due to the advice given to staff and their successes in heeding it.

MSA operators are likely to be most sensitive to offences where they, or their staff, are the potential victims. Most, though far from all, of the preventive efforts so far in the case study MSAs had been directed at reducing their risks. Indeed, recorded crime rates might well have been much higher without the MSAs' efforts. While there may in some cases be some scope for further MSA improvements, for crime prevention in relation to operators' property and personnel, it is likely that there is rather more scope for further preventive work in relation to the public as victims. On the whole, the MSA users' losses are greater and they are less likely to be visible as victims. MSA operators at their best are strongly committed to customer care. One part of this could include improved provision for the safety of those customers and their belongings while on MSA property.

Though the crime issues identified in this report are located on MSAs, MSA operators are far from the only organisations whose practices and policies impact on the risks faced by both customers and MSAs themselves. The following sections highlight some preventive opportunities, challenges and possibilities for a range of different organisations, including the MSA operators but not only them. We begin with what might be done at existing MSAs, then move on to ways in which crime might be designed out of planned MSAs, and then turn to other agencies and organisations whose products and practices might be changed in ways that would reduce crime at MSAs.

General issues in preventing crime at existing MSAs

Crime patterns vary by MSA. A starting point in determining how to reduce crime will involve analysing the data on existing patterns. The police do have data that can usefully be drawn on, though it requires some time and effort to extract them. We initially hoped for three years' data relating to all crime types. It was not possible to extract them. When extracted the data required checking and correcting for coding errors. Some text fields had to be read and special codes created to subject the data to aggregate analysis. Police data are a useful resource for smart crime prevention – to check what the crime problems are, to understand them and to inform ideas about what might be done to reduce them. Strong, consistent recording practices using pre-coded variables whenever possible would make analysis of the sort undertaken here much more straightforward. Some potentially useful analyses were not possible because of lacunae in the data. For example, the coding did not permit comparison of patterns of incident at individual MSAs by the side of the carriageway on which the incidents occurred.

In addition to police data on incident numbers, it would have been useful to have consistent denominator data to calculate rates. Throughput of traffic, MSA sales figures, footfall, lorry park numbers of overnight stays and car park numbers visiting would have been ideal. None of these was obtainable for the MSAs studied. Indeed, it is likely that operators would want at least some of these figures kept confidential for commercial reasons. An MSA operator with strong records on individual MSA usage combined with strong police data would be able to examine the patterns of crime across their entire operation to identify where preventive efforts are most needed. They might also have access to a range of data on crime and disorder related issues that do not necessarily come to the attention of the police, such as criminal damage, shrinkage, staff harassment, etc.

Police posts at MSAs are often located at their fringes and infrequently used. Greater police visibility could be achieved by providing space for officers to park, rally and refresh themselves at MSAs in more prominent places, where and when offending peaks – perhaps in car parks in late afternoons and early evenings and lorry parks at night. In the daytime, reassurance to public and staff at MSAs might be enhanced by uniformed officers eating in MSAs. The less predictable that police attendance is, the more difficult it becomes for offenders to anticipate and avoid the perceived increased risk that can be expected from police presence.

Most MSAs make some use of security patrols. The specific patterns of offending by time and place within MSAs identified in this report suggest patterns of deployment that would maximise impact.

Crime at MSAs affects the operator, staff and users. The MSA operator has an interest in its own losses and in the welfare of staff. They also arguably have a responsibility for user care. MSA managers have diverse responsibilities competing for prioritisation. Routine attention to crime prevention could be improved by making reported crime one of the performance indicators used by central management.

Car parks

A recent review of the Secured Car Park Award Scheme (Smith *et al.* 2003) found that design modifications could reduce crime in high-crime car parks and maintain low levels in low-crime car parks. Police architectural liaison officers and crime prevention officers can advise on what is required to obtain an award. The scheme's self-assessment manual can also be drawn on in efforts to improve security (ACPO, no date). Smith *et al.* found that those parking in car parks that conformed to 'secured by design' principles – in particular where lighting was good, they were clean, layout was good, CCTV was installed and staff were present – were also less likely to be concerned about being victimised.

Given the particular temporal patterns of thefts from vehicles at MSA car parks – notably the concentration of incidents on weekdays in the late afternoon and early evening – providing for enhanced guardianship at peak times may reduce crime by increasing perceived risks to offenders. Increased guardianship could be provided either by dedicated high-visibility patrols or by agreeing that prominent vendors and other service providers operate at these times to provide natural surveillance.

Forecourts

There is a widespread problem of fuel drive-offs on a range of sites for forecourts. BOSS (the British Oil Security Syndicate) estimated losses of £12 million nationally for 2001, down from £17.1 million in 2000. There seems no reason to suppose that the issues are especially marked at MSAs. The figures suggest something of a problem, but not out of proportion to other service stations or the volume of traffic dealt with at MSAs. The kinds of measures research suggests might be effective in reducing fuel drive-offs include, for example, pay-first policies (probably not practical at service areas), clear lines of sight for the till operator where payment is made (including their proximity to un-obstructed windows), good lighting, CCTV and signage indicating that CCTV is operating and number plates are recorded (see LaVigne 1994).

Detailed and systematic signed records of fuel drive-off incidents would bring at least two specific benefits. First, they would provide a disincentive to collusive frauds since staff members making the report would have to endorse the report form and repeat reports could be interrogated in detail to see if there were any suspicious circumstances. Second, detailed analysis of incident patterns would be possible, enabling for example the identification of individual pumps where offences were most common and the times when the incidents occurred. This could inform specific pump closure decisions at quiet sales times when risks of fuel drive-offs are also high.

Well-publicised police crackdowns at MSAs, applied randomly at MSA forecourts with high rates of fuel drive-off, may be expected to produce a preventive impact beyond their operation. Less expensively, police vehicles parked at forecourts experiencing spates of fuel drive-off may discourage offenders.

The low-volume but high-cost thefts of vehicles from forecourts where keys have been left whilst the customer pays for fuel may be addressed in part by posting reminders at pumps that drivers take their keys, preferably locking their vehicles when paying.

Lorry parks

Overnight thefts from curtain-sided lorries in lorry parks is a substantial problem. As with car parks, architectural liaison officers could usefully be asked to provide advice, attending to the rather specific patterns of thefts in lorry parks which are very different from those patterns of thefts from cars in MSA car parks. It would be useful to have a specific secured lorry park scheme, with awards, that could be promoted both to companies running fleets of trucks and operators of lorry parks.

The patterns of overnight offences in lorry parks may suggest benefits to gating or staffing access points, especially at night, to control the vehicular access needed for offloading the substantial volumes of goods currently often taken. Lighting and CCTV may increase per-ceived risk to potential offenders. Improving peripheral security, perhaps with locked gates at night, could reduce pedestrian access at high crime times. Encouraging drivers to park close together could make it more difficult for those wanting to slash curtains and offload goods. Randomised high visibility security patrols at night could increase perceived risk to those who might otherwise offend. Closure of non-motorway access roads could prevent local offenders from sneaking in easily from nearby neighbourhoods.

The likely association between thefts from lorries and organised stolen goods networks suggests that the police may benefit from concentrating efforts at detection and disruption of crimes in lorry parks and the subsequent disposal of goods taken. In these circumstances, non-closure of local access roads and use of automated number-plate recognition (ANPR) systems, for example to track the comings and goings of particular vehicles on nights where crimes are committed, may be preferable to efforts to inhibit crimes. There is a tension between immediate preventive efforts through assiduous application of situational measures and efforts at detection exploiting the repeat use made by organised offenders of good crime opportunities. Smart tags permitting the tracing of goods may be useful in the case of goods that are parked overnight in vulnerable locations, and that are readily open to resale in stolen goods markets.

A slight note of caution is needed here. A major organised group of offenders specialising in thefts from trucks using curtain slashing as their method became the target of sustained and successful specialist police squad attention. They were evidently most active for eight months in 1999–2000. During that period there was an average of one incident a month in the MSAs focused on here. In the following months, numbers rose. They increased again when news of the conviction with details of what was done in the offences and names and home addresses of those sentenced was posted on the Internet in spring 2001. In the following eight months there was an average of eight incidents per month. This suggests firstly that arrest per se may not be an effective way of containing crime, and secondly that the Internet may be a means of inadvertently disseminating information on crime opportunities and techniques to take advantage of them.

Main buildings

The different offences in MSA main buildings call for different preventive responses.

Theft from gaming machines

Gaming machines are especially attractive to thieves. They contain the most attractive object of theft – cash. Moreover, to allow pay-outs they are known to contain a substantial sum. The gaming machines area in MSAs is often set aside and hence provides some cover for the offender. Steps have already been taken by manufacturers to reduce the accessibility of the cash in machines to potential offenders. The machines clearly require very substantial peripheral security if they are to resist brute-force attacks. They might best be sited in locations where customers, and more particularly staff, are most likely to see them rather than tucking them away. It might be possible also to alarm machines with the sound going through to backroom staff. Advertising prominently the special measures taken to increase risk to the offenders may be effective in persuading some offenders that they do not comprise suitable targets.

Shop theft

The problems of shop theft in MSAs will be akin to shop theft problems in other self-service retail outlets. Preventing the crimes calls for similar measures, for example: care not to site attractive goods where they cannot be seen from the till; non-public display of high-value portable goods such as compact discs; locks on display cabinets; placement and elevation of till areas to maximise surveillance of the shop; use of tagging on crime-attractive products that customers will want to handle such as clothes; avoidance of forms of advertising that obstruct natural and shop-worker surveillance; care to take up staff references on appointment to avoid collusive theft (and fraud); use of till guards; and regular collection of cash from tills.

Personal theft

Handbags are attractive to thieves and are often quite readily available. It may be possible to provide more secure sites for their storage while customers are in the restaurant areas, for example, hooks under tables or under seats.

Overall perceived risks to the prospective offender within MSA buildings can be enhanced by layouts that maximise staff surveillance across their own and others' operational areas; by staff deployment patterns, for example to clean tables, that target surveillance; by front of building greeting practices that give customers a sense that they are being watched and watched over; and by managed pedestrian traffic that takes customers through areas where crime risks are high and hence natural surveillance is needed.

Burglary

Thefts from backrooms at MSAs could be made more difficult by fitting self-closing self-locking access doors wherever possible. Forced entries can be made more difficult with security upgrades and more risky by fitting alarms.

Designing crime out of new MSAs

It should be easier and less costly to build in crime prevention during the establishment of a new MSA than to make adjustments subsequently to a criminogenic environment. A low-crime MSA would need both to be designed physically and to be operated in ways that minimise crime opportunities while taking account of commercial imperatives such as the need to run self-service shops and forecourts. A low-crime MSA would also require continuous tracking of any emerging crime problems in order that modifications could be made to cut off any opportunities that emerge.

The following comprise a set of attributes that a low-crime MSA would need to incorporate.

General

- Maintenance of the MSA as a clean, orderly and graffiti-free area.
- Spatio-temporal deployment of security staff in accordance with characteristic patterns of crime in MSAs.
- Avoidance of situations where sales staff work on their own out of sight (and potential help) from colleagues.
- Encouragement of uniformed police usage of and presence at MSAs.
- Maintenance of detailed, structured records of incidents of crime and disorder that come to the attention of staff, to supplement those of the police.
- Regular liaison with local police to review crime patterns and identify emerging issues and ways to deal with them effectively.
- Controlled access from service roads.
- Performance management measurements at all levels that include numbers of crimes affecting the public and the MSA.

Car park

- Satisfaction of requirements for secured car park award.
- Maximisation of natural surveillance – for example, by locating the car park adjacent to the windows of MSA restaurant areas so that users can see the cars; by avoiding landscaping and planting practices that inhibit surveillance; channelling traffic so that drivers provide natural surveillance as they enter and leave the car park; by

providing safe walkways that enable natural surveillance; by permitting commercial activities in car parks, notably at typically high crime times; and by erecting wide-coverage CCTV and monitors that can be seen by the public within MSAs.

- Provision of perimeter security in locations where it is needed.

- Provision of adequate lighting.

Forecourt

- Maximisation of petrol pump surveillance opportunities from those operating the tills, especially of pumps delivering petrol, by lighting, placement of tills, clarity of lines of sight and CCTV.

- Signage indicating use of measures recording comings and goings from the service area and reminding drivers not to leave keys in their cars when paying for fuel

- Tannoy (public loud speaker) arrangements to communicate with customers, in particular to let them know they have been seen by welcoming them.

Lorry park

- Provision for surveillance from the MSA main building.

- Controlled single-point access, especially at night.

- Secure perimeter fencing.

- Recorded CCTV coverage of comings and goings.

- Security lighting.

- Parking layout minimising access to curtain-sided vehicles and maximising surveillance opportunities.

Main building

- Welcome desk.

- Through routes providing for natural surveillance, for example on the way to public lavatories.

- Advertised one-way mirror to games area, transparent surround to games area so that what happens within can be seen.

- Places to put handbags securely in the restaurant and lavatories.

- Self-locking doors to staff-only parts of MSAs.
- Mutual surveillance across zones in the MSA main building.
- Shop layout to facilitate surveillance.
- Non-open-display of high-value, high-theft items.

The study reported here used only reported crime. It is highly likely that much will be unreported. Within stores a proportion of the unreported crime will be unnoticed, for example shop theft. There will also be some shop theft and fraud that involves staff collusion (see Bamfield 1998) and some theft committed by employees that is either unnoticed or dealt with internally (see Beck and Willis 1995). In a low-crime MSA reported and unreported, internal and external crime needs to be minimised. There was a vanishingly small number of recorded incidents of internal and collusive crime in the data examined here, but there is no reason to believe that MSAs differ from other organisations in their susceptibility to it. Measures to reduce internal theft in a new MSA (both in the main building and on the forecourt), might include:

- clear rules for staff about what constitutes acceptable and unacceptable behaviour by them;
- checks on staff references on appointment;
- random bag checks for all staff when employees leave work at the end of a shift;
- clear procedures laying out consequences for employees if found to be involved in crime, including reports to the police, prosecution and pursuit of civil recovery;
- CCTV in storage areas and on tills;
- routine checks on any relationship between staff duty times and thefts/fraud cases.

Product and service design, and reducing crimes at MSAs

The issues raised in this section go beyond crime specifically at MSAs and refer to design issues relating to the specific crimes that have been found to occur at MSAs.

The theft of cars in which ignition keys have been left while the driver pays for petrol does not occur only on MSA forecourts. Cars might be designed to make it impossible to open the fuel cap while keys remain in the ignition (indeed some cars require the ignition key in order to open the fuel cap). The driver would then find it more difficult to provide the potential offender with the opportunity to steal the car.

The theft of laptop computers from parked cars raises more than one design opportunity. The first relates to cars. There seems to be a more or less continuous development of portable, anonymous, desirable, high-value, CRAVED products. Portable computers are simply one of a line of products of this kind. Building in scope for their incapacitation when stolen would reduce their attraction to thieves. This goes specifically for laptops but can be generalised also to future CRAVED products. The motor car is the container for many CRAVED products and is a site where they seem to be conspicuously accessible to thieves. There have, of course, been many developments improving the security of cars and their contents. Given the frequency with which CRAVED goods are targeted, the development and installation of some form of easily used and readily accessible car safe could provide drivers with the opportunity to lodge their most valuable possessions where they will be least vulnerable.

As with manufacturers of motor cars, manufacturers of gaming machines have been involved in continuous product design, part of which has focused on their accessibility to criminals. Offenders have found means to release the stock of cash in the machine and manufacturers have responded with design modifications to thwart them. The crudity of the methods used in the machine breaks found in this study is testament to the effectiveness of the design modifications made by manufacturers to prevent other methods. Nevertheless, there may be scope for improving the physical security of machines better to obstruct the 'brute-force' methods that were found here.

Tarpaulin covered lorries carrying CRAVED goods left unattended or unguarded are clearly good targets for crime. Several design possibilities arise relating to lorries, methods of improving peripheral security and methods of operating distribution networks. Lorries could have slash-proof tarpaulins or be otherwise redesigned to allow for ready accessibility of goods while providing for in-transit security. Development and provision of alarms, perhaps sounding in a device carried by the driver, might be made to alert the driver to potential thefts. Haulage companies might avoid carrying CRAVED goods in tarpaulin covered vehicles, especially where overnight stops are required. If they have to make such stops, they could try to identify places where their security can be assured overnight.

Conclusion

Even with the limited data that could be made available for this study, it is clear that crime in MSAs is highly structured and patterned, and that the observed patterns are created through differing opportunity generators. This situation presents a range of preventive opportunities, though not all fall under the control of any single body. The range of potential beneficiaries, potential change agents and potentially responsible bodies creates implementation challenges.

Levels of crime were found to vary between and within MSAs. It will clearly make sense to prioritise preventive efforts at the MSAs with relatively high levels of crime and, within them, on the most significant crime problems.

It seems likely that much crime could quite economically be designed out of newly developing MSAs not only with an eye to physical layout, but also by focusing on routine operating procedures.

Some of the crime problems encountered within MSAs might be more effectively and efficiently addressed by company fleet operators, hauliers, vehicle designers and likely hot product manufacturers than by MSA operators or by them alone.

Note

1   This study formed part of a review of the future of the Central Motorway Police Group. The latter, which includes officers from Staffordshire, Warwickshire, West Mercia and West Midlands, has responsibility for policing the motorways around Birmingham. The work was carried out under the direction of the CMPG Executive Board. Chief Inspector Phil Marsh of CMPG played an essential role in the work reported here.

References

Association of Chief Police Officers (ACPO) (n.d.) *The Secured Car Park Award Scheme: Guidelines for Self-Assessment*. Home Office, ACPO and the British Parking Asociation.

Bamfield, J. (1998) 'A breach of trust: employee collusion and theft from major retailers', in M. Gill (ed.), *Crime at Work*, Vol, 2. Leicester: Perpetuity Press.

Beck, A. and Willis, A. (1995) 'The enemy within', *Security Management Today*, 4 (9).

Brantingham, P. and Brantingham, P. (1995) 'Criminality of place: crime generators and crime attractors', *European Journal of Criminal Policy and Research*, 3 (3): 5–26.

Clarke, R. (1999) *Hot Products: Understanding, Anticipating and Reducing Demand for Stolen Goods*, Police Research Series Paper 112. London: Home Office.

CMPG (2002). *A Strategic Review of the Central Motorway Police Group*. Staffordshire Police, Warwickshire Police, West Mercia Police, West Midlands Police and the Highways Agency.

LaVigne, N. (1994) 'Gasoline drive-offs: designing a less convenient environment', in R. Clarke (ed.), *Crime Prevention Studies*, Vol. 2. Monsey, NY: Criminal Justice Press.

Smith, D., Gregson, M. and Morgan, J. (2003) *Between the Lines: An Evaluation of the Secured Car Park Award Scheme*, Home Office Research Study 266. London: Home Office.

Chapter 6

Vehicle excise duty evasion in the UK

Melissa J. Smith and Barry Webb

The problem of vehicle excise duty

What is vehicle excise duty?

Vehicle excise duty (otherwise known as road tax) is a tax on vehicle ownership (Smith 2000). Almost all owners of vehicles used on the road must buy this tax and display a tax disc inside their front windscreen. If caught driving without a valid disc, the owner is liable for prosecution and can be fined up to £1,000.

To purchase VED, motorists need first to have a valid insurance and MOT certificate. They can choose to pay VED either annually or six monthly. The cost of VED currently ranges from £60 to £165 and is dependent on vehicle type, type of fuel used and the vehicle's carbon dioxide emission level (for new vehicles registered from March 2001). The different levels of payments are structured to encourage the use of 'environmentally friendly' vehicles and fuels.

Current levels of evasion in the UK

Despite the threat of prosecution, many motorists neglect to purchase VED. The numbers of those evading VED is monitored by regular national roadside surveys. Licence plate numbers of traffic throughout the country on different road types (e.g. motorways, minor roads, A roads) are recorded either by contractors or camera and compared with DVLA records to determine whether the vehicle is licensed or not. These surveys allow for reasonable sized samples of the vehicle population on the road to be analysed: in 2002, for example, over 700,000 vehicles were observed (Department for Transport 2002).

Figure 6.1 shows the roadside survey results of vehicles on the road with no VED from 1984/5 to 2002 in England and Wales in two different forms: as a proportion of the total traffic and as a proportion of total vehicle stock. The proportion of total traffic refers to the proportion of all vehicles observed evading VED. As shown in Figure 6.1, using this type of calculation it appears that there has been little change in VED evasion – from 2.9% (1984/5) – 2.8% (2002). The proportion of those in stock accounts, however, for the possibility that some vehicles are counted more than once in the roadside survey. To elaborate, generally those who drive with valid VED travel longer distances than those who drive without VED. Therefore in this type of survey there is a possibility that the same *licensed* vehicles may pass more than one survey site (because they travel longer distances) and are thus more likely to be double counted in the survey. If a licensed vehicle is double counted, it may over-represent the numbers of those which are licensed and under-represent the numbers of those unlicensed. However, the in-stock measurement takes this possibility into account and statistically adjusts for it after comparing the average number of repeat sightings of evading vehicles with the average numbers of repeat sightings for licensed vehicles. This measurement is thus a more reliable estimate of the problem.

Figure 6.1 displays three important findings. First, vehicles evading VED have increased from 4.8% (1.1 million vehicles) to 5.5% (1.76 million vehicles) of the vehicle stock. Although not statistically

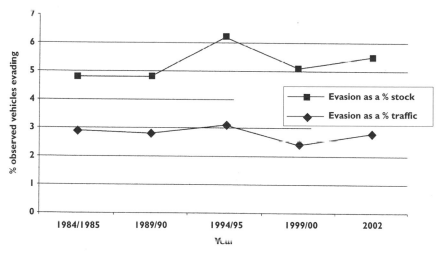

Figure 6.1 VED evasion as a percent of all observed traffic and of stock, in Great Britain, 1984/5–1999/2000

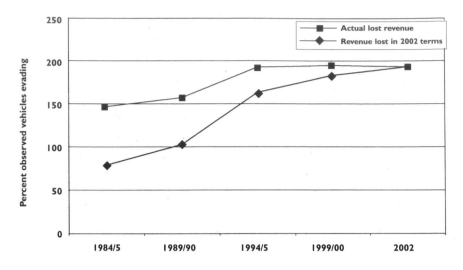

Figure 6.2 Estimated loss in revenue (£ million) from VED evasion 1984–2002

significant, this increase is still a point of concern. The peak observed in 1994/95 may be a consequence of a peak in the cost of insurance in those years (discussed below). Secondly, there is a higher rate of evasion 'in stock' compared with the rate 'in traffic' (which is to be expected, given the double counting adjustment that the in-stock measurement takes). Thirdly, the increasing disparity between the two measures suggests that vehicles without VED are used increasingly less frequently than licensed vehicles and are subsequently double counted less in traffic. If this trend is to continue, it may be harder to detect and capture those evading VED in the future. Equally, though, it suggests that VED evaders are sensitive to the risk of capture, and so may be more easily deterred in the future.

Despite only a small increase in the prevalence of evasion (0.7% in stock) over the last 17 years, revenue lost from VED evasion has increased substantially (Figure 6.2). In 2002, £193.4 million was lost in revenue, compared with around £79 million in 1984/5 (which, adjusting for inflation, equates to £147 million in 2002 figures[1]). This increase in lost revenue may be due to an increase in the number of vehicles on the road and the VED levy, as well as increased evasion rates.

Regional differences

Overall, VED evasion rates for the UK show an increase over the 17-year period. However, these roadside survey results also display marked

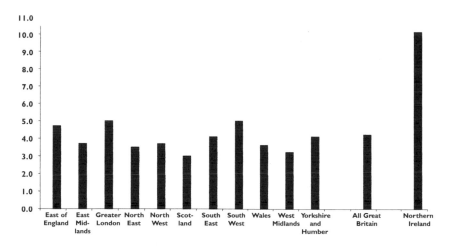

Figure 6.3 Regional variations in VED evasion rates (in stock) in the UK, 1999 and 2002

regional variations in evasion rates. Figure 6.3 shows regional levels of VED evasion in 2002 (figures are for private and light vehicles in stock). The regions with the highest rates of VED evasion in 2002 are Northern Ireland (10%), London (5%) and the South West (5%). Those with the lowest rates are Scotland (3%) and the West Midlands (3%).

VED evasion across different vehicle types, ages and lengths of time unlicensed

There are also differences in evasion rates across the range of vehicle types. Vehicles monitored for VED evasion in the roadside survey include private and light goods (cars, vans and small trucks), heavy goods, motorcycles and buses.

Of these vehicles, motorcycles suffer much higher rates of VED evasion than any other vehicle class. The 2002 roadside survey showed that although motorcycles made up only 0.5% of all sightings on the survey, the evasion rate for motorcycles accounted for 25% of stock. In comparison, private and light goods made up 89.6% of all sightings and their evasion rate was 4.2% of stock. This difference in evasion between the two vehicle classes is highlighted in Figure 6.4.

As shown in Figure 6.4, although motorcycles have a much higher VED evasion rate than private and light goods vehicles, both vehicle classes show a similar pattern of VED evasion with age. That is, older vehicles are more likely to show higher levels of VED evasion. Private

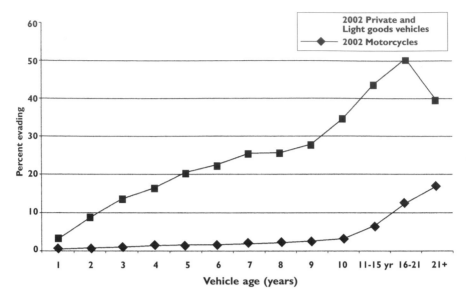

Figure 6.4 VED evasion rates for motorcycles and private and light goods vehicles 2002, by age of vehicle

and light goods vehicles aged two years have an evasion rate of 0.8% whereas those aged within the 16–21 year bracket have an evasion rate of 12%. Using these same age groups for motorcycles, 9% of two-year - old motorcycles evade VED and 50% of 16–21-year-old motorcycles.

Finally, examining the lengths of time people evade VED helps to build a more comprehensive picture of the behaviour and motives behind VED evasion in the UK.

Figure 6.5[2] shows that most people evade VED for short periods of time. Sixty per cent of those evading do so for four months or less (PLGs). Many people in this category may have inadvertently let their VED lapse because they have forgotten, or just 'haven't got around to it yet'. Alternatively, they may be 'skipping' a few months, in the knowledge (however true or untrue) that the risk of getting caught is relatively small.

In contrast, 10% of evaders driving PLGs evaded VED for more than one year. This 10% are most likely the 'hard-core' evaders – those that have no intention of paying VED. They may also be those that do not have insurance/MOT or are involved in other forms of vehicle crime. Interestingly, a greater proportion of motorcycle evaders evade for one year or more (35%) compared with PLG motorists. This suggests that an evasion culture may be more pervasive for motorcyclists than PLG

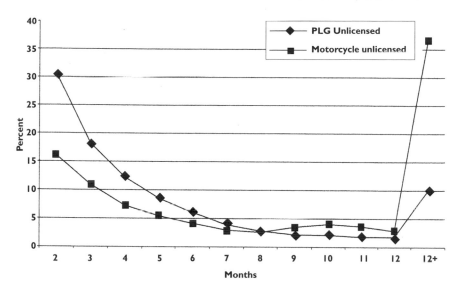

Figure 6.5 Time periods of evasion for PLGs and motorcycles, 2002

motorists. One reason for this may be that fear of having the tax disc stolen leads many motorcyclists to avoid displaying the disc and, in doing so, they develop a rather different perception of the risks of VED evasion from other motorists. Changing the behaviour of the long-term evaders will inevitably be more difficult than the 'month skippers'.

Factors contributing to VED evasion

There are a variety of factors which may motivate motorists to evade VED. However, two of the most likely factors are the high costs of motoring and the existing loopholes within the registration and licensing system.

Motoring costs

The average driver is faced with a multitude of motoring costs. Not only are they required to pay VED either every six months or once a year, but there are also insurance, MOT, fuel, servicing and repair costs to pay. On their own, these costs might not seem a lot. Added together, they can cost the average motorist a considerable amount of money. In fact, figures released in March 2004 show that the average cost of running a car is around £102 per week (RAC Insure 2003).

The relationship between running costs and evasion is complex, and is mediated by income levels among other factors. On average, motoring costs amounted to 13% of income in 2001/02 (see Figure 6.6). RAC research found, however, that some owners spend up to 25% of their income on motoring costs (RAC Insure 2003). The motivation to reduce costs through, for example, VED evasion will be much higher in these groups.

Figure 6.6 shows motoring costs from 1984 to 2002 (Office of National Statistics, 1984–2002). These motoring costs include the vehicle's running costs, as well as purchase price of the vehicle, parking fees, tolls, permits, driving lessons, garage rent and motoring subscriptions. As shown, the financial burden of owning and running a vehicle has greatly increased over the last 17 years, with motoring costs nearly doubling as a proportion of weekly disposable income. This may in part be a consequence of an increase in car ownership. Between 1991 and 2001, car ownership increased by 4% in Great Britain (DfT 2003). The number of households running two or more cars has also increased. In 1990, 23% of households owned two or more cars and in 2000 this figure was 26% (DfT 2003).

Figure 6.6 also shows some interesting trends in the different expenses that make up motoring costs. VED costs, as a proportion of income, have remained relatively stable over the last 17 years. However, the picture is a somewhat different when other running costs (e.g. insurance, spares and accessories, fuel, repairs and servicing) are examined (as a proportion of disposable income). These costs have increased over this time period.

Teasing out insurance from running costs shows that insurance costs peaked in 1994/5 (Figure 6.7). This pattern bears similarities to the pattern of VED evasion in Figure 6.1, which also peaked in 1994/95, suggesting that substantial change in insurance costs may be reflected in increased VED evasion rates. Given that VED cannot be bought without insurance, it seems highly possible that VED evasion is at least in part a consequence, intended or otherwise, of insurance evasion.

High insurance costs might also explain the particularly high rate of VED evasion in Northern Ireland. Northern Ireland has the highest VED rates in the UK – an evasion rate of 10% compared with England's rate of 5.2%. It also suffers higher insurance premiums. The average amount spent on insurance per week in 1999–2000 in Northern Ireland was £6.80, in contrast to £4.30 spent on average per week in England (DfT 2001).

As shown previously, older vehicles suffer from higher rates of VED evasion, and motorcycles have a higher rate of VED evasion than all

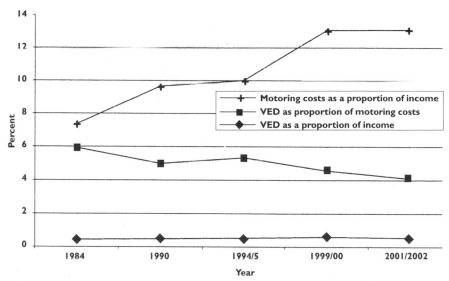

Figure 6.6 Average VED and motoring costs as a proportion of the average weekly disposable income
Source: Family Expenditure Surveys 1984/5–2001/2

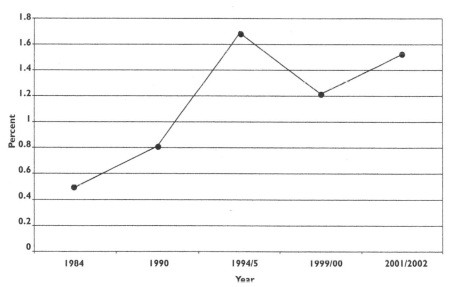

Figure 6.7 Average insurance costs as a proportion of average weekly disposable income

other vehicle types. The insurance premiums for these groups are also high, especially in comparison with the vehicle value. In 2002, the average insurance premium for motorcycles was £275 (Motorcycle Action Group 2003), while those for a Ford Focus car averaged £360 (AA 2003). The insurance premium for motorcycles shown above was thus around 75% of that for a car, yet an average motorcycle's value is far less than a car – only one in five motorcycles is worth more than £4,000 (MCE, 2002). Insurance costs which appear high in relation to the actual value of the vehicle may therefore deter motorists from buying insurance, which disenfranchises them from buying VED. Furthermore, not only are insurance costs likely to be much higher in comparison with the vehicle's value, but these vehicles are also likely to be owned by poorer motorists who are less able to afford VED.

In sum, although the increase in VED costs over time is not likely to have greatly impacted financially on the average vehicle owner, the dramatic increase in running costs, especially insurance, is more likely to have made a substantial impact on owners' wallets. This situation will provide the motivation for vehicle owners to try and reduce or evade as many motoring costs as possible, resulting in higher rates of VED evasion.

Although increasing motoring costs may provide the *motivation* for motorists to evade VED, without an *opportunity* to do so the crime cannot be committed. Loopholes in the current registration and licensing system provide many opportunities.

Designing out VED evasion – the registration and licensing system

The licensing and registration system was first developed amid public concern about dangerous driving. In 1903 under the Motor Car Act, it became a legal requirement that all vehicles should be registered with their local county council. Over time, changes have been made to this system, including the introduction of tax discs (1921), compulsory third-party insurance (1930), compulsory driving tests (1935) and MOT tests (1960). The huge increase in vehicle ownership resulted in the creation of a national Driver and Vehicle Licensing Centre (later to be named the Driver and Vehicle Licensing Agency, DVLA) which recorded and maintained records of all vehicles in the UK. Although the DVLA took control of the licensing and registration system, the demands placed on this system have increased and with it an increase in the number of opportunities for vehicle crime.

A key problem with the current registration and licensing system is the extent to which details held centrally by DVLA about vehicles and their current keepers are accurate (Laycock *et al.* 2002). There remains some question of exactly how inaccurate the DVLA database is. The DVLA estimate that errors may be found in up to one million records on their database (Home Office 1998) whereas anecdotal evidence from police indicate that where DVLA have supplied information on the registered keeper, this information has been found to be incorrect for a minimum of 10% of queries (PA Consulting 2003). Other agencies that rely on the DVLA database have found that 10–25% of parking penalty notices sent out using the database information were sent to the wrong person or address (*Observer*, 10 November 2002). Although the exact inaccuracy rate is not known, all the estimates suggest it is sufficient to create opportunities for significant levels of VED evasion, driving without insurance and MOT, and vehicle theft as the following will illustrate.

When a vehicle is first registered, basic information on the vehicle is collected (e.g. make, model, number plate, etc.) and stored at the DVLA. When the vehicle is relicensed, sold, scrapped or altered in any manner this information is supposed to be updated.

Inaccuracies that have been found in this record include vehicles recorded as on the road even though they have actually been scrapped, vehicles recorded as unlicensed even though they are actually licensed (and vice versa), and mismatches between vehicles and their current and previous vehicle owners. These inaccuracies can arise at many different stages of a vehicle lifecycle. For example, if a vehicle is sold, both the vendor and the purchaser are expected to notify the DVLA that they had sold and bought the vehicle respectively. Prior to 2004, if either party failed to notify the DVLA, the DVLA would remain unaware of this change and the new owner would be able to drive around in their newly purchased vehicle without paying VED since they could claim they had just bought the vehicle (even if it was some time ago) and were planning on buying the VED.

People were also able to report that their car had been scrapped to avoid paying VED. Scrap yards are required to notify DVLA when they dispose of a vehicle. However, not all scrap yards do so. This resulted in vehicles that were legitimately scrapped being labelled on the DVLA's database as still on the road, while others could be fraudulently reported as scrapped even though they were still being driven. A further problem was the delay between a motorist purchasing VED and the time it took for the DVLA system to be updated. This could take up to six weeks. Knowledge of these delays led many motorists who were caught by police or other enforcement officers to use the excuse that the VED was 'in the post'.

Without checks on a buyer's identity at the point of sale, motorists could evade VED by registering their vehicle to a false name and address. By registering to a false name and address, the motorist could not only avoid speeding and parking fines, but they could also claim if caught driving without VED that they were not the owner and escape paying an instant fine.

These problems in the DVLA records have been the subject of many complaints, especially from those who enforce VED using methods which rely on the DVLA record being accurate. The increasing use of Automatic Number Plate Readers (ANPR) is an example of such a method. ANPR systems are arranged so that when a vehicle drives past a camera, the number plate is read and compared with databases of registration marks wanted for various crimes. If the vehicle's registration mark 'hits' on one particular database, the police or DVLA can then apprehend the vehicle. One of these databases is a record provided by the DVLA of those with unpaid VED. However, because the DVLA is not always notified of keeper changes or scrapped vehicles and because of the mismatches in unlicensed vehicles that are actually licensed, the police have found that many of the stops made for VED evasion using ANPR are unfounded. As an example, the Metropolitan Police found that hits triggered from the DVLA's 'no VED' database were only 25–30% accurate (Metropolitan police, personal communication, 21 May 2003).

Table 6.1 shows the key changes being introduced to the registration and licensing system which are likely to impact on VED evasion. Specifically, Table 1 shows the changes being introduced, explains what each change is and how and why we would expect it to reduce VED evasion.

These changes are likely to reduce VED evasion by ensuring that the system has a greater ability to capture the details of the current vehicle owners, thus deterring potential offenders, and allowing faster and more efficient detection of actual evaders. Changes such as EVI and the increased enforcement regimes should explicitly increase capture rates.

The following analysis shows when and by how much we might expect this programme to reduce VED evasion. Figure 6.8 below shows three possible scenarios. First, we forecast how VED evasion rates might look had none of the changes been implemented. This assumed a 'best-case' scenario (Scenario 1). Second, we forecast how the rates might look if only continuous registration and no other changes are made. And

Table 6.1 Changes to the licensing and registration system likely to impact on VED evasion

Initiative	How it will work	How will it impact on VED evasion
Continuous registration (January 2004) and new buyer checks (January 2005)	Owners remain liable for their vehicles until the vehicle is registered with another keeper or reported scrapped, exported or stolen. Those who do not relicense will be issued with Fixed Penalty Notices.	Sellers encouraged to pass on new keeper details to the DVLA. Buyer checks reduce possibility of buyer giving false name or address. Threat of fines deters owners from evading VED.
	New buyers must provide confirmation of their identity and address when registering and licensing their vehicles.	Long term, details of vehicle ownership and vehicles scrapped on DVLA's database will be more accurate. This increase in accuracy will be especially marked in ownership details of older vehicles, which are more likely to be inconsistent because of address and ownership changes than younger vehicles.
Harmonised V5 (Jan 2004)	Vehicle registration information differs across countries. These barriers will be broken down, and there will be more information sharing.	Improved database ownership details, although it will depend on the level of information sharing between countries.
New enforcement regime (end 2004)	Fourfold increase in wheelclamping (approximately 200,000 vehicles clamped) and national roll out of ANPR from April 2004. Increased Statutory Off Road Notification (SORN) enforcement for vehicles that have been declared not in use and therefore off road by their owners, from 15% to 100%.	Speed up detection of unlicensed vehicles and enable more unlicensed vehicles to be identified. Reductions in the numbers of vehicles that are declared off road, even thought they are actually in use. Visible enforcement will increase the perceived risk of detection and act as a deterrent.

Table 6.1 continued

Initiative	How it will work	How will it impact on VED evasion
Virtual database (plans for 2005)	Each motor database system, e.g. motor insurance, MOT, DVLA databases, linked to others electronically. This may be a 'real-time' link.	Improved accuracy of vehicle records, as vehicle details are checked and updated at every opportunity. Increase in the speed and capacity of enquiries (e.g. police) that can be made, meaning more evaders will be identified at a faster rate than at present.
Electronic vehicle identification (2007)	Electronic chips can be placed in vehicles. When the vehicle drives past an electronic reader, the vehicle is identified. If the chip information does not match the database, or if the vehicle on this database is 'flagged', authorities alerted and the vehicle stopped.	Increases the risk of detection of VED evaders.

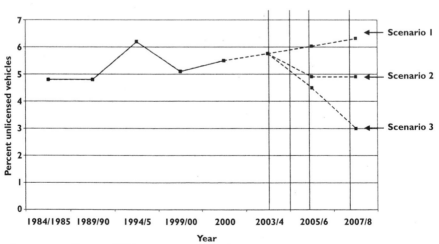

Figure 6.8   Future VED evasion 'in stock' rates

finally, we show how the VED evasion rates might look if all changes detailed in Table 6.1 are implemented.

Scenario 1 – VED evasion rates if nothing is implemented

The average age of the vehicle stock is growing. In Great Britain, 44% of vehicles were more than six years old in 1992–4. In 1999–2001, this figure had risen to 51% (Office of National Statistics 2004). Given the findings that VED evasion is higher in older vehicles and that the trend in the financial burden of running a motor vehicle is increasing, we would expect VED evasion to increase further if no intervention had been implemented. We might expect VED evasion in stock to continue its upward trend, increasing from the current 5.5% to 6.3% by 2007.

Scenario 2 – continuous registration only implemented

Given that continuous registration is the only substantial change implemented to date, we forecast how VED evasion rates might look if no other changes were to take place.

The purpose of continuous registration is to monitor keepership change more effectively. It is therefore more likely to impact on VED evasion committed by new keepers rather than existing keepers. The introduction of continuous registration was accompanied by a well publicised message that the DVLA can now track and fine the new current vehicle owners. This increased awareness that owners can now be traced and fined more easily may encourage new vehicle owners to renew their VED more promptly.

Scenario 2 is based on the fact that approximately five million vehicles change hands every year. Given that the average VED evasion rate is approximately 5.5% (based on 2002 roadside survey data), the maximum by which continuous registration could reduce VED evasion is 275,000 vehicles per annum (5.5% of 5 million). By 2006, the evasion rate would subsequently lie around 5%. As the problem of VED evasion in recently sold vehicles is resolved, this trend would be expected to remain stable at the lower level.

Scenario 3 – all initiatives implemented

The third scenario is based on the assumption that all changes including increased enforcement through greater use of ANPR and wheel-clamping, the creation of a single virtual database and EVI will be implemented.

Experiences with the ANPR system in Northampton led the police to sapprehend 10% of 'hits' against the 'no current VED' database produced by DVLA. National roll-out of ANPR is expected during 2004. Assuming that other forces across the country have a capability similar to Northampton, the number of evading vehicles could be reduced by 130,000 through increased capture rates in addition to the reduction in evasion by continuous registration. This could result in an evasion rate of 4.5% by the end of 2005.

As enforcement becomes more intensive and targeted over time, more evaders are likely to be caught. Furthermore, more people might be deterred from evading VED providing that an effective communication strategy (such as that accompanying the implementation of continuous registration) is put in place. This has the potential to influence particularly those who evade for only short periods of time – the so-called 'month skippers'. These short-term evaders, evading for less than four months, constitute 60% of total evaders. Assuming that these changes impact on approximately half of these short term-evaders, this could possibly result in a decrease in evasion to 3% by 2007.

Finally, measures such as EVI will result in further reductions in evasion in forthcoming years as it captures the more determined evaders.

Resulting loss in revenue

These three scenarios result in different losses in revenue to the government (see Figure 6.9). Figure 6.9 takes into account the increasing numbers of vehicles on the road and assumes no substantial change in the tax levy.

Figure 6.9 shows by the end of 2007/8[3]:

1   Had no interventions taken place, over £230 million per year, at today's prices, could have been lost from VED evasion (Scenario 1).
2   If no measures other than the current continuous registration are introduced, VED evasion could result in losses of up to £170 million per year (Scenario 2).
3   If all measures are to be introduced, VED evasion would result in losses of under £100 million per year and should decrease further into the future (Scenario 3).

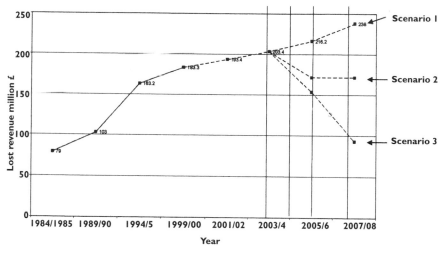

Figure 6.9 Predicted future trends

Future recommendations

The extent to which these outcomes are achieved depends, among other factors, on how well these measures are implemented. When designing crime prevention approaches in general, issues surrounding implementation need to be considered and addressed as they can be vital in ensuring the success of the approach. In this particular case, implementation issues that need to be addressed include publicity, the partnership approach and timing.

Communication strategies will be vital to make the most of the interventions planned. Research has shown that publicity can have a positive impact on anti-crime projects (Bowers and Johnson 2003). For vehicle crime campaigns, the aim of the publicity should be to increase the perception of risk among offenders and potential offenders by publicising that something is actually being done and that people are actually being caught. This message, if widespread, should help to deter some offenders.

Secondly, an effective partnership approach is important. The success of these changes will depend upon how well agencies such as the DVLA and the police work together. While the DVLA and police already collaborate, the DVLA database inaccuracy may hinder police confidence in VED evasion 'hits' received on ANPR. Once issues such as these are addressed, the DVLA will be able to work more effectively with the police in capturing VED evaders.

Finally, the accuracy of the projections we have produced here is dependent upon timing. If the proposed changes are delayed, not only will this affect the projections, but there is also the risk that evasion could escalate as potential offenders have more time to find ways around the new system. Experience from other car theft initiatives, for example steering column locks, is that it is much better to introduce a full package of measures quickly than it is to introduce them in a piecemeal fashion over a period of time. The former strategy has the ability to eradicate a culture while the latter does not (Webb, 1994).

Summary and conclusion

This chapter has provided an illustration of how crime prevention researchers can apply their skills to practical problems to assist policy-makers in focusing their efforts and galvanising attention to the problem. Because there are so many variables that are beyond our control (such as the economic climate, numbers of vehicles on the road and so forth), the forecasts produced here should not be taken as absolute or precise. However, they are sufficient to enable policy-makers to see what might be achieved if they get implementation of these measures right and prevent VED evasion by designing it out through changes in the regulatory system.

VED evasion is a serious problem in the UK. The latest roadside survey in 2002 revealed that 5.5% of the nation's total vehicle stock did not have valid VED. While it is a national problem, some areas suffer higher rates of evasion than others, notably Northern Ireland, and vehicles aged around 16–21 years are generally more at risk of evasion as are certain vehicle types (e.g. motorcycles). Finally, the majority of those that evade VED appear to do so for relatively short periods of time, usually four months or less. Some of these anomalies and indeed the motivation to evade VED itself could well be explained by the high costs of motoring, particularly insurance, which has increased over the last 17 years. In evading insurance costs, motorists are unable to obtain VED.

While the high costs of motoring may well provide the motivation for evading VED, the opportunity to evade VED has arisen through the loopholes in the licensing and registration system itself. The system was designed over 100 years ago. While alterations have been made to the system over time, weaknesses have emerged in the current system. For example, these have allowed people to scrap or exchange ownership without notifying the DVLA. As a result, the inaccuracy in the DVLA record makes enforcing VED compliance a difficult task.

This chapter has shown that if current plans for tightening the system are implemented, VED evasion could drop from the current 5.5% to 3%. Financially, this could reduce the current amount of revenue lost by nearly half – from the current £194 million down to £100 million.

Aside from these, there may be other benefits to be gained from this programme. These measures may not only affect VED evasion; they also have the potential to affect other crimes. For example, many of the 'hard-core' evaders are also likely to be evading MOT and insurance requirements, and indeed may be wanted by the police for other crimes. A pilot study of ANPR capabilities in the UK found that some drivers originally stopped for evading VED were also found to have committed other offences such as burglary, drugs or auto crime (PA Consulting 2003). Thus, by increasing their likelihood of capture there may be a reduction also in other terms of vehicle-related crime. The programme of change discussed here, therefore, promises to have an impact beyond the targeted problem.

Notes

1   See McCusker (2001).
2   Based on analysis of DVLA data from the month of September 2002.
3   Revenue lost each year is shown in Figure 6.9 as actual values – not adjusted to 2002 values.

References

AA (2003) *The AA's Ford Focus Survey 2003*. Retrieved from: http://www.theaa.com.

Bowers, K. and Johnson, S. (2003) *The Role of Publicity in Crime Prevention*. London: Home Office.

Department for Transport (1984/5) *Transport Statistics: Vehicle Excise Duty Evasion in Great Britain in 1984/85*. London: HMSO.

Department for Transport (1990) *Transport Statistics: Vehicle Excise Duty Evasion in Great Britain in 1989/90*. London: HMSO.

Department for Transport (1995) *Transport Statistics: Vehicle Excise Duty Evasion in Great Britain: 1994/95*. London: HMSO.

Department for Transport (2000) *Transport Statistics: Vehicle Excise Duty Evasion: 1999*. London: HMSO.

Department for Transport (2001) *Focus on Personal Travel*. London: HMSO.

Department for Transport (2002) *Transport Statistics: Vehicle Excise Duty Evasion: 2002*. London: HMSO.

Department for Transport (2003) *Transport Statistics for Great Britain edition 2003*. Available from: http://www.dft.gov.uk/stellent/groups/dft_transstats/documents/page/dft_transstats_025215.pdf.

Home Office (1998*). Road Policing and Traffic: HMIC Thematic Inspection Report 1998*. Retrieved from: http://www.homeoffice.gov.uk/hmic/roadpol.htm

Laycock, G., Burrows, T. and Morgan, R. (2002) *Crime Prevention and the UK Vehicle Registration and Licensing System*. Published on the Jill Dando Institute website: www.jdi.ucl.ac.uk.

McCusker, J. (2001) *Comparing the Purchasing Power of Money in Great Britain from 1264 to Any Other Year Including the Present*. Economic History Services. Retrieved from: http://www.eh.net/hmit/ppowerbp/.

MCE 2002). *Biking in the UK: A Young Man's Game?*, 18 December. Retrieved from: http://www.insuremce.com/news/index.asp#news16.

Motorcycle Action Group (2003) *Motorcycle Action Group (MAG-UK) 2002 Survey Results*. Retrieved from: http://www.mag-uk.org/index2.html.

Observer (2002). 'Chaos hits London traffic charge plan', 10 November. Retrieved from: http://observer.guardian.co.uk/politics/story/0,6903,837031,00.html.

Office of National Statistics (1984/5) *Family Spending: A Report on the 1984/5 Family Expenditure Survey*. London: Stationery Office.

Office of National Statistics (2000) *Family Spending: A Report on the 1999/00 Family Expenditure Survey*. London: Stationery Office.

Office of National Statistics (2004) *Regional Trends, No. 38*. London: Stationery Office.

PA Consulting (2003) *Engaging Criminality – Denying Criminals Use of the Road*. Home Office.

RAC Insure (2003) *RAC Motoring Index, Quarter 4, 2003*. Retrieved from: www.rac.co.uk/pdfs/2314insureindex.pdf.

Smith, Z. (2000) *Vehicle Excise Duty Evasion in Rural Areas*, Briefing Note 10. London: Institute for Fiscal Studies.

Webb, B. (1994) 'Steering column locks and motor vehicle theft: evaluations from three countries', in R.V.G. Clarke, (ed.), *Crime Prevention Studies*, Vol. 2. New York: Willow Tree Press, pp. 71–91.

Webb, B., Smith, M. and Laycock, G. (2004) 'Designing out crime through vehicle licensing and registration systems', in M.G. Maxfield and R.V. Clark (eds), *Understanding and Preventing Car Theft*, Crime Prevention Studies, Vol. 17.

Chapter 7

Predicting the future or summarising the past? Crime mapping as anticipation

Shane D. Johnson, Kate J. Bowers and Ken Pease

Reducing uncertainty about when and where crime is likely to occur facilitates its reduction, by limiting opportunity at crime-prone times and places and by detecting offenders at work. 'Sting' operations illustrate the extreme case wherein crime opportunities are engineered. Their attractiveness inheres in the predictability of time and locale of crimes. Sting operations will always be exceptional, not least because of the possible charge of entrapment of offenders through the creation of attractive opportunities. For volume crime generally, crime mapping has, over the last decade, afforded the most common means by which uncertainty about the distribution of future crime can be reduced. The standard general approach taken has been to map the past and to assume the future will resemble it.

This chapter considers whether crime prevention (through opportunity reduction and/or detection) could be deployed with greater accuracy than conventional mapping approaches allow. The belief that this should be possible derives from a raft of research showing how crimes are patterned spatially and temporally. If one conceives each crime event as in its own right a communication about the future, and the task of prediction being to synthesise those communications optimally to predict crime, there emerges a more ambitious agenda for the mapping enterprise. Predicting future patterns requires an understanding of the sequenced way in which things typically occur, which can be summarised as a set of principles and operationalised. This can only be achieved with the availability of good data and through the execution of systematic empirical research. The chapter focuses on domestic burglary, but support for the generalisability of the approach taken is evidenced at its end. Before moving to the original work, we will provide a brief overview of resource targeting in crime reduction to date.

Conventional approaches to the assessment of crime prediction

A number of approaches are used to identify areas of high crime risk. For instance, some initiatives, such as the New Deal for Communities programme, allocate resources on the basis of area-level indicators of deprivation. Such an approach has some limited appeal, given the almost linear relation between (area-wide) levels of deprivation and rates of burglary (see, for instance Johnson *et al.* 1997). However, in a context where resources for crime prevention are limited, such an approach is inefficient. Allocating resources to areas wastes them on individuals and households at low risk in high-risk areas, and denies them to those at high risk in low-risk areas. Furthermore, the easy equation of deprivation with crime risk appears perverse at the individual household level. For instance, research has found that it is often more affluent types of housing that are targets of burglary within deprived areas (e.g. Budd 1999), and thus concentrating crime prevention effort in certain areas and on certain households on the basis of proxy indicators of area-level crime risk (such as deprivation) is misguided.

A more elegant and precise way of identifying areas of high crime has evolved over the last ten years with the proliferation of geographical information systems (GIS) and the advent of police recording systems that support the geo-referencing of crime records. Using a GIS and these data, analysts have been able to generate so-called (retrospective) 'hotspot' maps of increasing aesthetic sophistication. Similar in appearance to the types of analytical displays generated by meteorologists to describe weather pressure systems, hotspots of crime delineate areas of past high crime, typically shaded in dark red, and the areas of low crime (or cold spots) usually shaded in a lighter colour. Understandably, such maps have found considerable favour with academics and practitioners alike, not least because of their ability to convey a wealth of information in a readily interpretable (or misinterpretable) way. The geographical resolution of the hotspots identified is limited only by the accuracy of the data available and the parameters of the mathematical model used to generate the maps. Where recorded crime data are accurate to a resolution of one metre, as is often the case, this means that maps may be generated with a high level of geographical precision. In principle, this should allow a practitioner's attention to be directed to the specific locations where it is most required.

Whilst it is beyond the scope of this chapter to describe how hotspot maps are generated in any detail, we will briefly discuss the basic method to facilitate understanding of how what is proposed differs from it. The technique most commonly used involves the generation of a two-dimensional lattice to represent the area of interest. As shown in Figure 7.1, a two-dimensional lattice (Figure 7.1(b)) is overlaid upon a study area (Figure 7.1(a)). This comprises a series of (x*y) cells, each with identical proportions. The challenge of delineating a hotspot lies in the derivation of a set of values, one per cell, that reflects the intensity of crime risk at each location. Thus a methodology and mathematical algorithm is required that can generate risk intensity values for every cell. One technique commonly used to do this is called the 'moving window'. Here, a circle with a predetermined radius (referred to as the *bandwidth*) is drawn from the midpoint of each cell (Figure 7.1(c)), and each of the events that falls within the circle is used to generate the risk intensity value for that cell. The risk intensity value for each cell is determined by the number of crime events (in Figure 7.1, four for the cell considered) that occurred within the circle and how far away they are located from the midpoint of the cell. Those closest to the midpoint are typically assigned a greater weighting than those further away. To illustrate the method, three of the cells in Figure 7.1(c) have been shaded to indicate the intensity of risk at those locations. Those shaded darkest exhibit the highest risks. An example of a hotspot (quartic) function (Bailey and Gatrell 1995) is described by the following equation:

$$\lambda_\tau(s) = Y \sum_{di \le \tau} \frac{3}{\pi \tau^2} \left(1 - \frac{d^2_i}{\tau^2} \right)^2 \tag{7.1}$$

where $\lambda_\tau(s)$ = risk-intensity value for cell s
τ = bandwidth
d_i = distance of each point (i) within the bandwidth from the centroid of the cell.

The bandwidth used to generate the hotspot and the mathematical equation used to generate the risk-intensity values vary, but the basic rationale is the same.

The study of hotspots of crime can reveal much about patterns of

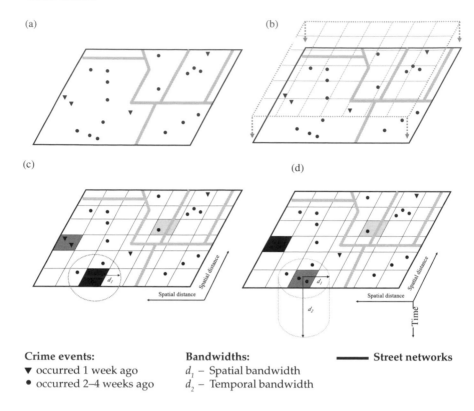

(a) (b)

(c) (d)

Crime events:
▼ occurred 1 week ago
● occurred 2–4 weeks ago

Bandwidths:
d_1 – Spatial bandwidth
d_2 – Temporal bandwidth

——— **Street networks**

Figure 7.1 Two-dimensional and three-dimensional hotspot lattices (a) study area; (b) study plus lattice; (c) lattice and retrospective moving window; (d) lattice and prospective moving window.

criminal activity and the relationship between levels of crime and other factors, such as deprivation and land use. This is important for our general understanding of how and where crime manifests itself. However, practitioners, including the police, also use the products of retrospective hotspot research to allocate resources. Here, the assumption is that the hotspots of yesterday will be the hotspots of tomorrow. Where this tactic is adopted, police (or other) resources are deployed according to the geographical constellation of historic criminal events, summarised in the form of a hotspot. This approach may be effective were the geographical pattern of crime to prove stable and unchanging, but we already know that this is not always the case (for a discussion of the flux of crime, see Barr and Pease 1990).

Surprisingly, given the near ubiquitous acceptance of these methods, there has been little evaluation of the predictive efficiency of extant hotspotting techniques. In one cautionary study, Townsley and Pease (2002) found that even hotspots based on data from the very recent past may be of limited value. This will be a particular problem where resources are deployed and tactics revised on a daily basis, because it is over small units of time that the dynamics of the flux of crime are most likely to be apparent. Expressed in a slightly different way, while some (large) areas may suffer from enduring high rates of crime one year to the next, the specific locations at which crimes occur are likely to vary considerably on a day-to-day basis. Since any police officer can only be in one small place at a time, the point is crucial. These more precise locations are less likely to be specifically highlighted using retrospective hotspot analysis – either because the geographic level of resolution used is too imprecise, or because the aggregation procedure employed to generate the maps masks differences in within-area risks. The former would be a problem where the cells used in the lattice model are too large, the latter where the bandwidth is too large. Thus it should be clear that the calibration of the model is of critical importance. Despite this, the choice of cell size and bandwidth used is typically somewhat arbitrary. Researchers often select parameters that produce attractive maps. We suggest that an approach more informed by theory and data capturing crime sequences is required. In the following sections we discuss an attempt to meet this goal. We begin by summarising some recent research that has examined the spatial and temporal patterns of crime in a new way, and then discuss how the findings may be used to inform predictive crime mapping.

Is the risk of burglary communicable?

What follows has its origins in three different fields of academic research. The first element considers criminal behaviour in terms of a model developed in behavioural ecology, *optimal foraging theory*. According to this theory (for an account, see Krebs and Davies 1987), when hunting for resources (e.g. food), animals aim to maximise the resources acquired while simultaneously minimising the consequent chance of getting injured (or eaten!) and the search time (or effort) involved. To what extent do offenders behave in this way?

The second element, from the discipline of criminology, concerns repeat victimisation – the finding that prior victimisation is an excellent predictor of future risk (for a review, see Pease 1998). Interviews with offenders reveal simple reasons why repeat burglaries occur. Typical responses include the following: that the house was known to be associated with low risk (to the offender); that the offender was familiar with the layout of the house; and the target was easily accessible (Ericsson 1995). The overwhelming evidence from the research undertaken, at least for domestic burglary, is that the same perpetrators are responsible for the bulk of offences against the same target (Farrell and Pease 2002). We suggest that repeat offending of this kind is a form of optimal foraging. After all, the offenders in question are aware of both the likely rewards of returning to the property and the potential risks of doing so. Considered in these terms, the best targets to select would be those where the likely yield was high and the probability of getting caught low.

Where repeats occur as a direct result of a prior offence, either because the same offender returns to the same property or because information about the property is shared amongst offender networks, the risk of victimisation at a particular home can be seen to be heightened as a result of the crime event itself. Thus the risk of crime is boosted (Pease 1998). In relation to crime prevention, the implications are clear – the crime event should trigger preventive action focused on the burgled home.

However, what of those as yet unvictimised? Returning to optimal foraging theory, consider that while an animal hunts in or surveys an area, it is likely to learn much about neighbouring or surrounding areas including the abundance of food, the presence of predators and so on. If offenders are optimal foragers, then we would expect the equivalent to be true. For instance, having burgled one property, they should develop their knowledge of nearby homes, such as the existence of escape routes and probable levels of physical security. From this line of reasoning, we hypothesised that burglaries would cluster in space and time, occurring within close proximity of one another in short spaces of time. If this were true, then the risk of victimisation may be conceptualised as being communicable, in much the same way as a disease. Crucially for the research described below, this spatial and temporal pattern of crime would differ from a geographical hotspot of crime, for which the only defining feature is the closeness of events in space over the past period considered. In the case of geographical hotspots, the sequenced interaction between precisely when and where crimes occur is essentially irrelevant.

To test the above hypothesis, we drew on research from a third discipline, epidemiology. Specifically, we analysed burglary data for the county of Merseyside using methods developed for the study of communicable diseases. Two types of analysis were used, but the rationale for both is essentially the same. To illustrate using a test developed by

Knox (1964), the number of crimes that occur within a series of specified distances (e.g. 0–100m) and times (e.g. 1 month) of one another are compared with what would be expected on the basis of chance. The chance or expected distribution is generated using the actual data (for details, see Johnson and Bowers 2004). Where there is an over-representation of events occurring close in space *and* time, this reflects space-time clustering. That is, burglaries occur within short distances and times of one another more frequently than we would expect if the spatial and temporal distribution of events were simply random.

Importantly, the analyses conducted can be used not only to detect space-time clustering but also the periods and distances over which victimisation has an impact. The methods allow us to answer the question – if a burglary occurs at one home, over what geographical distance is the risk of victimization communicated, for how long does this heightened risk endure and how does it decay? This is of clear importance, particularly in the current research, as knowing precisely how one burglary event influences the risk at other locations can help us to determine the bandwidths used when generating a risk surface.

To summarise the results, we found that crime *does* cluster in space and time, thereby exhibiting the key feature of communicability (Johnson and Bowers 2004). In particular, we showed that following an initial burglary event, there was a heightened risk of burglary to houses within 400 metres of the burgled home for a period of approximately one month. Similar results have been found in Australia (Townsley *et al.* 2003), and this phenomenon has been labelled 'near-repeats' (Morgan 2001) to reflect its extension and clarification of the phenomena of repeat victimisation. Put otherwise, repeat victimization is a special case of the space-time patterning of burglary.

Further analyses were conducted to examine the spatial distribution of near-repeats to see if they occur in the same places from one month to the next. The results showed that rather than occurring in the same places over time, as would be expected if they were simply an expression of a geographical hotspot of crime, they tended to occur in one area and subsequently in another, nearby area (Johnson and Bowers 2004). This is a finding whose importance it is difficult to exaggerate, as it highlights the flux of crime, and suggests a slippery aspect to the geographic placement of crime subversive of conventional hotspotting. This pattern is, of course, not considered in retrospective hotspot techniques. Rather, the geographical location of clusters of crime is there assumed to be predominantly anchored to specific locations.

Visualising patterns of risk

As with the research concerned with repeat victimisation, the findings have clear implications for crime prevention practice. These are probably best realised by improving the prediction of the future locations of crime, or what we have called *prospective mapping* (Johnson and Bowers 2004; Bowers *et al.* 2004). To explore this, we have developed a new algorithm for generating risk surfaces which, like hotspots, can be displayed using a GIS. At this stage, we have adopted a simple approach which uses only the basic rules generated by our earlier research. Part of the reason for starting with a simple approach was to test the robustness of the rationale. Specifically, if traditional hotspotting is less efficient because it is retrospective, then we should realise greater predictive accuracy even using a crude variant of existing techniques. If we were to start our endeavour using a more complicated approach, it would be difficult to determine whether an increase in predictive accuracy could be attributed to the underlying theory or the complexity of the algorithm used.

To generate prospective maps, we used a variant of the moving window technique discussed above. The novel feature was that the amount of time that had elapsed since each event occurred was considered as well as the distance between the crime events and cells. When defining the model used, we considered carefully the size of the cells in the two-dimensional lattice. Rather than opting for the highest resolution of cell size possible (e.g. 1m × 1m) we used dimensions that would be useful in an operational policing context. While the optimal size is difficult to determine, it is clear that if a cell is too large it will be too imprecise and much effort would be wasted in policing low-risk places within an area. Overly large cells would also suffer from the Modifiable Areal Unit Problem (Openshaw 1995), which occurs when the aggregate pattern across a series of smaller areas does not reliably reflect the patterns typical for the (smaller) areas themselves. For instance, if we calculate a risk-intensity value for one large area which encapsulates two smaller areas with very different risks, the true risks for neither of the smaller areas will be accurately reflected by the risk-intensity value for the aggregated area. Thus it is wise to use a cell size that enables differences in relative risk across (and within) cells within the lattice to be revealed accurately. However, it is also wise to avoid cell sizes that are simply too small. For instance, it is unlikely that a method which used one million cells, each 1m × 1m, would reveal more useful intellligence than a method in which the cells were say, 50m × 50m. Moreover, areal units such as the latter are perhaps more operationally relevant in the policing context – approximating, for instance, to typical lines of sight. For this reason we used a cell size of 50m × 50m, although we acknowledge that other dimensions could be used and may be more appropriate for other purposes.

The next issue that needed to be resolved concerned bandwidth. As is illustrated in Figure 7.1(d), we used two bandwidths in the present research. The first, the spatial bandwidth, was set at 400m to reflect the distance over which our results suggested that the risk of victimisation is communicable. This is the distance over which our findings suggested that a crime event would influence the risk of victimisation at other locations.

The second type of bandwidth was concerned with the time elapsed since crimes had occurred. This bandwidth was conditional upon the first, as a burglary event should contribute to the risk intensity value of a cell only if it occurred within 400m of that cell. For the temporal bandwidth, we used a period of one month as this reflected the period of time over which our results suggested that the communicability of risk endured. Of course, it is important to point out that the bandwidths selected were based on research for the area studied. If the same procedure was used for another geographical area, we would recommend that the model should be calibrated to reflect the patterns evident for the area concerned, if different.

A further methodological difference between our approach and that used in retrospective hotspotting lay in avoiding use of the distance from the midpoint of the cell and the relevant burglary events in the derivation of the risk intensity values. We felt that the usual approach can be misleading. Consider that for retrospective hotspotting a risk-intensity value is calculated for the midpoint of the cell and this value is then allocated to all other points within that cell. If risk-intensity values were computed for all points within a cell it is unlikely that they would be identical. Thus using the value for the centroid of the cell gives the impression that the risk of victimisation is uniform across the entire cell. This is unlikely to be true. This problem will be amplified as the cell size increases. Instead of using the exact Euclidian distance between all events and the cell midpoint, we used the number of cells, the actual unit of analysis considered, between the event and the cell considered. Thus if a crime occurred within the cell under consideration, the distance would be zero (actually, for computational reasons 1); if it occurred within an adjacent cell, two, and so on. By adopting this approach we feel that the risk intensity values for each cell reflect more accurately the risks across the entire cell rather than at one single point.

The formula used to derive the risk intensity values for the prospective map was as follows:

$$\lambda_\tau(s) = Y \sum_{ci \le \tau \cap ei \le \upsilon} \left(1 + \frac{1}{c_i}\right) * \frac{1}{e_i} \qquad (7.2)$$

where $\lambda_\tau(s)$ = risk-intensity value for cell s
  τ = spatial bandwidth
  υ = temporal bandwidth
  c_i = number of cells between each point (i) within the bandwidth and the cell
  e_i = time elapsed for each point (i) within the temporal bandwidth.

To illustrate the differences between equations (7.1) and (7.2) and the rationale underlying retrospective hotspotting and prospective mapping, the same three cells that are shaded in Figure 7.1(c) to reflect the risk-intensity values at those locations are also shaded in Figure 7.1(d). It is evident that when time is taken into account (as is the case with the prospective mapping function), the risk-intensity values (reflected by the density of the shading) for the three cells change. Thus, of the three cells considered, the cell on the left edge of the prospective map has the highest risk-intensity value, whereas this is not the case for the retrospective hotspot.

How predictive is prospective mapping?

The next step was to generate a prospective map and compare this to a retrospective hotspot. To do this, we used two months' burglary data for the county of Merseyside. Having generated the two maps it was necessary to compare the predictive efficiency of the maps in a meaningful way. Surprisingly we were unable to find examples of how to do this in the extant research literature. This perhaps reflects what might be described as an imbalance within the crime mapping research literature favouring the production of attractive maps over concerns with the predictive utility of alternative approaches. Consequently, we developed a series of simple metrics that can be used to evaluate the predictive efficiency of hotspot maps. Two will be used here and may be summarised as follows (Bowers *et al.* 2004):

1 *hit rate* – the number of future crimes that are captured by the defined hotspot area;
2 *search efficiency rate* – the number of crimes successfully predicted per km².

Of course, in both cases the results will be affected by the area considered in the analysis. If the entire surface area of a map is considered to be 'hot', then naturally all crimes will be successfully captured! Considering the two measures, the hit rate will simply increase as the area considered 'hot' is extended. In contrast, however, the search efficiency rate is affected not only by the number of crimes captured but also by the area considered. For instance, if an increasingly large area is considered 'hot' but no more crime is captured, the search efficiency rate will decrease, indicating a trade-off between the effort expended and the capture rate. The advantage of using a standardised index like this is that it allows different procedures to be meaningfully compared.

Considering the results of our earlier research, the analysis indicated that the prospective map was more accurate than the retrospective hotspot, successfully identifying a greater number of burglary events (62% vs 46% of events respectively) that occurred in the two days that followed the historic period used to generate the maps. In that analysis we generated only one map of each type and hence the possibility exists that the results may not have been representative. Consequently, for the current chapter we generated three maps of each type, one for each of three different days of the week.

A further question that currently remains unanswered and hence addressed here concerns the duration over which different types of map accurately predict where crimes will occur in the future. That is, does the predictive efficiency of the maps deteriorate over time and, if so, for how long into the future does a map remain useful?

To clarify this, we assessed the accuracy of the two maps for the seven days following their construction. To do this, we used burglary data for the same geographical grid in South Liverpool used in our earlier research (Bowers *et al.* 2004). The dimensions of the grid used were approximately 5km by 5 km. Two months' historic data were used to generate the maps, and data for a further month were used to evaluate the predictive accuracy of the maps.

Figures 7.2(a) and 7.2(b) exemplify the two types of map (the prospective in Figure 7.2(a) and the retrospective in Figure 7.2(b)). The cells shaded darkest (approximately 20% of the cells for each map[1]) are those for which the risk intensity values are highest. The figure also shows the spatial location of the crimes occurring within the next seven

(b) Retrospective

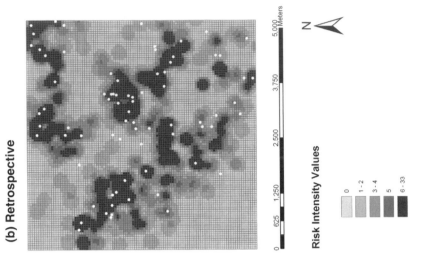

(a) Prospective

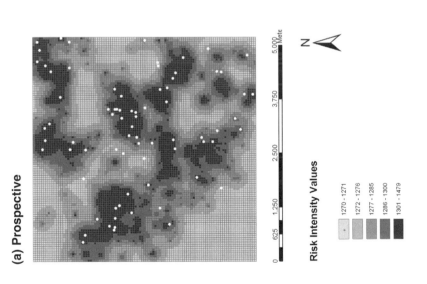

Figure 7.2 Prospective and retrospective maps

days. As is evident from Figure 7.2 the maps are to some extent similar. However, closer inspection reveals differences. For instance, at the bottom centre of the two maps, the prospective map captures two events that are not identified in the hotspot map. Similarly, more burglary events are captured in the top left of the prospective map than in the hotspot map. To establish the accuracy of the maps we compared their effectiveness for four different time periods (2 days, 3 days, 7 days and 1 month). The results, shown as Table 7.1, indicate that the prospective map is more accurate for all comparisons. It is also apparent from this analysis that the predictive accuracy of the maps generally decreases over time. The very limited shelf-life of these maps neatly illustrates the assumption central to this paper, namely that crime risk moves about.

It is also clear from Table 7.1 that the areas highlighted by the two maps cover different surface areas, the hotspot map covering the largest geography. Thus to examine the accuracy of the maps in a more meaningful way we computed search efficiency rates for the two maps. In addition, as we envisage that the maps would be routinely updated in operational policing, for this analysis we focused on the effectiveness of the maps over a seven-day period. The results summarised in Figure 7.3 confirm that for the different periods considered, the prospective map is consistently more accurate than the retrospective hotspot. The difference achieved statistical significance ($z = 3.01$, $p < 0.005$, two-tailed).

Table 7.1 Percentage (and numbers) of crimes predicted by prospective and retrospective hotspot maps

	2 days	3 days	7 days	1 month	Area covered (m²)
Day one					
Retrospective	48% (11)	60% (18)	56% (35)	60% (166)	5,890,000
Prospective	61% (14)	70% (21)	66% (41)	64% (177)	5,612,500
Day two					
Retrospective	71% (12)	67% (20)	63% (39)	59% (170)	5,947,500
Prospective	77% (13)	73% (22)	68% (42)	62% (187)	5,577,550
Day three					
Retrospective	75% (15)	77% (20)	57% (35)	60% (171)	6,085,000
Prospective	80% (16)	81% (21)	61% (38)	62% (176)	5,620,000

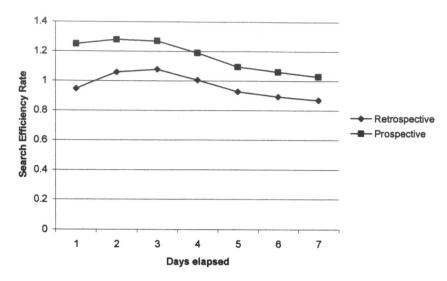

Figure 7.3   Search efficiency rates for prospective and retrospective maps

It is also clear that both maps, but particularly the prospective map, are more accurate at predicting crime patterns for the immediate future. The prospective map is most accurate at predicting where crime will occur for the three days that follow the generation of the risk surface, after which the accuracy of the map declines. This suggests that if used in an operational setting, maps generated on a weekly basis would generate sub-optimal predictions, which could result in resources being directed to the wrong places at the wrong times. Thus the results suggest that new maps should be produced (at least) every three days. In practice (see below), we envisage new maps being incorporated into the briefing of each new policing shift, as being the most timely and helpful transmission of information which is typically now given to patrolling officers in a less helpful and accurate form.

Considering interpretation of the search efficiency rate in more detail, one useful way of thinking about this metric is that it readily translates into the number of burglaries that could be prevented each day if a one kilometre 'hot' square was policed or targeted for crime reduction. Thus, for the prospective map, directing crime reduction resources across a 10 km² square with the highest risk intensity values should lead to the prevention (or detection) of approximately 13 burglaries each day (91 per week), whereas for the retrospective hotspot the equivalent figure would be around 10 burglaries (70 per week). Expressed in a slightly different way, the prospective mapping algorithm is around ((13 − 10)/10 =) 30% more accurate than the retrospective hotspot at identifying the future locations of burglary events.

Many remaining challenges

So far we have developed a method of predicting the future locations of crime – a prototype system. The next steps are clear:

1 to explore ways in which to improve the accuracy of the system and extend it to all offence types;
2 to evaluate its utility in an operational context.

In relation to the former, we are pursuing a number of approaches. These include the recursive calibration of the model for different areas or times, perhaps based upon the degree to which crime appears to cluster in space and time in that area. As discussed above, and is illustrated by a comparison of equations (7.1) and (7.2), the model used to generate the prospective maps is very simple (particularly compared with the retrospective hotspot equation). Thus an obvious next step is to increase the sophistication of the mathematical model, or to examine the impact of changing the parameters of the equation. Obvious refinements include the metric in which the risk is to be expressed, the shift-specific element in prediction (i.e. is a map from the most recent eight hours better than one for the clock-equivalent shift one day before), and how best to incorporate the decay in risk which is only crudely indexed in the work reported here. There is also the issue of patrolling distances between high-risk areas. Maps with dispersed risk points will be more difficult to patrol than those with fewer hot spots, so it must be ensured that what is gained in predictive accuracy is not lost in non-productive transit times between risk areas.

A further related question concerns the generality of our earlier findings in relation to other types of crime. That is, how do other types of crime cluster in space and time? To examine this issue, we conducted some further original analyses for three types of crime that we have previously not examined. For simplicity, we will report only the basic analyses. Table 7.2 contains Mantel Z-scores for the four different crime types analysed. A Z-score of 2 or more indicates that the events cluster significantly in space and time, and thus it is evident that while there is some variability, all of the crime types considered below cluster in space

Table 7.2 Mantel Z-scores for different crime types

	Mantel Z-score
Burglary dwelling	5.53
Burglary other	6.89
Theft from car	7.26
Theft of car	4.35

and time. This means that the finding that crime is communicable in a similar way to a disease is not restricted to dwelling burglary alone.

While the results presented here for other types of crime are preliminary, they are important as they suggest that the prospective mapping approach discussed may also be effective for other types of crime. A comparison of the individual Z-scores also suggests that space-time clustering may be most evident for the crime type 'theft from car'. In fact, the Z-score for this type of crime was significantly greater than those for all of the other types of crime ($p < 0.01$, in all cases, two-tailed). Thus it is possible that prospective maps may be of even greater utility for crimes such as this.

While we believe that the system can be improved, no doubt considerably, the operational advantage offered by the current technique in comparison with traditional methods more than warrants our urgent desire to conduct a field test. Field-testing the system may itself enhance our understanding of how it might be improved and patterns predicted with greater efficiency. A number of possibilities exist. Perhaps the most obvious would be to use the system to deploy police resources, with new maps generated on a shift-by-shift basis. In the extreme scenario of a highly accurate system, directing officers to the (future) 'scenes of the crime' has the potential to serve the dual function of preventing crimes that have yet to occur and of detecting those in progress. It is, of course, unlikely that the system will be accurate enough to enable this goal to be fully realised in the short term, but the aspiration is not unrealistic.

To establish how useful this approach will be in different locations it is important to determine the extent to which victimisation risk is communicable across different locations and countries. Townsley *et al.* (2003) have demonstrated that burglary clusters in space and time in Australia, but as far as we are aware analyses of this kind have not been conducted in other countries. To address this issue and to extend the research more generally we have established an international collaborative network, funded by the British Academy and the

Netherlands Institute for the Study of Crime and Law Enforcement (NSCR). Working with our project partners, George Rengert and Jerry Ratcliffe in the USA, and Wim Bernasco and Henk Elffers in the Netherlands, this will allow us to see if the communication of victimisation risk is an international phenomenon and consider the role of contextual factors in some detail. Working with academics with considerable expertise in crime mapping, geography and offender behaviour should also enable the development of still more accurate models for predicting future risk.

Considering the application of prospective mapping in crime prevention, given limited police resources, alternative approaches to high visibility policing and sting operations require attention and development, particularly those that would allow the police to work effectively with their crime prevention partners. The adaptation of target-hardening strategies would be the natural place to start. For instance, prioritising not only victims of crime but also those (currently) non-victims that are placed at a heightened risk as a result of an initial event would seem sensible. Protecting those within 400m of every burglary event is perhaps an unhelpful suggestion,[2] and hence the more precise prediction of which properties will be at the greatest risk in the near future using a system such as that discussed here should offer a considerable advantage.

A further tactic that the authors strongly advocate in harness with the approach outlined here is the use of publicity directed at offenders. Research conducted in both the UK (Johnson and Bowers 2003) and US (Kennedy et al. 2001) demonstrates the power of publicity in crime prevention. For instance, in an evaluation of 21 burglary reduction projects (for a summary of the programme, see Kodz and Pease 2003), Johnson and Bowers (2003) found that reductions in burglary were coincident with the timing of publicity focused on the activities of the different schemes. It is important to note that we refer here to the active publicising of strategies that are or will be launched to prevent or reduce crime, and not that which is directed at victims (with the aim of reducing risky behaviour). There is little evidence to suggest that the latter has any effect on levels of crime. In the context of the current discussion, publicity (overt or subtle) may be used to advertise the fact that policing attention is directed towards an area. For example, recently decommissioned liveried police cars could be parked in vulnerable areas, vulnerable cars in key areas stickered with advice by Neighbourhood Wardens, and so on.

To summarise, in this chapter we have discussed recent research concerned with the communicability of victimisation risk. We have focused particularly on how the findings can be used to develop new mapping techniques for predicting when and where crime will happen next. The work is in its early stages yet the results suggest that the new method offers considerable gains in predictive efficiency because of the shifting location of crime concentrations. We aim to refine the methods and to field test the suitability and effectiveness of the resulting system in an operational setting.

Notes

1 Due to the distribution of the risk-intensity values, it was not possible to split the cells into exact quantiles.
2 Although, for 'communal' target-hardening measures, such as 'alley-gating' schemes, this might not be so out of the question.

References

Bailey, T.C. and Gatrell, A.C. (1995) *Interactive Spatial Data Analysis*. Harlow: Longman.

Barr, R., and Pease, K. (1990) 'Crime placement, displacement, and deflection', *Crime and Justice: A Review of the Research*, 12: 277–318.

Bowers, K.J., Johnson, S.D. and Pease, K. (2004) 'Prospective hot-spotting: the future of crime mapping?', *British Journal of Criminology*, 44(5), 641–658.

Budd, T. (1999) *Burglary of Domestic Dwellings: Findings from the British Crime Survey*, Home Office Statistical Bulletin 4/99. London: Home Office Research and Statistics Directorate.

Ericsson, U. (1995) 'Straight from the horse's mouth', *Forensic Update*, 43: 23–25.

Farrell, G. and Pease, K. (eds) (2002) *Repeat Victimisation*. Monsey, NY: Criminal Justice Press.

Johnson, S.D. and Bowers, K.J. (2003) 'Opportunity is in the eye of the beholder: The role of publicity in crime prevention', *Criminology and Public Policy*, 2 (3): 201–228.

Johnson, S.D. and Bowers, K.J. (2004) 'The burglary as a clue to the future: the beginnings of prospective hot-spotting', *The European Journal of Criminology*, 1(2), 237–255.

Johnson, S.D., Bowers, K. and Hirschfield, A. (1997) 'New insights into the spatial and temporal distribution of repeat victimisation', *British Journal of Criminology*, 37 (2): 224–244.

Kennedy, D.M., Braga, A.A. and Piehl, A.M. (2001) *Reducing Gun Violence: The Boston Gun Project's Operation Ceasefire*, National Institute of Justice Research Report. US Department of Justice.

Knox, G. (1964) 'Epidemiology of childhood leukaemia in Northumberland and Durham', *British Journal of Preventative and Social Medicine* 18: 17–24.

Kodz, J. and Pease, K (2003) *Reducing Burglary Initiative: Early Findings on Burglary Reduction*, Home Office Research Findings 204. London: Home Office.

Krebs, J.R. and Davies, N.B. (1987) *An Introduction to Behavioural Ecology*, 2nd edn. Oxford: Blackwell.

Morgan, F. (2001) 'Repeat burglary in a Perth suburb: indicator of short-term or long-term risk?', in G. Farrell, G. and K. Pease (eds), *Repeat Victimisation*, Crime Prevention Studies, Vol. 12, Monsey, NY: Criminal Justice Press, pp. 83–118.

Openshaw, S. (ed.) (1995) *Census Users' Handbook*. Cambridge: GeoInformation International.

Pease, K. (1998) *Repeat victimisation: Taking Stock*, Crime Detection and Prevention Series Paper 90. London: Home Office.

Townsley, M. and Pease, K. (2002) 'Hot spots and cold comfort', in N. Tilley (ed.), Crime Prevention Studies, Vol. 13. Monsey, NY: Criminal Justrice Press, pp. 59–69.

Townsley, M., Homel, R. and Chaseling, J. (2003) 'Infectious burglaries: a test of the near repeat hypothesis', *British Journal of Criminology*, 43: 615–633.

Part 4
Case Studies in Crime Science for Detection

Chapter 8

DNA fast-tracking

Barry Webb, Chloe Smith, Andrew Brock and Michael Townsley

Introduction

This chapter examines the impact of an initiative between a major UK police force and the Forensic Science Service (FSS) to speed up the investigation of domestic burglary where DNA is captured from the scene. Known as fast-tracking, the initiative aimed to reduce the time taken to capture, analyse and match DNA against the national DNA database and the subsequent police response to 'hits'. The initiative was part of a wider strategy, aimed at reducing the incidence of domestic burglary.

Using a range of data we examined the impact of fast-tracking on the speed of dealing with cases, the outcome of investigations and the impact on crime.

We concluded by making several recommendations about how the process could be improved.

Background

The issue of timeliness in processing DNA was first raised in 1996 (Tilley and Ford). It was recommended by this review that police forces and the FSS should reduce the time between the collection of DNA at the scene of crime, a match being made and the suspect being arrested (DNA fast-tracking).

The 2000 review *Under the Microscope* (HMIC 2000) found, however, that the majority of police forces had not addressed this issue of timeliness. It revealed widespread weaknesses in strategic exploitation of forensic science generally, and a lack of knowledge concerning ACPO policy on forensic science, even among senior detectives. Performance data was also found to be inaccurate and unreliable, creating significant difficulties in examining the outcomes and success of police use of forensic science.

Follow-up research in 2002 to assess the extent to which the police had responded to *Under the Microscope* reported that 'things are improving but sometimes too slowly despite the large amounts of money invested' (HMIC 2002). In relation to using DNA effectively, the report concluded that, 'timeliness is a matter of concern and there are still significant delays in most forces assessed in commencing an investigation following receipt of the identification'.

While there appears a prima facie case for encouraging fast processing of DNA, there has been little research to demonstrate whether and how this impacts on the investigative process and outcome. Prime and Hennelly (2003) explored the potential impact, reviewing available relevant research and theorising on the ways in which speeding up DNA processing could work. Based on the limited research available (much unpublished), the paper suggests that improved timeliness could result in earlier identification which in turn might quicken offenders' apprehension and incarceration. The quality of evidence may be improved through locating informants quickly and eliminating suspects sooner. Improved speed could increase the chance to recover stolen goods, obtain more and earlier confessions and encourage operational staff to pursue the case with more purpose.

In summary, faster turnaround of DNA analysis could lead to suspects being exonerated swiftly and offenders being apprehended faster, with more decisions to remand in custody rather than bail being taken on the basis of availability of DNA evidence putting suspects at the scene of crime. If it achieves these things, fast-tracking DNA could, in turn, reduce crime by reducing the length of time offenders are at liberty to continue committing offences (Prime and Hennelly 2003; Phillips and Brown 1998). High rates of offending have been found while on police bail (see e.g. Morgan and Henderson, 1998). Furthermore, offenders on bail awaiting DNA evidence may be more prolific than those on bail for alternative reasons (because of their perception of more certain conviction), thereby further raising the importance of faster DNA processing.

These potential consequences and benefits of faster DNA processing have yet to be demonstrated. The fast-tracking initiative in this UK police force provides a unique opportunity to test the extent to which these outcomes have been achieved, and suggest how practice might be changed to maximise the benefits of DNA fast-tracking.

DNA fast-tracking initiative

This UK police force has been implementing DNA fast-tracking since October 2002.

The fast-tracking initiative aims to reduce the duration of each stage of the investigative process in which DNA is involved, setting some very challenging targets for scenes of crime officers (SOCOs), the FSS, Scientific Support centrally in the force and Operational Command Unit (OCU) response to identifications. It is important to stress that the initiative is not restricted to FSS processing activity. It includes each stage of the investigative process, from scene of crime attendance right through to post-match police activity. As such, it is an ambitious initiative requiring some very close and innovative collaborative working arrangements between these various parts of the force and between the force and the FSS.

Key elements of the fast-track process are as follows.

1   SOCOs attend 100% of burglary dwelling scenes, and as soon as possible with the aim of being the first to attend to avoid scene contamination. The SOCO recovers any biological material found at the crime scene, e.g. blood, saliva, hair and semen.
2   The best sample is chosen and delivered to the FSS by midday the following day.
3   The FSS has a seven-day target turnaround time from receiving the sample to reporting back to the force scientific support unit on results and any matches.
4   In the event of a match against a person on the national DNA database, an intelligence package is produced by the force Scientific Support Unit. This process involves researching and delivering information about the suspect to the appropriate OCU intelligence unit within 24 hours of match information being received.
5   Once received, the OCU has a target of 36 hours to action the intelligence package and arrest the suspect or, if not located, place on the Police National Computer (PNC).
6   In the event of an arrest, the FSS aims to turn around a sample of the suspect's DNA for evidential purposes within 24 hours. This element was not introduced until after March 2003.

The flow diagram in Figure 8.1 summarises the fast-tracking process and associated target times.

As Figure 8.1 shows, in those cases where a DNA match is achieved, if all the targets are met, a suspect could be arrested within 13 days of the burglary being reported to the police.

The whole process is very tightly managed by a central coordinating group supervised at superintendent level. The group comprises representatives from each OCU, the FSS and Scientific Support centrally. It receives regular performance information, and holds OCUs and others responsible for each stage to account for any failure to meet the targets. The process is akin to the COMPSTAT process, a management process credited with achieving the large crime reductions in New York (O'Connell 2001), albeit applied here in a supportive rather than punitive style.

Aims of the research and methodology

The aims of the study were to assess the impact of the fast-tracking initiative on the investigative process. In particular, we focused on three questions:

1   What has been the impact on latency of action? Latency of action was measured through quantitative analysis of performance data collected by the police and FSS.
2   What has been the impact on the conduct and outcome of investigations? If latency of action has been improved, it is plausible this might also have an impact on the outcome of investigations (see Prime and Hennelly 2003, discussed above).
3   What was the impact on crime? This is a more difficult outcome to measure, particularly since fast-tracking is just one of eight different initiatives that constitute the wider anti-burglary initiative programme. If, however, fast-tracking improves either the speed with which offenders are captured and incarcerated and/or the numbers of offenders captured, one might expect to see an impact on crime overall.

In answering these questions, the evaluation draws on:

* case tracking data collected by the FSS and the police on the duration and outcome of each stage of the investigative process in relation to incidents of domestic burglary where DNA has been captured from

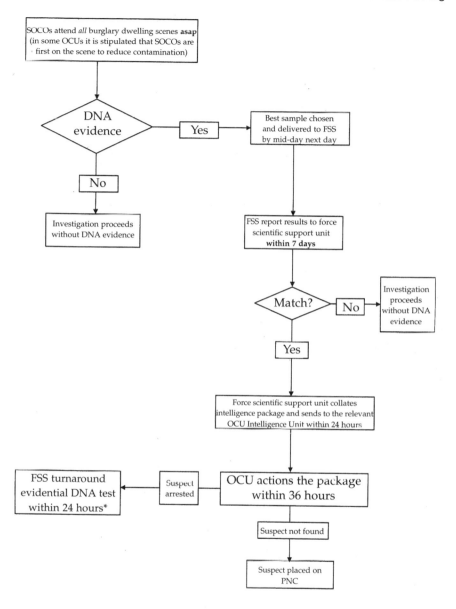

*This element introduced after March 2003.

Figure 8.1 Summary of fast-tracking process and associated target times

the scene: 784 cases dealt with in the first five months of 'fast-tracking' (November 2002 – March 2003) were compared with 140 cases in a benchmark period (November 2001);

- recorded incidents of domestic burglary in the West Midlands, 1999–2003;
- analysis of the offending histories of offenders captured via DNA left at burglary scenes;
- interviews with operational detectives and SOCOs; and
- direct observations.

Impact on latency of action

Figure 8.2 shows the average number of days taken to deal with the various stages of burglary investigations for both the fast-track and benchmark periods.

Figure 8.2 shows that overall the average length of time taken for an offender to be arrested and charged has reduced by 48%, from 89 days to 45 days, and time taken to appear in court has reduced by 38%, from 191 days to 118 days. Figure 8.2 shows faster action at every stage of the process, with the exception of time taken between a submission being received by the FSS and a match being delivered to the force. The reasons for this are discussed below.

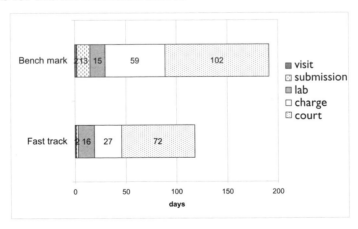

Notes

Outliers removed where possible. It was not possible to remove outliers for time taken to visit the scene and time taken to make the submission to the FSS. Values have been rounded. The number for 'visit' in fast track is not visible on the figure. It is 1.

Figure 8.2 Impact on latency: mean number of days for each stage

This fast-track initiative has resulted in some very significant improvements in the speed with which investigations of burglary are conducted. The time taken to submit the sample, the time taken by the police to charge after a match is made and the time taken for offenders to appear in court after charge are all significantly reduced. Offenders are, on average, appearing before the court over two months (73 days) earlier than they might otherwise have done.

Notwithstanding this very considerable achievement overall, there were at each stage a number of cases which took a disproportionately long time to deal with. These 'outliers' seemed particularly to affect the time to match stage in the lab which shows little change, on average, from the benchmark period. The reason for this is that in 14% of fast-tracked cases which produced a hit, the scene DNA sample arrived in the lab and was loaded to the national DNA Database prior to a CJ sample being taken from the suspect. This is often the case with DNA matches as new suspects are continually being added to the National DNA Database. Inevitably there is therefore a delay in returning the DNA match in these cases. This type of match was monitored during the fast track period but not included in the benchmark period. When these cases are removed, the mean speed of returning a hit to the force speeds up from 15 to 9 days, an improvement in performance in line with other stages of the investigative process.

In relation to police action 'post-match', there has been a more consistent response across the force but many cases still take a long time to action. For example, 25% of cases still take more than 48 days to clear. The stable match-to-charge times over the five-month period suggests this is a more intractable problem meriting further work to understand what it is about these cases that makes them so difficult to clear.

The final point to note is the faster time for offenders to appear in court. This is curious given that action post-charge was not subject to fast-track management. It may be that the fast-track initiative has diffused beyond the immediate targets set. For example, it may have engendered greater enthusiasm among officers which has somehow affected other criminal justice processes. However, it is to the impact of fast-tracking on the conduct and outcome of investigations that we now turn.

Impact on the outcome of investigations

During the study we examined the impact of fast-tracking on the conduct and outcome of investigations. It is important to point out that it was not the value of DNA evidence itself that we were concerned with here, but its speedier availability. Prime and Hennelly (2003) describe a number of ways in which reducing the latency of action might plausibly have a beneficial impact on the outcome of investigations. The two case studies below, illustrate the kind and complexity of impact fast-tracking can have on investigations.

Case study 8.1

There was a series of burglaries in a commercial business area. Police ran a plain clothes operation and a suspect was caught.

As the suspect was caught 'red-handed', he had no choice but to admit the offence. While he was in custody, an intelligence package arrived which had been fast-tracked from a blood sample taken from the scene of a domestic burglary committed the week before. The DNA provided an immediate match as the suspect was on the DNA database.

The arrival of the intelligence package provided grounds for the suspect to be refused bail and remanded in custody. As a result of this, the series of burglaries ceased.

The suspect was subsequently linked to three other burglaries by DNA, which he admitted. He also admitted 12 other burglary offences, which he asked to be taken into consideration. He admitted the offences at court and received a prison sentence.

Case study 8.2

A series of 15–20 burglary dwellings were identified with a similar modus operandi and in a similar location. Police were confident the same offender committed the burglaries but the offender remained unknown.

A suspect was apprehended for one of these offences following a report from a member of the public of a burglary in progress. On the same day that the suspect was arrested an intelligence package arrived giving full DNA match to another domestic burglary.

The suspect initially denied the burglary for which he was arrested but when the DNA evidence from the intelligence package was put to him he admitted both offences and asked that a further four be taken into consideration.

As a result of this, the offender was remanded in custody and his driving licence revoked, returning him to prison. Analysis of crime trends indicated that the identified series stopped after his arrest.

While in custody awaiting sentence for the above, a further intelligence package was produced linking him to another domestic burglary. The offender admitted the offence and asked for a further eight offences to be taken into consideration. He appeared in court and was sentenced to four years' imprisonment.

These case studies illustrate how the *speed* of DNA processing influenced events post-arrest. In neither case did DNA evidence lead directly to the arrest, but speedier processing of previous incidents produced a weight of evidence which would not otherwise have been available when the suspect was in custody, leading to the incarceration of the offender, which may not otherwise have been the outcome.

The following further describes the experience and views of operational officers on the impact of fast-tracking on investigations and its value in improving the availability of evidence at the time of arrest.

Improved interviewing

Some officers felt that fast tracking both dramatically improves the effectiveness of interviewing suspects and encourages suspects to confess earlier.

> Fast-tracking allows us to investigate the offence while it is fresh in our minds. It is easier to question the offender also, because it is harder for them to say, for example, they don't remember what they were doing [at the time of the offence] when it is only a few days ago. (Detective sergeant)

> When they [offenders] are confronted with DNA evidence so quickly, it is easier to get them to plead guilty. (Detective sergeant)

Evidential fast-tracking

Twenty-four hour evidential conversion fast tracking was introduced after March 2003, so any impact will not be reflected in the data analyses discussed later. At the time of these interviews, however, officers had experience of this service and unanimously considered it potentially an extremely useful tool to prevent the offender receiving bail.

Increased job satisfaction, commitment and morale of police officers

Increased job satisfaction and morale were universally identified as an outcome of the fast-tracking initiative. This is a consequence not just of the speedier availability of DNA, but of the way in which the whole programme has been managed, giving clear messages from the top about priorities and 'joining up' the investigative process more effectively.

> When you get the intelligence package so quickly, you take greater ownership of the investigation. When they [investigating officers] know it [the intelligence package] is coming, they can't wait to get their hands on it. (Sergeant)

A number of the SOCOs also indicated that fast-tracking had a significant impact on their job satisfaction. Specifically, they felt more part of the investigation.

> From a personal perspective, I believe that DNA fast-tracking is great. You see the results straight away and the crime and the victims are still fresh in your mind. It is more rewarding and you feel like you've done your job and made a difference [...] I also believe that police take greater ownership when they receive idents [identifications of offender] quickly. (SOCO)

The kind of commitment and enthusiasm fast-tracking generates is illustrated in the following comment from another SOCO:

> On quiet days, we will often check the incoming log so we can get to the crime scene before the Police Officer notifies us, or even gets there. This can save valuable time and preserve the scene. Sometimes we can get to the scene within 20 minutes of the crime being reported. (SOCO)

Attrition

The conventional way in which the efficiency and effectiveness of criminal investigation and the criminal justice system are measured is through the attrition rate. The attrition rate refers to the extent to which cases fail to proceed to the next stage of investigation. A zero attrition rate in relation to burglary, for example, would mean that every reported crime results in an offender being detected, appearing before a court and receiving a sanction of some kind. A low attrition rate is therefore something to aspire to, indicating that a high number of cases are retained through the criminal justice system from offence to receiving sanction. For example, an attrition rate of 0 is equivalent to a retention rate of 100%. This section examines attrition by comparing retention rates before and during fast-tracking, to explore more objectively the impact of fast-tracking on the outcome of burglary investigations.

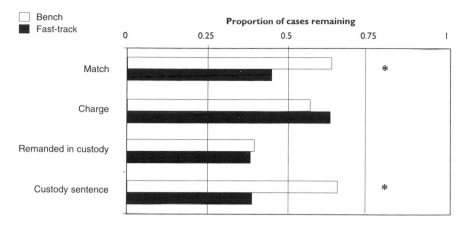

Note *indicates a significant difference with 95% confidence.

Figure 8.3   Retention rate for benchmark and fast-track periods

Figure 8.3 shows the retention rate for those cases where DNA was captured from the burglary scene for November 2001 (the benchmark period) and November 2002–March 2003 (the fast-track period). The baseline for Figure 8.3 is the number of cases producing a DNA submission (benchmarked at 1). The proportion of these submissions producing a match is then shown, followed by the proportion of those matches producing a charge, and finally the proportion of those charges resulting in (a) an offender being remanded in custody and (b) a custodial sentence. The number of cases used for this analysis is shown in the appendix. Cases resulting in elimination have been excluded from this analysis.

The only statistically significant changes in Figure 8.3 are the proportion of submissions producing matches and the proportion of charged suspects receiving a custodial sentence. Both show the retention of cases decreased during the fast-track period. These are not, however, stages which you would expect to be affected by fast-tracking. Charge and remand rates, however, could more plausibly be affected by the speedier availability of DNA, as our interviews with officers indicated, and indeed the charge rate is the only process in Figure 8.3 to show improvement although this fails to reach statistical significance. There appears no change in the rate at which charged suspects are remanded.

One of the difficulties in interpreting changes in attrition rates in this analysis is the considerable monthly variation in rates. Figure 8.4

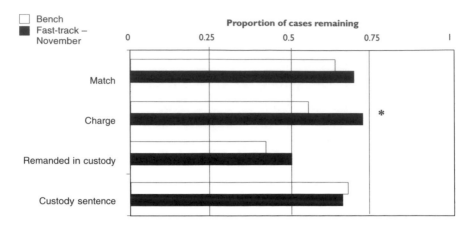

Note *indicates a significant difference with 95% confidence.

Figure 8.4 Retention rates for November benchmark and November fast-track

compares the November fast-track month with the November benchmark period, and shows how the picture changes as a result.

All stages of the investigative process show improvement when the November fast-track is compared against the benchmark, with the improvement in converting matches to charges reaching statistical significance. The reason for this improved picture is that November is the best performing month in the fast-track period. Comparison with the subsequent four fast-track months (Figure 8.5) reveals that November has the highest proportion of submissions producing matches, the highest proportion of matches resulting in a charge, and the highest rate of custodial sentencing both at remand and in the courts.

One possible explanation for the better performance in November is that the initiative was launched with much enthusiasm, energy and expectation, and this has diminished over time. This, however, is not reflected in latency of action which shows no sign of deteriorating. Also, the primary reason why the match rate is so much better in November is that the number of submissions in November is much lower than for other months, including the benchmark month. The number of submissions in March is more than twice the number for November, again not what you would expect if enthusiasm were waning.

Another reason why November shows better performance than the benchmark month is, because there is so much variability between months, it may be just by chance that November fast-track results look better than the November benchmark. This seems to be the case

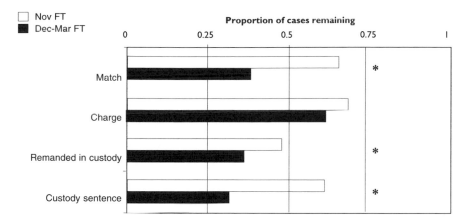

Note *indicates a significant difference with 95% confidence.

Figure 8.5 Comparison of retention rates within the fast-track period.

particularly for the match rate and the rate at which offenders are incarcerated. The proportion of charged offenders that are remanded, for example, varies from 31–50%, compared with 40% in the benchmark month.

However, charge rates show there is less variability and more consistent change in one direction. The rate at which hits against the DNA database are converted to charges is better in every fast-track month than the benchmark month, producing the better rate overall in Figure 8.3. Although this does not reach statistical significance, the consistently higher rates do at least suggest a change in the right direction at this stage of the investigative process as a result of fast-tracking.

Guilty pleas

Officers interviewed felt that the speed of apprehension helps effective interviewing. It is therefore plausible that reducing the latency of action could increase guilty pleas. The case-tracking database includes a count of the number of cases in which a B23 request is made. This is a request for analysis of DNA taken from an arrested suspect for *evidentiary* purposes and consequently not required if an offender pleads guilty. If offenders were pleading guilty more often, then it seems likely that fewer cases would require further and costly DNA analysis for evidentiary purposes, reflected in fewer B23 requests. We found no evidence of this.

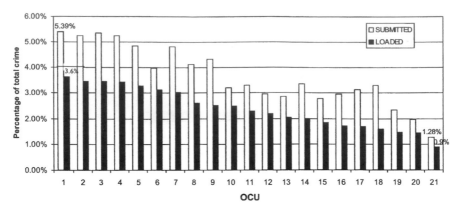

Figure 8.6 DNA capture rates from burglary dwelling scenes, by OCU

DNA capture rates

One issue that emerged is variability, and the need to develop a better understanding of why some cases take much longer than others to process, why submission rates are substantially lower in some months than others or why remand decisions vary so much. Another example of variability is shown in Figure 8.6. This shows that OCUs vary greatly in the rates at which they capture and submit DNA to the FSS, and the proportion of these submissions that were good enough to be 'loaded' onto the DNA database. The capture rate in terms of 'loaded' DNA for the best performing OCU was nearly 4% of scenes while the worst was less than 1% of scenes (these exclude submissions of samples that were subsequently eliminated to the victim).

It would be worthwhile undertaking further work to understand why OCUs vary so much in their capture rates, and introduce measures to bring the poorer performers up to the standard of the better ones. If, for example, it was shown that SOCOs in good OCUs spend more time at certain scenes and that this produces DNA that might otherwise not be found, then the question of focusing SOCO resources and working out how to be more selective in scenes searched is raised. Focusing on scenes of repeat burglary, for example, would be justified on the grounds that research shows these are most likely to have been committed by more prolific offenders (Pease 1998).

A related point, which is also worth examining, is the strategic combination of DNA with other forensic traces such as fingerprints and footprints. It was suggested during the interviews that some offenders might be more DNA aware and that it was relatively easy to avoid leaving obvious DNA traces by not leaving blood, cigarette butts, cans of drink or half eaten food. Other forms of trace would be less easily avoided. Again, this would require the focusing of SOCO resources on offences likely to have been committed by prolific offenders.

In summary, the only consistent change in the attrition analysis is in proportion of matches that convert to charged suspects. These rates are better under fast-tracking, although the difference does not reach statistical significance. The available evidence does not suggest that more guilty pleas are produced under fast-tracking. Decisions affecting the incarceration rate of offenders do not seem to have changed, although there is so much variability here that it is hard to judge when just one month of benchmark data is available.

Impact on crime

> The major benefit of fast-tracking is it allows us to respond quickly to prolific offending [...] this quick response reduces the number of offences [...] Whereas before we waited months, now we can have them [offenders] in a matter of days. (Detective sergeant)

The finding that latency of action has improved and possibly also charge rates means that it is worth now examining whether fast-tracking has had any impact on crime. The analysis to follow searches for evidence of such an outcome, through the analysis of recorded burglary and the offending rates of offenders captured.

Analysis of burglary rates

Figure 8.7 shows burglary dwellings recorded and detected across the police force area between April 2001 and March 2003. Fast-tracking was implemented across the force during the last five months of this period, November 2002 – March 2003.

After peaking in the period November 2001 – January 2002, the number of recorded burglaries across the force area has steadily decreased until the fast-tracking period when the number of recorded burglaries *increased*, particularly in January and March 2003.

Burglary detections increased by 3.7% during the fast-tracking period from November 2002 – March 2003 compared with the same period in the previous year. However, Figure 8.7 shows that this is a reflection of an upward trend in detections that has been taking place in the force since April 2001.

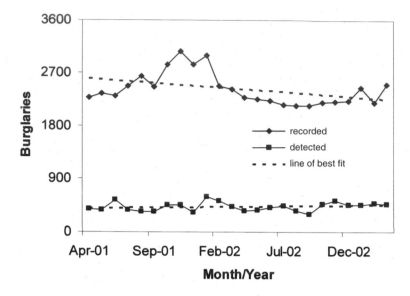

Figure 8.7 Recorded burglary dwellings in the police force area: April 2001–March 2003

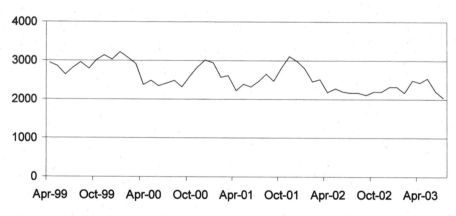

Figure 8.8 Burglary dwellings in the police force area: April 1999–July 2003.

The fast-tracking initiative was introduced in November 2002 to tackle a seasonal peak in burglaries that had been found to take place in the winter months every year. An analysis of burglary figures over a longer period of time is therefore necessary to identify any change to this pattern. Figure 8.8 plots monthly numbers of burglary dwellings over a four-year period, April 1999 – July 2003, and shows this seasonal peak quite clearly.

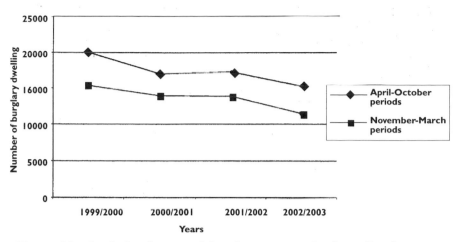

Figure 8.9 Analysis of seasonal burglary patterns in the police force area, 1999/2000 – 2002/2003.

Figure 8.8 shows higher levels of burglary in the November–March periods of each year. This peak seems to have 'flattened' during the period fast-tracking was operational. To examine the impact of fast-tracking on this in more detail, Figure 8.9 plots the number of burglaries recorded in the five peak months of November–March and in the seven 'trough' months of April–October in the years 1999/00, 2000/01, 2001/02 and 2002/03.

While the final November–March point is much lower than November–March periods in previous years, the trend has been consistently downwards over the four years. Moreover, the greater reduction in the final November–March period is reflected also in the final April–October period in 2002, before fast-tracking started. However, closer analysis reveals that burglary in the final November–March period is lower than expected on the basis of the previous three years. Burglary in November–March in the previous three years is, on average, 20% less than burglary in the preceding April–October periods. In the final November–March period when fast-tracking was operational, burglary was 25% lower than in the preceding April–October period. This suggests that burglary has reduced by 5% more (735 fewer burglaries) than would have been expected.

Fast-tracking, however, was just one of a number of measures introduced to reduce burglary in the area. An opportunity to disentangle the effect of fast-tracking from the other initiatives comes from the fact that OCUs vary greatly in their performance in meeting fast-track targets. One would therefore expect this variation to be reflected in different burglary rates. The three graphs shown in Figure 8.10 show recorded and detected burglary between April 2001 and March 2003 for two OCUs considered by the force to be good performers in relation to fast-tracking (Figures 8.10(a) and 8.10(b)) and one OCU considered a poor performer in meeting fast track targets (Figure 8.10(c)). Of the three, it is only the third 'poor performing' OCU which shows any convincing evidence of a reduced burglary 'peak' during the fast-track period.

It is quite difficult to discern the impact of fast-tracking on burglary. One reason for this must be that DNA is only captured from around 5% of burglary dwelling scenes, and around 3% of scenes produce DNA that is loaded onto the national DNA database. The penetration of the burglar population via DNA is therefore likely to be limited, unless DNA picks up some very prolific burglars.

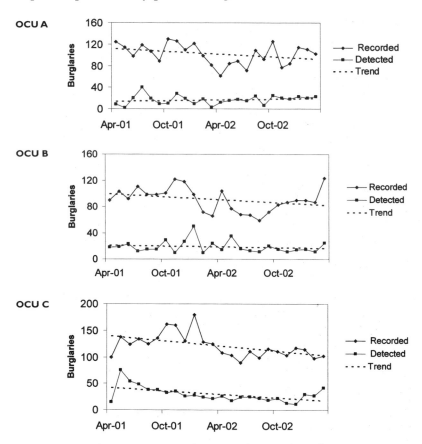

Figure 8.10 Burglaries in OCUs of varying fast-track performance

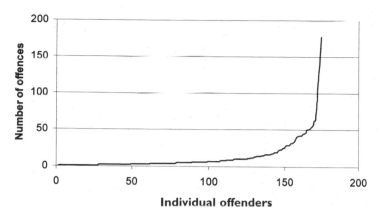

Figure 8.11 Number of offences committed by DNA-captured burglars in 12 months prior to their capture.

Analysis of offenders

The criminal histories of 178 offenders captured in the fast-track period were examined using the force intelligence system. This revealed that these offenders were responsible for a total of 2,365 offences in the 12 months prior to their capture. This equates to, on average, each offender committing one crime every month. As Figure 8.11 shows, however, this statistic is misleading and hides some very prolific offending. Figure 8.11 shows the number of offences each offender was known to have committed.

Figure 8.11 shows that half (49%) of these 178 offenders had each committed six or more offences in the previous 12 months. Eleven offenders were each responsible for more than 50 crimes in the period, and six (3% of all offenders) committed 660 crimes – 28% of all offences. The range of offending included theft of vehicles, theft from vehicles, taking a vehicle without the owner's consent, shop theft, assault, robbery and drug offences as well as burglary. Many of these offenders are prolific and well worth capturing therefore, and capturing fast.

While many are prolific offenders, they are not necessarily all prolific burglars, but are versatile offenders committing a variety of offences. Domestic burglary made up just 16% of all 2,365 offences and over half of these 178 offenders had no record for burglary in the previous 12 months. Of those 80 offenders who had, 46% had committed just one burglary dwelling. Figure 8.12 shows the number of domestic burglary offences each offender was known to have been involved in.

While Figure 8.12 clearly shows some very prolific burglars in the group (for example three offenders were responsible for 36% of all the

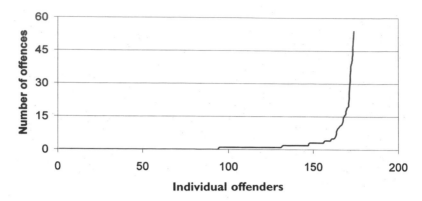

Figure 8.12 Number of domestic burglaries committed by DNA-captured burglars in the 12 months prior to their capture

burglary dwelling offences) the picture that emerges is one of a very prolific but generalist group of offenders. The impact of their capture and incarceration is likely to be diffused across a range of crime types and difficult to discern in relation any one particular crime type.

Conclusions and recommendations

There is little doubt that the fast-tracking initiative has reduced the latency of action in relation to domestic burglary investigations. The time between reporting of a burglary which produces a DNA identification to charging a suspect has reduced by 48%, from an average of 89 to 45 days. Offenders appear in court more than two months earlier than they would otherwise have done. It is also very clear that this is a popular initiative with operational officers, who feel it gives clear direction and good operational support to the capture and processing of prolific offenders. Morale and job satisfaction have improved as a result.

In addition to speeding up the process, more matches also result in a charge (although this improvement does not reach statistical significance). There is no evidence that more charged offenders are being incarcerated either through remand or court sentencing, although the monthly rates are so variable that drawing firm conclusions on the basis of just one month's benchmark data is difficult.

It is hard to find any evidence that the speedier capture of DNA-identified offenders has reduced burglary. This is probably because (a) DNA is captured from so few burglary scenes, and (b) the offenders captured are usually generalists and not burglary specialists. Nevertheless, it is clear that many offenders caught in this way are prolific offenders – well worth capturing since their faster incarceration will be felt across many crime types.

In view of the fact that DNA left at burglary scenes does enable prolific offenders to be identified and captured faster, there are good reasons for trying to improve the impact of the initiative. The following suggestions draw on the findings from the analyses above and interviews with officers.

Managing the programme

The importance of intensive management of the process was evident from our observations and was highlighted by operational staff as well. The data-driven, micro-level performance management approach increases accountability and stresses the priority senior managers place on the initiative. Participants felt these processes promoted urgency in action at an operational level and this has a 'knock-on' effect to other areas of the investigative process.

> ... there has been a knock-on effect of fast tracking to other areas of the process. The key to fast tracking's success is the change in business processes. (Scientific Support)

Feedback to SOCOs

While there has been considerable effort in 'joining up' the investigative process and the contribution of detectives, SOCOs and the FSS, one issue that remained for SOCOs was the lack of feedback on the outcome of investigations.

> Although we are left largely to operate independently, we rarely receive any feedback from the police once we have done our part. (SOCO)

> If there is one thing I would like it would be some feedback from police. The only time we ever hear anything [regarding the outcome of an investigation] is if we chase it ourselves. (SOCO)

It was universally suggested that receiving feedback would improve job satisfaction further. Such feedback would be invaluable in improving learning amongst SOCOs, and should perhaps be considered as part of a strategy to reduce the variation between OCUs in submission rates.

Management and monitoring arrangements within OCUs

Another observation was that those OCUs identified as 'good performers' had developed their own databases (typically a simple Excel spreadsheet) and had an officer specifically appointed to monitor the investigation process once an identification was received. This officer was responsible for ensuring deadlines for action were achieved and that investigating officers were accountable. At both OCUs, this officer reviewed the status of the investigation daily. This was not the case in the 'poorer' performing OCU, which had neither a specific officer allocated nor a database to monitor this process.

Improving the outcome of investigations

DNA capture rates

DNA is captured from just 5% of burglary scenes. The scope for improving this capture rate is worth examining.

The variation between OCUs in capture rates indicates both the need and possibility of learning from the better performers to understand how the level of the poorer performers might be raised. Do more experienced SOCOs, for example, operate more effective search strategies developed with experience that might be explicated and disseminated? Spending more time searching for DNA at the scenes of repeat burglaries may also pay dividends since these are likely to involve more prolific offenders.

Additionally, there was disagreement among the interviewees about whether the rule demanding SOCO attendance at all scenes is useful.

Offender capture rates

Around 30% of matches still fail to produce a charge. One explanation from interviews is that many offenders live chaotic lifestyles, often with no stable home address. This makes it extremely difficult to find them, particularly in the 36-hour window within the fast-track programme. This problem merits attention as it limits the effectiveness not just of fast-tracking but of any initiatives designed to improve the detection and incarceration of prolific offenders.

One area worthy of attention in trying to locate prolific offenders is the way in which they 'reveal' themselves, for example via more trivial offences such as driving off from petrol stations without paying or parking offences (Chenery et al. 1999). Paying attention to these offences may facilitate the capture of those difficult-to-find offenders for more serious crimes.

Incarceration rates

Fast-tracking, by improving the availability of DNA evidence at the time of being charged, provides an opportunity to increase the incarceration rate of offenders through remand and thereby make a more substantial impact on crime. More than 50% of suspects charged with DNA evidence that puts them at scenes of crime, however, are still being released and therefore at liberty to continue to commit further offences, which we know many of them will do. It would be worth examining the circumstances in which decisions to remand are made, the role played by the availability of DNA evidence and the scope for enhancing that role.

'Lambda' and improving the use of DNA in capturing prolific offenders

Finally, there is a need to integrate research on criminal careers, especially rate of offending (lambda[1]), with DNA developments. Some tentative attempts at such integration have already been made (Leary and Pease 2003), but these are admittedly crude and provisional. The more thorough and comprehensive understanding of offending rates of individuals and crime switch patterns across a criminal career we have, the better will we be placed to optimise DNA prioritisation in terms of capturing prolific offenders and reducing crime.

The authors would like to thank Stuart Bell, Peter Goodman, Derek Forest, and Bob Green for their help and support in the DNA fast-track evaluation.

Note

1   Lambda is the term used in the criminological literature to refer to individual offending rates.

References

Chenery, S., Henshaw, C. and Pease, K. (1999) *Illegal Parking in Disabled Parking Bays: A Means of Offender Targeting*, Policing and Reducing Crime Briefing Note 1/99. London: Home Office.

HMIC (2000) *Under the Microscope*. London: HMIC.

HMIC (2002) *Under the Microscope Refocused*. London: HMIC.

Leary, R. and Pease, K. (2003) *DNA and the Active Criminal Population*. Jill Dando Institute of Crime Science, University College London.

McCulloch, H. (1996) *Police Use of Forensic Science*, Police Research Series Paper 19. London: Home Office.

Morgan, P. and Henderson, P. (1998) *Remand Decisions and Offending on Bail: Evaluation of the Bail Process Project*, Home Office Research Study 185. London: Home Office.

O'Connell, P. (2001) *Using Performance Data for Accountability: The New York City Police Department's CompStat Model of Police Management*. Retrieved on 21 May 21 2004 from: http://www.businessofgovernment.org/pdfs/Oconnell_Report.pdf.

Pease, K. (1998) *Repeat Victimisation: Taking Stock*, Crime Detection and Prevention Paper 90. London: Home Office.

Phillips, C. and Brown, D. (1998) *Entry into the Criminal Justice System: A Survey of Police Arrests and Their Outcomes*. Home Office Research Study 185. London: Home Office.

Prime, R. and Hennelly, L. (2003) 'Effects of the Timeliness of DNA Processing'. London: Home Office (unpublished).

Tilley, N. and Ford, A. (1996) *Forensic Science and Crime Investigation*, Crime Detection and Prevention Paper 73. London: Home Office.

Appendix

The table below shows the number of cases in the FSS/police force case tracking database which were used to calculate the retention rates in this report.

	Nov	Dec	Jan	Feb	Mar	Total	Bench
Submissions	102	128	155	171	228	784	140
Matches	76	49	63	77	114	379	90
Eliminations	18	3	7	15	22	65	4
Charged	42	29	33	40	65	209	49
Custody–police	21	9	16	14	24	84	20
Custody–court	27	7	15	12	21	82	32

Chapter 9

Cognition and detection: reluctant bedfellows?

Peter Stelfox[1] and Ken Pease

> I've learned from my mistakes, and I'm sure I can repeat them.
> (Peter Cook[2])

There has been surprisingly little empirical research into the way in which individual officers approach the task of investigating crime. One would expect detective memoirs to emphasise the individual skills of their authors, perhaps coyly expressed to avoid the charge of arrogance. In fact, those memoirs sampled for this chapter (with qualified exceptions – see, for example, Muncie 1979; Maple 1999)[3] instead emphasise routine and systematic approach over individual brilliance. The senior officer investigating the Crippen case informs his readers:

> In telling you of these cases of mine, I shall show you, as far as I can, just how the CID man works. The first thing I want to say is that the real detective is by no means like the detective of fiction, who is always successful – in the end. Hard thinking is necessary. But with hard thinking must go hard graft as well. Dogged persistence has brought far more criminals to book than flashes of genius. (Dew 1938: 167).[4]

What research there is, together with the policing experience of the first author, suggests that, despite the commonality of the organisational resources of investigation, officers go about the task of investigating crime in different ways. These styles are interpreted in terms of 'effectiveness' (Nicol *et al.* 2004). Having recourse to peer judgements as a measure of effectiveness is itself a reflection of the absence of more task-oriented criteria. Variation in personal style is no doubt inevitable in all but the most repetitive work, perhaps augmented by the fact that there is no commonly accepted corpus of knowledge within the police service which informs officers' actions in the process of detection. The strong craft tradition of the police service means that officers learn how to carry out investigations on the job and as a result they develop a range of heuristics which research has found to differ between officers (Adhami and Browne 1996). These approaches have the primary defensive justification that they allow custom and practice to be invoked in the event of later criticism. They also have the more important virtue common to all heuristics of bringing a complex problem within human cognitive limits. That said, it will be argued that the choice of heuristic must be made explicit and its drawbacks fully understood. Heuristics enable officers to make sense of crime scenes and the accounts of victims and witnesses and to take action. In this they are no different to other occupational groups which have been found to develop experiential working rules for the processing of information. However, there are a number of dangers for the police in using this type of reasoning. The most obvious is that decisions are influenced by factors which are not relevant to the situation but which leak from officers' experience or from the wider police culture into the decision-making process. Some ready examples are provided in the form of racism, sexism and homophobia, all of which have at one time or another been found to have had an influence on the decisions taken by the police. But it seems likely that this problem operates at a more subtle level than crude prejudice. Officers may have a wide range of both conscious and unarticulated beliefs which influence their thinking as to a decision whether a crime has occurred or who should be included in the suspect set. A good example was provided by the public inquiry into the serial killings of Dr Harold Shipman where a number of officers closely involved with the first police investigation into his activities (which concluded that there was no evidence of wrong doing) said that their decisions had been influenced by a belief that a doctor would not intentionally kill patients.

A further danger for the police in the use of heuristics is that officers may be unwilling or unable to adapt their decision-making methods when their menu of heuristics is inadequate. This seems most likely to occur when officers are faced with complex, low-frequency types of crime such as homicide where their experience is likely to be limited. There may be a tendency for them to try and adapt the heuristics they have learnt in other situations to deal with the new one they face. The approach to understanding heuristics as a component of monitoring and training taken in this chapter is wholly compatible with the recommendations about Senior Investigating Officer (SIO) training and development made by Smith and Flanagan (2000).

In what follows, the examples used will almost exclusively come from the study of murder investigations, because of availability and the fact that this is the area of work in which the first author is engaged. The literature on such investigations tends to be helpfully prescriptive about processes that are necessary components of investigation (ACPO Crime Committee 2000) or whose absence is identifiable as a 'weakness' (Nicol *et al.* 2004). The current authors thus recognise that there are good reasons why the literature of detection has developed as it has, and nothing in what follows should be taken to indicate dissatisfaction with the quality of that literature. Indeed, more of it would be helpful. Rather, the attempt here is to bring to bear some of the literature on human reasoning which does not feature, as far as the writers' literature search has taken them, in the research on criminal investigation. Because it has not so featured, the links hypothesised are necessarily speculative. The reasons for wishing to develop the research literature in this direction, in spite of the tentativeness of the links proposed, are as follows:

1   The level at which guidance of investigations is couched is of necessity general. Each component decision in the investigative process is guided by a 'mental model' of the situation as conceptualised by the investigator. Within the investigative process thousands of individual decisions, most no doubt inconsequential to the outcome, are made. An understanding of reasoning processes at this micro-level would ensure that sound practice at the macro-level is translated into effectiveness.

2   While the source of suspect identification in murder investigations comes typically from an eye witness, the offender or a confidante of the offender, in rather over a quarter of cases it is made by police inference.[5]

3   Heuristics are search strategies which are defensible when their roots in logic are sound. When used by fallible people in the hurly-burly of life, they are not.

Adhami and Browne (1996) identify six skills central to the SIO task. They are:

• deciding on a mechanism for managing information;
• deciding suspect parameters;

- determining lines of inquiry;
- linking crimes;
- communicating information within the team;
- motivating the team.

The characteristics of human reasoning outlined below are tentatively and provisionally believed to be directly relevant to the first four of the skills set out by Adhami and Browne (1996), and indirectly to the final two.

Typical human biases and heuristics

Some 40 years ago, the second author was privileged to be at University College London when Professor Peter Wason's seminal work on human reasoning was being undertaken. A contemporary grew up to become Professor Phil Johnson-Laird, who collaborated with and developed the Wason work. These two scholars inspired the belief that an understanding of human cognition was of fundamental importance to the way in which the criminal justice system operates. This has emerged (too infrequently) in published work (see, for example, Fitzmaurice and Pease 1981, 1986). The Wason-inspired body of work (along with other leading research on heuristics and biases in decision-making) seems to be entirely absent from bibliographies on police detection. Correspondingly, crime detection does not feature prominently among the real-world applications mooted in at least the literature of human reasoning of which the writers are aware. It may turn out to be the case that errors of cognition are of no concern to the working detective, but this would be surprising since inference from data lies at the core of the task of detection. Smith and Flanagan (2000) in a Home Office research report promisingly entitled *The Effective Detective* select their sample of effective detectives on the basis of peer judgements. Whatever reservations one may have about this method of identifying effective detectives, Smith and Flanagan's placement of 'the assimilation and assessment of incoming information' (p. v) as central to judged effectiveness seems plausible. Since the assimilation and assessment of incoming information is at the heart of the study of reasoning, the conclusion of its irrelevance (or marginal relevance) to policing should be reached only as a last resort. To reach such a conclusion prematurely would be to close off the potential contribution of a rich vein of research evidence. The writers' view is that constituent decisions within a criminal investigation tend to be overlooked because of two features. These are:

1   The large extent to which the perpetrators of serious crime are swiftly identifiable by dint of evidence which is at hand or comes readily to hand after routine police action. This has long been recognised (see Chatterton (1975) for an early demonstration). This means that *perceived* decisions are largely limited to the appropriate deployment of resources in the early stages, and to preclude criticism in the event that the crime turns into a 'whodunit'.

2   The 'combinatorial explosion' of possibilities once the most obvious alternatives are discounted – the decision being in which part of the haystack to begin searching for the needle. In this context, segmentation of the search space (as recognised by Adhami and Browne 1996) is a central task, about which the work on cognitive heuristics has less to say. Work in other traditions within cognitive psychology is relevant (and as consistently neglected) but cannot be dealt with in this chapter. Interested readers should first consult Bruner *et al.* (1951).

These two features are characteristic of murder investigations from which examples in this chapter are drawn, but have relevance for volume crime more generally. The differences, which yield massive corresponding differences in rates of detection, are taken to be quantitative rather than qualitative, the obviously relevant factors including the resources allocated to an investigation and the extent of public cooperation which can reasonably be anticipated. Marlow (1989) obtained data from the diaries of a random sample of detectives and from agency records of 11,190 reported crimes. Marlow concluded that provided there were sufficient personnel to process the readily detectable crimes and to question the offenders, increases in detective manpower and technological improvements yielded only marginal gains in clear-up rates.

To restate, the purpose of the present chapter is to sketch out some putative connections between our understanding of human thinking and reasoning and the investigative task. Presuming a police and criminological readership unfamiliar with the reasoning literature, the emphasis will be placed on noting some of the basics of that literature and speculating on relevance. That literature shows complex and subtle influences on reasoning adequacy. On that basis, if no other, the chapter advocates a research programme rather than use of 'off-the-shelf' reasoning problems in investigation contexts.

The task of investigation can be described in terms of three central decisions:

- Is the incident classifiable as a crime, and if so, which crime? That most police officers would regard this as only infrequently problematic may say more about sources of information than any underlying 'reality'. For example, which missing people, and how many of those on whom coroners record open verdicts, have in fact been murdered? A serious crime initially not so treated will lead to severe criticism of the police officer responsible, as was recently the case in the investigation by the Inspectorate of Constabulary of the disappearance of two Cambridgeshire schoolgirls, Holly Wells and Jessica Chapman. The girls had been murdered. One senior officer's delay in treating the event as a critical incident was singled out for censure (Flanagan 2004: para. 5.42).[6]

- What is the evidence which allows the exclusion of people from the population of possible offenders and the provisional identification of an individual as the putative offender? The premature exclusion of the real offender from the population of possible offenders is a staple of crime fiction writers (see, for example, Christie 1970), and sometimes a major problem in investigations. The building block of murder investigations which are not swiftly solved on the basis of confession or overwhelming witness evidence from the TIE process (Trace, Implicate or Eliminate). If the search space within which the TIE process is deployed excludes the perpetrator, the process is a waste of time. Perhaps the best-known example is the derailing of the investigation into the murders committed by Peter Sutcliffe, the 'Yorkshire Ripper', occasioned by hoax audiotapes purporting to come from the killer, spoken in a strong North-Eastern accent.

- What is the evidence which enables a case to be built against the putative offender? Having established that the incident is a crime and having identified a suspect, the police are required to present sufficient evidence to satisfy a court of the person's guilt. The essential problem for the police here is to distinguish between information and evidence. During investigations the police amass information about the incident from a variety of sources and they can use it all to form judgements about the identity of suspects. However, the rules of evidence place strict criteria on the type of information that courts will allow and so, as a general rule, not all of the information that the police use to identify suspects can be used as evidence. For example, the police may have intelligence on the suspect, a list of previous convictions, the opinions of victims, witnesses and other police officers as to his or her trustworthiness, anonymous information, fingerprint and forensic evidence that does not meet evidential standards, etc., all of which may persuade the police that they have the right suspect but none of which is likely to be accepted as evidence by a court. Establishing what evidence there is can therefore be a significant problem of investigation (Maguire and Norris 1992). The importance of the switch of emphasis from information gathering to case development will be commented on below.

The sequential nature of suspect identification and case building against the putative offender requires two very different casts of mind. One feature of miscarriages of justice involves the premature shift from the first to the second, perhaps most famously in the events at 10 Rillington Place which led to the hanging of the innocent Timothy Evans (see Kennedy 1985). One of the Wason problems illustrates the point in human reasoning generally. In the '2-4-6' task the experimenter says that sequence is an example of a rule (s)he has in mind. The task of the subject is to pronounce other triples and the experimenter will inform the subject whether or not they are instances of the rule. The typical behaviour of subjects (see Wason 1960) is to propose triples like '8-10-12' and '14-16-18'. Being told these are correct, they opine that the rule is 'numbers ascending in twos'. Even *after* being informed that this was not the rule, more than half the triples selected conformed to the original rule. In brief, people tried to verify their proposed rule rather than falsify it or choose other rules. There are four components to verification bias (Tweney and Chitwood 1995). They involve the failure to:

1   seek disconfirmatory evidence;
2   utilise disconfirmatory evidence when it is available;
3   test alternative hypotheses;
4   consider whether evidence supporting a favoured hypothesis supports alternative hypotheses as well.

The phenomenon of verification bias seems common, and has been used to understand the process by which scientists explore possible experimental outcomes (see Gorman 1995). Certainly when the second author has given the 2-4-6 task to groups of police officers, they show the bias to roughly the same extent as other experienced and intelligent people. It is perhaps salutary to recall that the first application of DNA forensically was to exculpate the prime suspect (only later to identify

Colin Pitchfork as the murderer after taking samples from nearly 4,000 local men (see Rudin and Inman 2002). Even the great Sherlock Holmes seems prone to verification bias. In 'The Stockbroker's Clerk', for example, Holmes is visiting Watson's new practice. The exchange can be paraphrased as follows:

> *Holmes*: Your neighbour is a doctor.
> *Watson*: Yes, he bought a practice as I did.
> *Holmes*: An old-established one?
> *Watson*: Just the same as mine. Both have been ever since the houses were built.
> *Holmes*: Ah, then you got hold of the best of the two.
> *Watson*: I think I did. But how do you know?
> *Holmes*: By the steps, my boy. Yours are worn three inches deeper than his. (Conan Doyle 1993: 75)

Holmes asserts that Watson's practice is the better, thus providing another instance of the rule he had in mind (worn steps mean more patients). Because this is fiction, he is right. Of course, it is equally possible that Watson's neighbour's predecessor had been able to afford to replace his very worn steps whereas Watson's predecessor had not.

Consider the task of the investigating officer alongside the phenomenon of verification bias. He/she is being asked to make a judgement by tracing and eliminating alternatives, before moving into verification mode. This is done against a background of limited resources and the pressures that go therewith. It would not be surprising if the general human tendency to verify rather than test conspires with organisational pressures to yield premature movement from investigation to verification mode. We contend that an understanding of the verification bias, its prevalence in human thinking generally, and its potentially pernicious impact on policing is something that must be borne in mind in training and monitoring the investigative task.

To this point, the literature on investigation has been superficially outlined, followed by a mere note of the existence of the literature on heuristics and biases. The two have to this point been brought together only in the example of verification bias. In this section, a few more of the more well-established phenomena will be outlined, with instances (factual or literary) of how they may be relevant to crime investigation. Two points already made must be stressed at this juncture:

1   The investigator will not feel as though these phenomena are relevant, both because an adequate formulaic approach will be

effective in most cases where it is applied; and because common heuristics and biases will remain unrecognised because they are so ingrained. Indeed some investigators regard them as existing because they offered our forebears advantages in Darwinian natural selection (see Cosmides 1989)

2   The examples presented here come as illustrations of possible effects, as yet not systematically demonstrated in crime investigation. Our hope is for such a programme of research to be mounted, alongside tentative introduction of the topics into police training.

The caveats entered, we progress to a selection of the phenomena common in human reasoning

Illusory correlation

In a classic experiment demonstrating this phenomenon, Chapman (1967) and Chapman and Chapman (1969) provided people with information concerning several hypothetical patients suffering from mental disorder. This included a drawing of a person made by each patient. People then estimated the proportion of patients whose drawings exhibited various features. They dramatically overestimated the extent to which people suffering from a particular disorder exhibited 'expected' features. For example, paranoia was thought to be reflected in suspicious eyes, and men with worries about 'manliness' were deemed to draw men with broad shoulders. The implication of this concerns the development of expertise of an investigating officer. The review process which now follows murder investigations should perhaps incorporate explicit tests of the presumptions which led to suspect identification. In one (unsolved) murder of a prostitute reviewed by the first author, the suspicion lay against clients, as was the case in the Yorkshire Ripper investigation. It would be helpful to know the breakdown of responsibility for solved murders of prostitutes, so that illusory correlations about the relative frequencies in cases of this kind (for example about the relative frequency of murder by pimps, regular clients, one-off clients, etc.) could be avoided.[7]

Selection of evidence

The Wason selection task is the most intensively studied in human reasoning research (see Newstead and Evans (1995) for a review and selection of relevant work). It will be presented here first in its classic form. The subject is presented with four cards. On the upward facing side, there is a single digit or letter. On the four cards, the subject sees:

E T 4 7

They are told that each card has a letter on one side and a number on the other side. The experimenter asserts the rule: 'If a card has a vowel on one side then it has an even number on the other side.' The task is to decide which of the cards to turn over in order to decide whether the rule was true or false. Readers unfamiliar with the selection task may wish to decide which of the four 'cards' above they think they need to turn over to decide whether the rule is true or false, before reading on.

Most people faced with this example chose the cards showing the vowel and the even number, or only the card showing the vowel. The correct answer is that the cards with the vowel and the odd number should be turned over. If one finds an odd number on the reverse of the E, the rule is falsified. If one finds a vowel on the other side of the 7, the rule is falsified. Put generally, a rule of the form 'If p then q' will be falsified only by evidence from instances of p and not-q. Fortunately for the *amour-propre* of those who volunteer for psychological experiments, there are logically equivalent forms of the problem which are much easier to get right. For example, if cards have a destination on one side and a mode of travel on the other, which of the cards below need to be turned over to test the falsity of the rule 'Every time I go to Manchester, I travel by train.'

Manchester   Leeds   Train   Car

Most people correctly opt for Manchester and car (see Johnson-Laird *et al.* 1972). The key point of what was thought to be demonstrated here, a 'thematic facilitation effect', is that the errors made depend less on the formal logical properties of a problem than upon the mental model which one brings to bear upon the problem. This can be illustrated by a slightly different type of problem. Consider a store selling electrical goods with a rule such as 'Every purchaser of goods value £100+ gets a free radio.' Here, the cards have on one side the purchase amount, and on the other whether a free radio had been supplied.

£80 purchase   £120 purchase   radio   No radio

In this case, the cards to be chosen depend upon the perspective from which someone addresses the problem. If it is the customer keen to establish that the store behaves as it promises, the cards to turn over are '£120 purchase' and 'No radio'. If the former reveals 'No radio' and the latter a sum over £100, the store is not as good as its word. If, on the other hand, the perspective is that of the store manager, ensuring that a salesperson is not being over-generous, the cards to turn over are £80 purchase (in case it reveals 'Radio') or 'Radio' (in case it reveals a sum under £100).

What has all this to do with crime investigation? The anti-climactic answer is that it demonstrates that human reasoning typically proceeds on routes which fall short of the logical in predictable ways. As Wason (1983) notes:

> People all too readily succumb to logical fallacies, especially when trying to be persuasive ... Cognitive illusions ... may not be radically different from the circumstances and contingencies which are sometimes met in everyday life and which are quite irrational, eg incorrigible convictions about quite ordinary things, delusions of reference, and other transient symptoms such as falling in love. (pp. 59-60).

But the way in which logically identical problems are framed, and the guidance which can be offered on problem solution, will change the proportion of correct answers supplied, thus rendering training and monitoring relevant to the possible improvement of performance. That the framing of a problem can yield different outcomes can be illustrated by a device used by Kahneman and Tversky (2000). They presented people with one or other version of a problem as follows. The percentage of people opting for one or other course of action is given in brackets.

Problem 1. Imagine that you have decided to see a play and paid the admission price of $10 per ticket. As you enter the theater, you discover that you have lost the ticket. The seat was not marked, and the ticket cannot be recovered. Would you pay $10 for another ticket?
Yes (46%) No (54%)

Problem 2. Imagine that you have decided to see a play where admission is $10 per ticket. As you enter the theater, you discover that you have lost a $10 bill. Would you still pay $10 for a ticket for the play?
Yes (88%) No (12%)

Thus framing the same loss in terms of link to the lost item dramatically changes the proportion of people prepared to forgo the service to which the lost item entitled them. One can think of framing as relevant to many aspects of policing, not least the detection of crimes through detection of offenders in different crimes. The highwayman and murderer Dick Turpin was detected through the relatively minor offence of 'stealing a fine cock'.[8] The Yorkshire Ripper was detected for murder through the detected theft of a vehicle registration plate.[9] In the USA, the serial murderer known as Son of Sam was detected through illegally parking next to a fire hydrant.[10] Illegally parking in bays for the disabled is a strong marker for other kinds of criminality (Chenery *et al.* 1999). Put baldly, if offending is framed in terms of a general attribute called criminality, with offenders being versatile, investigation should be flexible across crime types. If offenders are thought of as specialists, the frame is set around a particular crime type. To oversimplify, the literature on criminal careers emphasises criminality as a general attribute, while the literature on crime reduction emphasises criminality as specialised by crime type. The frames are thus different, with incalculable consequences for the detection enterprise.

Risky choice

A phenomenon which merits mention but whose complexity precludes detailed discussion is that people are risk-averse when choosing among gains and risk-seeking when choosing among losses (see Kahneman and Tversky 2000 for a fuller exposition). For example, if asked to consider a terrorist attack, with 600 people in danger, an option in which 400 people will definitely die is regarded less favourably than the risky option wherein there is a one-third chance that no one will die and a two-thirds chance that all 600 will. The preference for risky choices when one is losing speaks to the SIO in investigations that seem to be going nowhere. Risky choices of course include the selection – perhaps under extreme pressure – of a search space for people to be interviewed which may exclude the perpetrator.

The knew-it-all-along effect

A well-established error is that we exaggerate with hindsight what we could have known by foresight. This is a familiar error (not recognised as such) among those of us who gamble. It is only after a horse/racing driver/soccer team on which we have gambled has lost that we recognise the importance of some factors which we failed to take into account and berate ourselves accordingly. Ingenious studies have been conducted where people are told of battles whose outcome they do not know, without being told of the outcome. Afterwards, those who are wrong do not sit easily with their own wrongness, but work on what they 'ought' to have taken into consideration which would have led to them being correct. Fischoff (1982) comments:

> In the short run, failure to ignore outcome knowledge holds substantial benefits. It is quite flattering to believe, or lead others to believe, that we would have known all along what we could only know with outcome knowledge. (p. 342)

This undoubted truth is bad news for those whose actions are retrospectively deemed culpable, not least SIOs. Fletcher (1986), ruefully quoting Byron, notes:

> When things go wrong, often through no fault of his own, [the SIO] is soon aware that 'A man must serve his time to every trade save censure – critics all are ready made' (p. 150)

The only wholly fair inquiry would occur where the inquirer did not know the outcome of the events into which she was inquiring until after the inquiry! It may be an advantage in reviewing murder inquiries for officers to be denied knowledge of the outcome. This is no doubt impractical considered at the national level, but cross-national reviews conducted under such a protocol would certainly yield interesting results.

In conclusion

The spectre of which we have been acutely aware while writing this chapter has been that of the experienced SIO who will not recognise at least some of the processes which we have described. It is worth reiterating the fact that we know that murders, as with much volume crime, if they are to be cleared up, are cleared up very quickly, and on the basis of information that comes to the officer without much effort on his or her part. However, a procedure has to be developed which addresses a situation which is contingent on failure in the short term. Just as early actions must be based on pessimism as to outcome, so the understanding of heuristics and biases in reasoning will come into its own after short-term failure. Having a repertoire of actions whose relevance are contingent on short-term failure is no less admirable for understanding investigator heuristics and biases than it is for, for example, full forensic investigation.

But policing is a practical business and investigators are practical people. Convincing SIOs of the limitations of their heuristics and of the desirability of having a repertoire of alternatives is one thing, it is quite another to address those limitations and develop alternatives that will be adopted in practice. Assuming that the cognitive abilities of the average investigator are no more nor less than the population as a whole we can anticipate that they will remain liable to make the same cognitive errors as the rest of us. Assuming also that the decision-making environment they work in is unlikely to change much, it can be anticipated that features which have been implicated in cognitive failures in the past, such as low information levels, limited resources and pressure to obtain quick results, are likely to recur. If the cognitive abilities of investigators and the environment they work in remain unchanged, what improvements are possible? In the short term, training may improve investigators' heuristics and the way in which they are used. There is currently no training available to investigators in how to make decisions. The literature touched on in this paper together with case studies of investigations would provide a sufficient basis for such training. In addition, improved decision support could be made available to investigators. The systematic debriefing of cases would provide a database from which statistical and case study material could be made available to SIOs. For example, the probability of the murderer of a prostitute being a stranger would assist SIOs in deciding which bit of the haystack they should start looking in first. In the longer term, research is required to identify more precisely the factors that are involved in cognitive failures during investigations and the types of systems and strategies that could be employed to prevent them.

Notes

1 The views expressed herein are not necessarily those of Greater Manchester Police.
2 See W. Cook (2002) *Tragically I was an Only Twin*. London: Century.
3 Qualified because the obvious force of Maple's personality is directed towards the development of adequate systems.
4 That said, Dew perhaps overemphasises the importance of his role in inducing Crippen and Ethel LeNeve to flee, and too little to Captain Kendall of the *Montrose*, without whose percipience Crippen would have reached Canada safely. It is difficult to be too hard on Dew, however. The

crowning achievement of his career was followed swiftly, as the book's dedication attests, by the death of his only son in the First World War.

5   In an unpublished study by the first author, in 8 out of 29 murder investigations this was the case.

6   Another chapter could be written about the decision as to proceeding on the basis of the consequences of being wrong in different ways. For example, treating an event as constituting a critical incident when it turns out not to be is one kind of mistake. Treating an event as not a critical incident when it turns out to be one is the other possible mistake. The consequences of the second will invite harsh criticism. Thus the first kind of mistake will be made much more often. This was illustrated by the Baxstrom case (see Steadman and Cocozza 1974) where the release of many prisoners designated dangerous resulted in few serious offences. The clinicians making assessments of dangerousness were avoiding the possibility of classifying the dangerous as safe, given the likely reaction to such a mistake. In police recording of crime, the same processes will lead to the under-investigation of less serious crime, and the presumption of seriousness where that is possible. The National Crime Recording System constitutes an effort to ensure that less serious crime escapes proper policing attention.

7   In a more prosaic example, crime reduction officers often use the example of the theft of lawnmowers from garden sheds to be a phenomenon of springtime, when the grass starts to grow. The second author has never been able to find evidence of this analysis of seasonality of offending, but the probably illusory correlation persists.

8   http://www.york-united-kingdom.co.uk/dickturpin/

9   www.bbc.co.uk/crime/caseclosed/yorkshireripper1.shtml

10   http://www.bbc.co.uk/crime/caseclosed/berkowitz1.shtml

References

ACPO Crime Committee (2000) 'MIRSAP Manual: Major Incident Room Standard Administration Procedures' (unpublished).

Adhami, E. and Browne, D.P. (1996) *Major Crime Enquiries: Improving Expert Support for Detectives*, Police Research Group Special Interest Series Paper 9. London: Home Office.

Bruner, J.S., Goodnow, J.J. and Austin, G.A. (1956) *A Study of Thinking*. London: John Wiley.

Chapman, L.J. (1967) 'Illusory correlation in observational report', *Journal of Verbal Learning and Verbal Behaviour*, 6: 151–155.

Chapman, L.J. and Chapman, J.P. (1969) 'Illusory correlation as an obstacle to the use of valid psychodiagnostic signs', *Journal of Abnormal Psychology*, 74: 271–280.

Chatterton, M.R. (1975) 'Organisational Relationships and Processes in Police Work: A Case Study in Urban Policing'. Unpublished PhD thesis, University of Manchester.

Chenery, S., Henshaw, C. and Pease, K. (1999) *Illegal Parking in Disabled Bays: A Means of Offender Targeting*, PRC Briefing Note 1/99. London: Home Office.

Christie, A. (1970) *Murder at the Vicarage*. London: Bantam.

Conan Doyle, A. (1993) *The Memoirs of Sherlock Holmes*. Oxford: Oxford University Press.

Cosmides, L. (1989) 'The logic of social exchange. Has natural selection shaped how humans reason? Studies with the Wason selection task', *Cognition*, 31: 187–276.

Dew, W. (1938) *I Caught Crippen*. London: Blackie.

Fischoff, B. (1982) 'For those condemned to study the past: heuristics and biases in hindsight', in D. Kahneman, P. Slovic, and A. Tversky (eds), *Judgement under Uncertainty: Heuristics and Biases*. Cambridge: Cambridge University Press.

Fitzmaurice, C.T. and Pease, K. (1981) 'On measuring distaste in years', in J. Gunn and D.P. Farrington (eds), *Abnormal Offenders, Delinquency and the Criminal Justice System*. Chichester: Wiley.

Fitzmaurice, C.T. and Pease, K. (1986) *The Psychology of Judicial Sentencing*. Manchester: University of Manchester Press.

Flanagan, R. (2004) *A Report on the Investigation by Cambridgeshire Constabulary into the Murders of Jessica Chapman and Holly Wells at Soham on 4 August 2002. Summary of Conclusions and Recommendations*. London: Home Office/Her Majesty's Inspectorate of Constabulary.

Fletcher, T. (1986) *Memories of Murder*. London: Weidenfeld & Nicolson.

Gorman, M.E. (1995) 'Hypothesis testing', in S.E. Newstead and J.St.B.T. Evans (eds), *Perspectives on Thinking and Reasoning*. Hove: Lawrence Erlbaum Associates.

Johnson-Laird, P.N. (1995). 'Inference and mental models', in S.E. Newstead, and J.St.B.T. Evans (eds), *Perspectives on Thinking and Reasoning*. Hove: Lawrence Erlbaum Associates.

Johnson-Laird, P.N., Legrenzi, P. and Legrenzi, M.S. (1972) 'Reasoning and a sense of reality', *British Journal of Psychology*, 63: 395–400.

Kahneman, D. and Tversky, A. (2000) *Choices, Values, and Frames*. Cambridge: Cambridge University Press.

Kennedy, L. (1985) *10 Rillington Place*. London: HarperCollins.

Maguire, M. and Norris, C. (1992) *The Conduct and Supervision of Criminal Investigations*, Royal Commission on Criminal Justice. London: HMSO.

Maple, J. (1999) *The Crime Fighter*. New York: Doubleday.

Marlow, A. (1989) 'The practice of detective work in a county force', *Criminologist*, 13: 130–135.

Muncie, W. (1979) *The Crime Pond*. Edinburgh: Chambers.

Newstead, S.E. and Evans, J.St.B.T. (eds) (1995). *Perspectives on Thinking and Reasoning*. Hove: Lawrence Erlbaum Associates.

Nicol, C., Innes, M., Gee, D. and Feist, A. (2004) *Reviewing Murder Investigations: An Analysis of Progress Reviews from Six Police Forces*. Home Office Online Report 25/04.

Rudin, N. and Inman, K. (2002) *Forensic DNA Analysis, 2nd edn*. Boca Raton, FL: CRC Press.

Smith, N. and Flanagan, C. (2000) *The Effective Detective: Identifying the Skills of an Effective SIO*, Police Research Paper 122. London: Home Office.

Steadman, H.J. and Cocozza, J.J. (1974) *Careers of the Criminally Insane*. Lexington, MA: Lexington.

Tweney, R.D. and Chitwood, S.T. (1995). 'Scientific reasoning', in S.E. Newstead and J.St.B.T. Evans (eds) *Perspectives on Thinking and Reasoning*. Hove: Lawrence Erlbaum Associates.

Wason, P.C. (1960) 'On the failure to eliminate hypotheses in a conceptual task'. *Quarterly Journal of Experimental Psychology*, 12: 129–140.

Wason, P.C. (1983) 'Realism and rationality in the selection task', in J.St.B.T. Evans (ed.), *Thinking and Reasoning: Psychological Approaches*. London: Routledge & Kegan Paul.

Index